PRAISE FOR SIMON GARFIELD

To the Letter

"Might stir you to send a handwritten note or two of your own. . . . Quirky stories abound. . . . Garfield is smart to celebrate letter-writing rather than lament its decline. He can tell that preaching against e-mail won't inspire anyone to choose the post office over pixels. But tugging at our heartstrings just might."
—*The Washington Post Book World*

"Thoroughly captivating . . . Garfield shows us the poetic nature of the written word. . . . An overdue homage to something we once took for granted but really was an art." —*The Tampa Tribune*

"Garfield's core argument . . . speaks powerfully to a broader urgency—the increasingly endangered species of meticulous, thoughtful self-revelation and deep mutual understanding through the written word in the age of reactionary responses and knee-jerk replies. He captures this beautifully." —BrainPickings.org

"Garfield is a bestselling writer of irresistible enthusiasm. [His] robust and propulsive engagement with letters as an essential embodiment of the human spirit and a driving cultural force makes for exciting reading and thoughtful speculation about the future of scholarship and communication." —*Booklist* (starred review)

"A book that goes on my 'keeper shelf.'. . . Buy it now, read it, and wrap it later!" —*Hudson Valley News*

"This endlessly informative book from one of Britain's best nonfiction writers provides a heartfelt reminder of just how much we'd lose . . . the book serves up any number of vivid examples from people famous and unknown." —*Reader's Digest*

On the Map

"Engaging . . . full of little conversation pieces."
—Janet Maslin, *The New York Times*

"Deep research and descriptive intensity. [Garfield] regales us with tales of such wonders as Britain's medieval Mappa Mundi . . . *On the Map* offers a world of revelation." —*USA Today*

"Delightfully meandering." —NPR.org

"This is an absolute must for map lovers everywhere."—*Chicago Tribune*

"*On the Map* is a treasure: exhilarating, witty, compulsively readable, and just plain fun." —*The Seattle Times*

S0-AHL-059

Simon Garfield is the author of fourteen acclaimed books of nonfiction, including *On the Map* and *Just My Type*. He lives in London.

Connect online:
www.simongarfield.com

© SARAH LEE

TO THE LETTER

A CELEBRATION OF THE LOST ART OF LETTER WRITING

SIMON GARFIELD

GOTHAM
BOOKS

GOTHAM

Published by the Penguin Group
Penguin Group (USA) LLC
375 Hudson Street
New York, New York 10014

USA | Canada | UK | Ireland | Australia | New Zealand | India | South Africa | China
penguin.com
A Penguin Random House Company

Previously published as a Gotham Books hardcover and in Great Britain by
Cannongate Books, Ltd.

First trade paperback printing, November 2014

1   3   5   7   9   10   8   6   4   2

Gotham Books and the skyscraper logo are trademarks of Penguin Group (USA) LLC.

The Library of Congress Cataloging-in-Publication Data has been applied for.

ISBN 978-1-592-40882-5

Printed in the United States of America
Set in Adobe Caslon Pro

To Justine

By Command of the Postmaster General.

NOTICE to the PUBLIC.

Rapid Delivery of Letters.

GENERAL POST OFFICE,
May, 1849.

The Postmaster General is desirous of calling attention to the greater rapidity of delivery which would obviously be consequent on the general adoption of *Street-door Letter Boxes, or Slits,* in private dwelling houses, and indeed wherever the Postman is at present kept waiting.

He hopes that householders will not object to the means by which, at a very moderate expense, they may secure so desirable an advantage to themselves, to their neighbours, and to the Public Service.

A slit in the door: a novel concept in 1849.

'We lay aside letters never to read them again, and at last we destroy them out of discretion, and so disappears the most beautiful, the most immediate breath of life, irrecoverable for ourselves and for others.'

– Johann Wolfgang von Goethe

'In an age like ours, which is not given to letter-writing, we forget what an important part it used to play in people's lives.'

– Anatole Broyard

'There must be millions of people all over the world who never get any love letters ... I could be their leader.'

– Charlie Brown

Contents

An early pillar box, circa 1853: 'Not a single letter has been stolen'.

Chapter One

The Magic of Letters

Lot 512. Walker (Val. A.) An extensive correspondence addressed to Bayard Grimshaw, 1941 and 1967–1969, comprising 37 autograph letters, signed, and 21 typed letters, with a long description of Houdini: 'His water torture cell simply underestimated the intelligence of the onlooker, no problem to layman & magician alike,' describing a stage performance by him where Walker was one of the people called on to attach handcuffs, and another at which he fixed Houdini in his own jacket, continuing with information about his own straight jacket, his 'Tank in the Thames' and 'Aquamarine Girl' escapes, and other escapology, including a handbill advertising 'The Challenge Handcuff Act', and promotional sheet for George Grimmond's 'Triple Box Escape'.

est. £300 – £400

Bloomsbury Auctions is not in Bloomsbury but in a road off Regent Street, and since its inception in 1983 it has specialised in sales of books and the visual arts. *Occasionally* these visual arts include conjuring, a catch-all heading that offers a glimpse into a vanishing world, and many other vanishing items besides, as well as sleight-of-hand, mind-reading, contortionism, levitation, escapology and sawing.

On 20 September 2012 one such sale offered complete tricks, props, solutions for tricks and the construction of props, posters, flyers, contracts and letters. Several lots related to particular magicians, such as Vonetta, the Mistress of Mystery, one of the few successful female illusionists and a major draw in Scotland, where she was celebrated not only for her magic but also for her prowess as a quick-change artiste. There was one lot connected with Ali Bongo, including letters describing seventeen inventions, and, improbably, 'a costume description for an appearance as The Invisible Man'.

There were three lots devoted to Chung Ling Soo, whose real name was William E. Robinson, born in 1861 not in Peking but in New York City (the photographs on offer suggested he looked less like an enigmatic man from the East and more like Nick Hornby with a hat on). One of the letters for sale discussed Chung Ling Soo's rival, Ching Ling Foo, who claimed that Chung Ling Soo stole not only the basics of his name, but also the basis of his act; their feud reached its apotheosis in 1905, when both Soo and Foo were performing in London at the same time, and each expressed the sort of inscrutable fury that did neither of them any harm at the box office. In order to cultivate his persona, Chung Ling Soo never spoke during his act, which included breathing smoke and catching fish from the air.

Between 1901 and 1918 Soo played the Swansea Empire, the Olympia Shoreditch, the Camberwell Palace, the Ardwick Green Empire and Preston Royal Hippodrome, but his career met an unforgettable end onstage at the Wood Green Empire – possibly the result of a curse laid by Ching Ling Foo – when his famous 'catch a bullet in the teeth' trick didn't quite work out as hoped. On this occasion, his gun fired a real bullet rather than just a blank charge, and, as historians of Soo are quick to point out, his first words on stage were also necessarily his last: 'Something's happened – lower the curtain!' Among the lots at the Bloomsbury sale were letters from assistants and friends of Soo claiming he had been born in Birmingham, England, at the back of the Fox Hotel, and that the death may not have been an accident. 'We who knew Robinson,' wrote a man called Harry Bosworth, 'say he was murdered.'

But the stand-out lot was the one involving the Radium Girl, the Aquamarine Girl, Carmo & the Vanishing Lion, Walking Through a Wall and the origins of sawing thin female assistants – the items relating to the life of Val Walker. Walker, who took the name Valentine because he was born on 14 February 1890, was once a star performer. He was known as 'The Wizard of the Navy' for his ability to escape a locked metal tank submerged in water during the First World War (a feat later repeated in the Thames in 1920, witnessed by police and military departments and 300 members of the press). After drying himself he received offers to perform all over the world. He subsequently escaped from jails in Argentina, Brazil, and, according to information contained in the auction lot, 'various prisons in Spain'.

Walker was the David Copperfield and David Blaine of his day. He appeared in shows at Maskelyne's Theatre of Mystery, next door to BBC Broadcasting House, the most famous European magic theatre of the time (perhaps of all time), surprising audiences with swift escapes from manacles, straitjackets and a 9-foot-long submarine submerged in a glass-fronted tank at the centre of the stage. And then there was the trick with which Walker secured his place in magical history: Radium Girl. This was known as a 'big box' restoration illusion, a process in which a skilled woman enters a cabinet and is either sawn in half or penetrated with swords, and then somehow emerges unscathed. Walker's role in this trick is fundamental; he is believed to have invented it in 1919, building the box himself and devising the necessary diversions and patter to make it the climax of his show.

The trick is one we've seen on stage or television for 95 years: an empty box on casters is displayed to the audience,

Britain's secret weapon: Val Walker contemplates his escape.

The Radium Girl illusion.

its sides and base are banged, an assistant climbs in and is secured by chains, the door is closed, knives or poles are inserted into pre-drilled holes, followed by sheets of metal that seem to slice the woman into three parts (feminists have consistently placed this trick in their Top Five). Weaned on cynicism and trick photography, we have become blasé about such things today, but Radium Girl was once quite something. The sheets and poles and swords are then (of course) all pulled out, the door is opened and the chains removed, and the woman is smiling and whole.

But then something even more dramatic happened: Walker got bored. He grew tired of the touring. He became envious of the acclaim and riches poured upon those he considered lesser talents, among them Harry Houdini. So one day Walker just quit. His professional disappearing act was, as might only be expected, an impressive feat: he gave up his Magic Circle membership in 1924, resumed his work as an electrical engineer, moved to Canford Cliffs, a suburb of Poole in Dorset with his wife Ethel, had a son named Kevin, and was never seen on a stage again. His gain, one imagines, but magic's loss.

At the end of September 1968, several decades after he retired from magic, Walker made one final appearance at a convention in Weymouth. But he came as a fan, not a star, and he had a particular purpose for being there, to see the

Radium Girl performed one more time. The magician was a man called Jeff Atkins, and Walker had rebuilt a new cabinet especially for him that summer in his garden. And it really was a last hurrah: Walker died six months later of a chronic and progressive disease (probably cancer), and many of his secrets went with him.

But not all: some of his letters remain, and are the source for much of the material you have just read, gleaned from browsing the files at Bloomsbury Auctions the day before the sale. His letters provide news of his great entertainments, but of a personal life that appears to have been conducted with modesty and decorum and a great care for others (until the end, as we shall see).

The more I read them, the more I wanted to know. Within a couple of days – from seeing the mention of Walker in the sale catalogue online, to skimming through these remnants of his life at the auction preview – I had fallen under the spell of a man I had never previously heard of. And I had become enveloped by a word he used more than once in his letters, his *milieu*, a world that relied for its buoyancy on deception, apparition and secrecy. But now the letters were letting me in.

Val Walker's correspondence, both inconsequential and profound, was doing what correspondence has so alluringly, convincingly and reliably done for more than 2,000 years, embracing the reader with a disarming blend of confession and emotion, and (for I had no reason to suspect otherwise, despite the illusory subject matter) integrity. His letters had secured what his former spiritualist medium colleagues could not – a new friend from beyond the grave. The folders now at auction not only prised open a subculture that was grow-ing ever more clandestine with the cloaky passage of time, but presented a trove of incidental personal details that, in other circumstances, would have bordered on intrusion. I sat in that auction room and wondered: what else could bring back a world and an individual's role within it so directly, so intensely, so plainly and so irresistibly? Only letters.

Letters have the power to grant us a larger life. They reveal motivation and deepen understanding. They are evidential. They change lives, and they rewire history. The world once used to run upon their transmission – the lubricant of human interaction and the freefall of ideas, the silent conduit of the worthy and the incidental, the time we were coming for dinner, the account of our marvellous day, the weightiest joys and sorrows of love. It must have seemed impossible that their worth would ever be taken for granted or swept aside. A world without letters would surely be a world without oxygen.

This is a book about a world without letters, or at least this possibility. It is a book about what we have lost by replacing letters with email – the post, the envelope, a pen, a slower cerebral whirring, the use of the whole of our hands and not just the tips of our fingers. It is a celebration of what has gone before, and the value we place on literacy, good thinking and thinking ahead. I wonder if it is not also a book about kindness.

The digitisation of communication has effected dramatic changes in our lives, but the impact on letter-writing – so gradual and so fundamental – has slipped by like an English summer. Something that has been crucial to our economic and emotional well-being since ancient Greece has been slowly evaporating for two decades, and in two more the licking of a stamp will seem as antiquated to a future generation as the paddle steamer. You can still travel by paddle steamer, and you can still send a letter, but why would you want to when the alternatives are so much faster and more convenient? This book is an attempt to provide a positive answer.

This is not an anti-email book (what would be the point?). It is not an anti-progress book, for that could have been written at the advent of the telegraph or the landline phone, neither of which did for letter-writing in the way that was predicted, certainly not in the way email has done. The book is driven by a simple thing: the sound – and I'm still struggling to define it, that thin blue wisp of an airmail, the showy heft of an invitation with RSVP card, the happy sneeze of a thank-you note – that the letter makes when it drops onto a doormat. Auden had it right – the romance of the mail and the news it brings, the transformative possibilities of the post – only the landing of a letter beckons us with ever-renewable faith. The inbox versus the shoebox; only one will be treasured, hoarded, moved when we move or will be forgotten to be found after us. Should our personal history, the proof of our emotional existence, reside in a Cloud server (a steel-lined warehouse) on some American plain, or should it reside where it has always done, scattered amongst our physical possessions? That emails are harder to archive while retaining a pixellated durability is a paradox that we are just beginning to grapple with. But will we ever glow when we open an email folder? Emails are a poke, but letters are a caress, and letters stick around to be newly discovered.

A story is told of Oscar Wilde: he would write a letter at his Chelsea home in Tite Street (or, looking at his handwriting, 'dash off' is probably more accurate), and because he was so brilliant and so busy being brilliant, he wouldn't bother to mail it. Instead, he would attach a stamp and throw the letter out of the window. He would be as certain as he could be that someone passing would see the letter, assume it had been dropped by accident, and put it into the nearest letterbox. If we all did this it wouldn't really work, but only people like Wilde had the nonchalant faith. How many letters didn't reach the letterbox and the intended recipient we will never know, but we can be fairly sure that if the method didn't work well, or if too many were neglected because they landed in manure, Wilde would have stopped doing it. And there are a lot of letters from Tite Street and elsewhere that have survived him to reach handy auction prices. There's no proper moral to this story, but it does conjure up a rather vivid picture of late-Victorian London: the horse-drawn traffic on the cobbled street below, the bustle, the clatter and the chat, and someone, probably wearing a hat, picking up a letter and doing the right thing, because going to the postbox was what one did as part of life's daily conversation.*

There is an intrinsic integrity about letters that is lacking from other forms of written communication. Some of this has to do with the application of hand to paper, or the rolling of the paper through the typewriter, the effort to get things right

---

* It's difficult not to mention Wilde's idiosyncratic postal system without also mentioning the exalted letter he could not send. *De Profundis*, written on 20 sheets of paper in Reading Gaol in the last months before his release in May 1897, is a study of sorrow, beauty and the position of the outcast, and it begins with plaintive regret: 'Dear Bosie, After long and fruitless waiting I have determined to write to you myself, as much for your sake as for mine, as I would not like to think that I had passed through two long years of imprisonment without ever having received a single line from you . . .'

What follows is an unapologetic account of an aesthete's life – his search for the exquisite in all things, his extravagances, his questing passions with Lord Alfred Douglas – and an account of the artistic consolations of a life devoted to Christ. Unable to send the letter from jail, he gave it to his friend Robbie Ross on his release, with instructions for it to be typed twice, whereupon certain passages were misread and excised. The original manuscript is held at the British Museum, where we may marvel at the succulent depths of his language and the calm certainty of his convictions.

'I have said of myself that I was one who stood in symbolic relations to the art and culture of my age,' Wilde writes. 'There is not a single wretched man in this wretched place along with me who does not stand in symbolic relation to the very secret of life. For the secret of life is suffering. It is what is hidden behind everything. When we begin to live, what is sweet is so sweet to us, and what is bitter so bitter, that we inevitably direct all our desires towards pleasures, and seek not merely for a "month or twain to feed on honeycomb," but for all our years to taste no other food, ignorant all the while that we may really be starving the soul.'

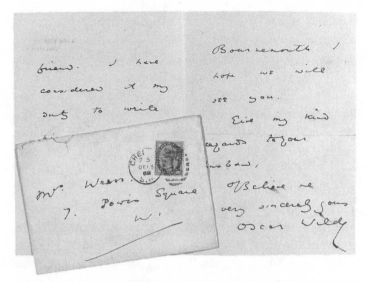

Oscar Wilde writes to Mrs Wren in 1888.

first time, the perceptive gathering of purpose. But I think it also has something to do with the mode of transmission, the knowledge of what happens to the letter when sealed. We know where to post it, roughly when it will be collected, the fact that it will be dumped from a bag, sorted, delivered to a van, train or similar, and then the same thing the other end in reverse. We have no idea about where email goes when we hit send. We couldn't track the journey even if we cared to; in the end, it's just another vanishing. No one in a stinky brown work coat wearily answers the phone at the dead email office. If it doesn't arrive we just send it again. But it almost always arrives, with no essence of human journey at all. The ethereal carrier is anonymous and odourless, and carries neither post-mark nor scuff nor crease. The woman goes into a box and emerges unblemished. The toil has gone, and with it some of the rewards.

I wanted to write a book about those rewards. It would include a glimpse of some of the great correspondents and correspondences of the past, fold in a little history of mail, consider how we value, collect and archive letters in our lives, and look at how we were once firmly instructed to write such things. And I was keen to encounter those who felt similarly enthused about letters, some of them so much so that they were trying to bring letters back. I was concerned primarily with personal letters rather than business correspondence or official post, though these two may reveal plenty about our lives. The letters in this book are the sort that may quicken the heart, the sort that may often reflect, in Auden's much-loved words, joy from the girl and the boy. I had no ambitions to write a complete history of letter-writing, and I certainly wouldn't attempt a definitive collection of great letters (the world is too old to accommodate such a thing, and lacks adequate shelving; it would be akin to collecting all the world's art in one gallery), but I did want to applaud some of the letters that managed to achieve a similarly gargantuan task – the art of capturing a whole world on a single page. *To the Letter* will begin its travels in Roman Britain, home of the earliest letters we have, with the discovery that the ancient method of opening and closing a letter – greetings and farewells – are those that we still use 2,000 years later. The letter hasn't really changed much in all that time. But now we may be at risk of letting it change irreversibly.

The auction took place on an autumnal Thursday only a few weeks after the close of the Olympics. A few yards from the auction room people queued to check their email at the Apple Store. Nearby, in Bond Street, there was Smythson, the posh stationer and leather goods shop. Its creative consultant Samantha Cameron, wife of the prime minister, had presumably been consulted on the display of a £50 box of Empire notecards with an Indian elephant motif, one of the many items in the shop keeping elegance alive against the touch screen odds.

But amidst these symbols of the new and the old stood something timeless. Like a good novel, an auction house promises escape, drama and revelation, and the prospect of greater truth. It also promises commerce, of course, the prospect of proud ownership on one hand and profit on the other, an equation as old as the Babylonian market stall. Occasionally a good sale also offers proper history and biographical insight, and perhaps an understanding of life hitherto denied to us. The conjuring sale was one such occasion. How else would these startling people be remembered in an age when conjuring has been largely reduced to Las Vegas and bar mitzvahs? There just isn't much call for illusionists in the digital age, not only because there are so many other ways to spend an evening, but because the Internet has long laid bare magic's hidden compartments. Illusionists have been obliged to become postmodernists, the masterful showmen Penn & Teller performing tricks and then instantly revealing how they were done, confident that the gap between knowledge and the ability to apply it in performance will safeguard their profession for a while.

I learnt from Walker's letters that the girl in the Radium Girl illusion concealed herself behind a panel before the blades went through, and that the box was deeper than we perceived, but this didn't make me a magician. I wasn't particularly interested in how the tricks were done. I was interested in who had done them, and why, and how these people lived their lives. By the date of the auction I had become determined to buy Walker's letters, and so, on that Thursday afternoon I exchanged my credit card details for a cardboard bidding paddle and sat in the middle of the room as the lots tumbled towards mine.

First there were books to
sell. These didn't have much
to do with magic, or not
directly. There was Dodgson,
Charles Lutwidge, known
to his readers as Lewis Carroll, *Alice's Adventures in Wonderland*, 1930, the Black Sun
Press, short split to head of
upper joint, glassine dust
jacket, chipped at spine ends
and corners, estimate £4,000
to £6,000 – unsold. There was
Wilde, Oscar, *The Picture of
Dorian Gray*, first edition in
book form, 1891, first issue

Walker in a straitjacket.

with misprint on p. 208 ('nd' rather than 'and'), darkened, corners bumped, estimate £750 to £1,000, sold for £700.

When it was time for the magic, one name kept recurring like marked aces. Bayard Grimshaw, who had died in
1994, was a recipient of a great many letters in the sale, and
he appeared to be one of magic's few super-groupies. He was
a magic correspondent for *World's Fair*, the weekly newspaper
for showmen, and he became friends with many of magic's
stars. Perhaps seeing a gap in market, and a gullible public,
he also became a performer himself, touting a mind-reading
act with his wife Marion. In so doing he achieved an illusion-
ist's connoisseurship and the trust of the Magic Circle, and
amassed a large hoard of oddments and correspondence. Perhaps he thought they would be valuable one day.

As a keen collector – stamps, tube maps, the usual male
detritus – I had been to a few auctions before, but none were
as sparsely attended as this. By the time the books had been
sold there were about 15 of us left, and I recognised half of

them from the preview the previous day. Most of those who had attended for the books portion had drifted away, and although a few others joined us on the phone and online, the prices rarely exceeded their upper estimate, which filled me with hope. And those who were there seemed predominantly interested in the props and physical tricks rather than documents. But just as I began to feel confident that I would get the Walker letters for a steal, or at least something near the lower estimate of £300, a few of the items started going for three or four times their estimate, and a handful went for more than £1,000. One of these was a vast hoard of card tricks, the earliest dating from 1820, an array of 'forcing decks', 'moving pip cards' and 'waterfall shuffle' packs, the names themselves so alluring that I had to check my urge to buy them on impulse.

The lot simply titled 'Mentalists' was a collection of letters relating to mind-reading, with a detailed account of an act performed by The Great Nixon, and one letter from 1938 suggesting that The Great Nixon was such a phenomenon that he might be worthy of investigation in a laboratory. The Great Nixon was a sham, of course, and only as great as his stooge in the audience. But such was the allure of the performers in this period that I imagined an audience where few were prepared not to believe; they wanted the trick not to be a trick, but to be magic. The world held enough impending horrors in 1938, so why be cynical when you could be amazed? It wasn't like today, when magic can only be a trick, and the pleasure is not in the illusion but in figuring it out.

The auction wore on, through several items featuring Madame Zomah and seven letters mentioning the Piddingtons.* Surely it was only a matter of time before Henry the Horse danced the waltz. But then it was my time, lot 512. The bidding started slowly. No one was interested in the Radium

---

* A married couple from Australia famed for their 'telepathy'.

Girl anymore, much less Aquamarine Girl. But then of course it picked up. The bidding was soon at £200. I had promised myself and my wife I wouldn't go above £400. It went to £260, then to £280. I was so hooked now that I didn't even lower my hand between bids when a higher counter-bid came in. I just kept on going. I didn't even know who I was bidding against – an anonymous voice on the phone taken by an auction house staff member. Then the bidding stopped, and I was the last one interested. The gavel came down at £300 to no reaction whatsoever, no gasps, no applause, just another lot sold, and immediately it was on to lot 513. But I had triumphed: I got his letters, and his letters got me.

When I got them home I read again how to saw a girl in half (a trick box, a very supple assistant, a pair of electronically controlled feet at one end) and also how to make it look as though a cabinet was smaller than it was (black tape, a crafty angle to the audience, an assistant who can really hold her stomach in). But not all knowledge can be written down, and the art of magic, rather than just an explanation of it, cannot be taught but must be learnt, by example and crushing hours of practice. Even a full written explanation, quite apart from breaking the Magician's Code, would be like showing someone the cockpit of a plane and expecting them to fly. But occasionally the letters would preserve a record of well-honed stage patter:

> Today I'd like to show you one of the most fantastic stunts you are ever likely to see. Behind this curtain we have a very odd looking telephone booth. There is nothing strange about the inside. Open it and show. Except that there are small holes bored thru the top and base. Honey [Miss Honey Duprez] goes inside the cabinet and we thread the ropes thru these holes to the outside. Music whilst you do this. Put mike back on stand. After threading is done take up the mike again. We are going to try a

INDOCILIS
PRIVATA
LOQUI

President: Francis White, M.I.M.C.
Vice-President: Claude Chandler, M.I.M.C.
Secretary: John Salisse, M.I.M.C.
Treasurer: Colin Donister, M.I.M.C.

THE MAGIC CIRCLE

Hearts of Oak Buildings
Euston Road, London, N.W.1

5th October 1966

John Salisse, M.I.M.C.
34, Eton Avenue,
London, N.W.3
Telephone: HAMpstead 1948

Dear Mr. McComb,

I have been requested by The Policy & Finance Committee to write to you regarding the complaint from Mr. Val Walker that you have infringed his copyright for a trick which he registered in August 1934.

The main crux of the complaint would appear to revolve around the following extract from the Patent :-

" In which a tubular member is pushed through a substantially centrally arranged opening in the wall of the cabinet and out through an opening in the other wall of the cabinet".

Though perhaps the Patent has expired, the registration of the effect in 1934 by Mr. Val Walker proves ownership by him at that date.

If you can produce evidence of this effect being in somebody's possession prior to 1934, then this may well be a point for discussion with Mr. Walker.

We would welcome your comments.

Yours sincerely,

JOHN SALISSE

Mr. Billy McComb,
"Long Branch",
Allum Lane,
ELSTREE, Herts.

A tricky judgment: The Magic Circle intervenes in 1966.

sequence of completely impossible effects. You'll notice a festive air about this place today ... It's the manager's birthday. He's just turned 25 ... he was 52 before he turned it.

Metal blades and an 18-inch square wooden tube are passed through the centre of the phone booth and, ostensibly, Honey Duprez. 'Pull out the tube and blades in the reverse order, crashing them to the back. Turn cabinet once to give girl time to collect knots and conceal them. Then with deliberate moves knock off the three catches and pull open box. Girl steps out. Let her come down front and bow. Then take her place and bow off after her.'

But the tricks were old and almost unperformable now; they belonged in a museum in Vegas. The descriptions reminded me of an old song Clive James wrote with Pete Atkin called 'The Master of the Revels', in which a showman has blueprints in his office of 'the first exploding handshake' and 'the charted trajectories of custard pies'. Where is Honey today? Where is that phone booth?

When it wasn't mourning the former careers and lost illusions of others, the bulk of Walker's correspondence was concerned with defending his own. Looking back at the end of a life, he had begun to worry about his reputation, and about how his cabinet tricks would be remembered after he was gone. Walker had heard that a young magician had begun performing a deep cabinet trick that sounded very like the Radium Girl, and that the trick had been supplied by another magician. Walker became convinced, without seeing the act in question, that the patent for his illusion – which he had registered in 1934 – was being infringed.

This became quite a battle; letters went back and forth for almost a year. 'I fear,' wrote John Salisse, secretary of the Magic Circle, 'that the thing may blow up into a holocaust.' As the letter trail advanced, so the secrets of the trick emerged. One expert witness claimed Walker's case was futile, 'unless you claim that the whole idea of the penetration of a living person originated with you.' I felt a sadness as I read about the subtleties of the art, and about the great care invested in each illusion. I felt that great magicians shouldn't be allowed to vanish just like that.

In the autumn of 1968, Val Walker briefly re-emerged into the spotlight. He attended a magic convention in Weymouth, where he watched a man called Jeff Atkins perform his Radium Girl for the final time. 'I can never be sure whether it was 1921 or 22 when I built the original in Maskelyne's workshop under the stage,' he wrote. 'PT Selbit watched it in rehearsal and sometime later asked if I minded him using the basic idea for a different effect, which I certainly did not. It was his Sawing Through A Woman that emerged, using the identical cabinet dimensions. I have been both saddened and amused at the plethora of variations on the theme which the public has had to swallow during the intervening 40-odd years. I do not think my version of a penetration has been bettered in this long time.'

Walker informed the weekly magic magazine *Abracadabra* that now he had returned to the fold he was already looking forward to the next convention in Scarborough in a year. But he didn't make it. His letters show a progressive illness: 'I'm not sure I can attend . . .', 'I may not be able to meet you, try as I might.'

A few days before he died, he sent his last letters from a hospital on the south coast. In one of them, at the close, he said he could be 'reached at the address above'. He didn't actually write the word 'at'. Instead, in February 1969, more than two years before what is widely acknowledged to be the first standard email between two computers, he used an old but generally unfamiliar symbol in its place. The symbol was @.

Chapter Two

From Vindolanda, Greetings

You set off on a clear March morning from the Lake District. You take the road north from Penrith, go east at Carlisle towards Brampton, and then head high into the Pennine Hills. The road undulates and the roads are empty, and a driver will wonder whether this isn't the stretch where car adverts are filmed. You keep going. There's a B road south, and when you pass a village called Twice Brewed you're tempted to stop the car to tweet a photo of the signpost. The road twists down to Winshields Farm and a guest house called Vellum Lodge, and then there you are, two coachloads of children ahead of you, at the historic site called Vindolanda, where the evidence of letters begins.

Here, between AD 85 and 130, a series of five forts made from timber and turf were built to defend the Stanegate, a wide belt of dirt road over the narrow neck of Britain, vital for the transport of men and supplies in the region. Londinium was a week away in the south, and it was perhaps a month to the heart of the empire in Rome. Vindolanda (its name is thought to mean 'white lawns') was one garrison among many: some 50,000 men were stationed around these ramparts, the unofficial northern frontier until Hadrian's Wall started going up about a mile above it in AD 122. The forts were a vital communication centre too, so perhaps we shouldn't have been surprised when, in the autumn of 1972, the archaeologist Robin Birley cut a trench to drain off excess water from the south-west corner of the Vindolanda excavation site and unearthed the first evidence of a Roman treasure trove.

What was more surprising was how well some things had survived. About 2.3 metres into the soil, Birley struck a leather sandal that was in such good condition it was possible to read the maker's name. He discovered other fragments of leather and textiles, and there were realistic dreams of further finds. Here was a moment that would, for decades to come, inspire young people to become archaeologists, a Tutankhamun moment 50 years on. But then the northern rains swept in, and Birley got another taste of the terrible challenges the Romans had faced in this remote valley. He was forced to close up the site for the winter.

Birley had digging in his blood. His father was Eric Birley, who, in 1929, had bought the Chesterholm estate on which the Vindolanda forts continued to stand and had made some of the key discoveries that had shaped the way we view the

The road to Vindolanda.

Romans' early defence of northern Britain. But although his
work had occasionally revealed
a few coins and chips of pottery,
there wasn't much in the way
of personal or domestic possessions that would enable us,
some 2,000 years later, to bring
the ancient world to life.

His son's excavation resumed
in March 1973. There was more
leather footwear, a gold earring,
a bronze brooch, keys, hammers,
rope, purses, tools for stripping
hide, oyster shells, and bones

Robin Birley on site.

from oxen, pigs and ducks. These things in the soil were found
enmeshed within bracken, heather and straw, and further preserved by what appeared to be excreta. The Romans may have
regarded all these objects as rubbish, and there were signs of
attempted incineration. But of course their rubbish isn't our
rubbish. The waterlogged conditions of the soil, the matted
foliage that enveloped it, and the man-made barriers from
repeated building on the site provided ideal conditions for
preservation.

There was something else amongst the detritus: lists and
letters. These took the form of thin wooden writing tablets,
some a sliver no thicker than a millimetre, most about 2mm,
sliced from birch, oak and alder, a few folded over as one might
fold paper for an envelope. Most appeared to be written with
ink, though some were denser and had been hollowed out to
hold a coating of wax to be inscribed with a metal stylus; in
some cases the stylus had carved beneath the wax and had left
a permanent mark on the wood. In 1973, a total of 86 tablets
was recovered, made up of about 200 fragments, more than

half with visible writing. The largest measured 8 × 6cm, the size of a credit card.

The word 'tablet' may suggest something solid and brittle, but these finds were as limp as wet blotting paper. Some fragments were sent to Kew Gardens for analysis, others to the department of photography at Newcastle University, and almost all ended up at the research laboratory at the British Museum. Here it became apparent that the tablets had lived a charmed life underground: had their discovery been made even two centuries earlier, our primitive capacity for scientific preservation would have distinctly limited their chances of longevity. As it was, the tablets encountered not only highly skilled conservationists, but a novel dehydration process developed on waterlogged wood only a few months before in Copenhagen and Paris.

'The wood was reasonably soft and easily split if handled without care,' according to Susan Blackshaw, who first handled the Vindolanda tablets at the British Museum, in *Studies in Conservation* in April 1973. She noted that the excavators had told her that the writing on the tablets was clearly visible when freshly exposed at the dig, 'but that it faded rapidly upon exposure to light and the atmosphere.'

The tablets were photographed with infrared film, after which Blackshaw set about trying to make the writing as legible as possible. They were written in Latin, and possessed what one early report in the journal *Britannia* called 'a fair range of styles and hands', from the competent workaday script to a real attempt at calligraphy. It also noted, 'It would be difficult to overestimate the potential value of a significant quantity of written material in Latin from this time and place.'

When the tablets arrived at the British Museum they were still soggy. A combination of methylated spirit and ether was used to dehydrate the wood, a complex process involving almost four weeks of soaking, evaporation and flattening.

Splintered tablets were delicately treated with resin. The tablets were then re-photographed with infrared film, and, according to Susan Blackshaw, 'it was thus established that the traces of writing were clearer after the treatment, and that no loss of writing had occurred.'

The contents of two tablets were then released to the academic community. The first, pieced together from four separate fragments and written with tall and slim letterforms, was an account of food supplies, almost certainly items purchased for consumption by the Vindolanda troops. The list confounded a common belief that the Roman soldiers ate little meat, although we do not know whether this was a standard diet or a spread for a feast.

In translation, with guesswork included, the tablet read:

> ... of spices ... goat ... of salt ... young pig ... ham ... of corn ... venison ... for daily ... goat ... total [in denarii] 20 ... of emmer ... total ...

Writing in the ruins: Vindolanda in 2013.

The second tablet, in two fragments, was a private letter sent to a soldier at the fort:

> I have sent [?] you x pairs of socks and from Sattia [?] two pairs of sandals; and two pairs of underpants, two pairs of sandals . . .

> Greet my friends [?] . . .ndes, Elpis, Iu. . .enus. Tetricus and all your messmates; I pray that you and they may enjoy long life and the best of fortune.

The notes accompanying the publication of these letters by the Roman scholars A.K. Bowman, J.D. Thomas and R.P. Wright were laden with uncertainties about the writing, the words and the meaning, as if they were completing a cryptic crossword: 'If *r* and *m* are correct, however, we must have a vowel here and only *a* seems feasible. If *ram* is the right reading, we may well have a pluperfect ending . . . this would be an epistolary pluperfect with the meaning of the perfect.'

But they were just at the beginning of the task. The soldiers at Vindolanda fought many battles – against the hordes from Scotland above them and the rebels below, against the exposures of winter – but now their descendants faced another: to explain how fragile remnants of buried script may direct light upon a brutally enchanting past.

Still inviting: news of a birthday party circa AD 100.

In the years and decades that followed the first discovery, archaeologists have unearthed more than 1,000 letters and other accounts from Vindolanda, and there will be many more to come. The process has been slow and wet; every time a new trench is dug – a hard enough feat beneath the stone forts that were built upon the original wooden sites until the Romans departed Britain more than three centuries later – it floods. The stable environment that has preserved the tablets for almost 1900 years in perfect anaerobic conditions is stubbornly reluctant to give them up. But the sodden archaeologists have delivered to us our earliest letters. We now understand far more of life in Britain under the Romans than we did before 1972, and far more about what it was like to be a Roman in Britain.

The Vindolanda heritage site, the very spot where goat and young pig were once consumed in sandals, lies in a part of wild Northumberland that is most easily reached these days by fossil-fuelled chariots made in Swindon or Japan. There are other routes – a wind-cheating, two-mile walk from a station where the fast trains don't stop – but the lure of getting 'the authentic Roman experience' in early March would, certainly for most travellers from London and the south-east, be merrily traded for arrival by car. There is plenty of authentic visitor experience to be gained upon arrival – a meandering stroll down a valley through the original stone wells, bathhouses, latrines, barracks, granaries, officers' residence and headquarters building, all cleaned and secured and certainly vivid enough to bring the place alive in young minds.

The small museum at the foot of the valley, newly outfitted in 2012, reflects perfectly the spirit of Vindolanda, not least the fact that it has completely subsumed an earlier construction. This was once the nineteenth-century cottage of Chesterholm, the home of the Anglican clergyman Anthony Hedley, the first excavator of the forts. The displays of sandals, pots, spears and gemstones give way to the writing tablets in a tall, darkened, climate-controlled cabinet of wood and glass, and one approaches it with hushed reverence and excitement. The letters are increasingly lucid:

> Masclus to Cerialis his king, greeting. Please, my lord, give instructions as to what you want us to have done tomorrow. Are we to return with the standard to [the shrine at?] the crossroads all together or every other one [i.e. half] of us? . . . Farewell. My fellow-soldiers have no beer. Please order some to be sent.

> Octavius to his brother Candidus, greetings. The hundred pounds of sinew from Marinus – I will settle up . . . I have several times written to you that I have bought about five thousand modii [about a peck] of ears of grain, on account of which I need cash. Unless you send me some cash, at least five hundred denarii, the result will be that I shall lose what I have laid out as a deposit, about three hundred denarii, and I shall be embarrassed. So I ask you, send me some cash as soon as possible. The hides [of] which you write are at Cataractonium [Catterick, a tanning centre] . . . I would have already been to collect them except that I did not care to injure the animals while the roads are bad. *

At the side of the glass cabinet a film explains that this is just the beginning of the great discoveries; the excavations continue at a deeper level and in further fields, and the initial cleansing, photography and deciphering are no longer outsourced to Newcastle but conducted at labs onsite, a busy and excited cottage industry. On the other side of the cabinet Robin Birley has made a personal 'Top Tablets' selection of the letters, including the request for beer quoted above, and the detailed listing of troop numbers on one particular day.

---

* Octavius was an import-exporter; the sinew he mentions is believed to have been an important element in the building of catapults. The word 'brother' in these greetings should often be read as 'comrade'.

Hushed and revered: the Vindolanda Museum displays its treasures.

There is also an account of preparations for Saturnalia, a discussion of the value of hunting nets, an intelligence report on the strength of the opposing British tribes, and a letter about making friends on the frontier.

Many more tablets are to be found at the British Museum. Partly it is their history that charms us – the reckless disposing of the letter in AD 90 or 95, the glee upon discovery of the same letter in the age of the moon shot and mobile phone. Partly it is the simplicity and brevity of the letters themselves, and their relentless politeness, with so much of each one concerned with greetings and farewells. Partly it is the sense of efficiency they convey: the successful conquest and running of this vast Roman outpost depended on these tiny, delicate scraps.

And partly it is because we see ourselves on those tablets. We all still need warm clothes, hearty food, reassurances of health. And, as is the case in at least one letter, we still value bedspreads.

We do not know precisely how the soldiers at Vindolanda received their mail, but it does appear to be an ordered process orchestrated initially from Rome and then adapted to the spreading network of Roman roads in Britain. The primitive Northumberland postal service would have seen deliveries along the Stanegate road supplemented by personal messengers to and from London (in this sense the fort may have served as a central sorting office). Indeed, the Vindolanda network may have been one of the testing grounds for the new postal carrier service. A book called *The Antonine Itinerary* suggests that postal carriers would have had a detailed system of inns or stables on a network of roads where they could rest or change horses, and these 'posts' – the markers along any route that signified a resting place, storage place or a place to feed and maintain horses – gave the mail network its other name. The roads carried far more than mail, of course, but there is evidence that successive emperors ordered that military mail should take precedence over, say, the movement of clothing or cattle – an early example of express delivery.

However it travelled, we can imagine the anticipation, delight and relief experienced by the recipients of mail at Vindolanda, just as we can still locate the emotions felt by their families as the wooden tablets were folded over and trustingly dispatched. And it is worth considering that the letters that have been discovered, possibly purposely discarded 2,000 years ago, were not those held most dear; those may have perished in the possession of the owner and, of no value to looters, been left to rot. What value, for instance, would anyone place on a collection of birthday letters?* 'Clodius Super to his Cerialis greetings. Most willingly brother, just as you had wanted, I would have been present for your Lepidina's birth-

* See Chapter Fourteen.

day. At any rate . . . for you surely know that it pleases me most whenever we are together.'

Beyond the fact that he was a centurion, and once requested a large supply of cloaks and tunics for his slaves, Clodius Super is little known to us. But Flavius Cerialis is a frequent presence in these tablets. An equestrian prefect (local governing general) of the 9th cohort of Batavians, he was married to Sulpicia Lepidina, who also features regularly. His presence enables scholars to date the tablets to AD 97–104. There was much coming and going among his men across the frontier, and there appears to be a lenient attitude towards sick and compassionate leave. The upper crust of his troops, if not the entire cohort, also appear to be generally well fortified: their larder included not only the goat and young pig from the earlier account, but specifically also pig's trotters, roe deer, goose, garlic paste, pickling liquor, anise, fish sauce, thyme, caraway, cumin, beetroot, olives, beer and wine (alongside the staples – wheat, cereal, butter, barley, eggs and apples). Several letters reveal a fair supply of kitchen utensils and what is believed to be a recipe from Lepidina's kitchen (involving an early *mise-en-place* food arrangement involving a small dish, a cup and a tray).

We learn that the soldiers' wardrobe contains a large ensemble of clothes and sandals of all weights for all weathers (*gallicu-lae, abolla, tunicae cenatoriae* – a Gallic shoe, a thick cloak, a fine wool tunic), along with decorative fabrics, blankets and *cubito-ria* – an elegant evening ensemble. There is certainly an element of fashion consciousness: use of the term *de synthesi* indicates items of clothing that were part of a collection, items that could be worn either as separates or as a coordinating costume.

But having hosted a birthday party of one's own, what should one wear to Claudia Severa's?

Claudia Severa to her Lepidina, greetings. On the 3rd day before the Ides of September, sister, for the day of the celebration of my birthday, I give you a warm invitation to make sure that you come to us, to make the day more enjoyable for me by your arrival, if you are present. Give my greetings to your Cerialis. My Aelius and my little son send you their greetings. [In another's handwriting:] I shall expect you, sister. Farewell, sister, my dearest soul, as I hope to prosper, and hail.

This letter alone carries an undue weight of history. The bulk of it was written by a scribe, almost certainly a man. But the signature is by another hand, believed to be Claudia Severa herself, the earliest example of a woman's handwriting in the Roman world.

The letters are usually isolated items, and only occasionally – as with notes to Flavius Cerialis and Lepidina – do they appear to form part of a logical sequence. But they should generally be considered as part of an ongoing correspondence, and the visible hiccups in these exchanges (the chiding for failing to reply) are as much a part of letters in the first and second century as they are of our own.

Solemnis to Paris, his brother, very many greetings.* I want you to know that I am in very good health, as I hope you are in turn, you neglectful man, who have sent me not even one letter. But I think I am behaving in a more considerate fashion in writing to you . . . to you, brother . . . my messmate. Greet from me Diligens and Cogitatus and Corinthus . . . Farewell, dearest brother.

Chrauttius to Veldeius his brother and old messmate, very many greetings. And I ask you, brother Veldeius, – I am surprised that you have written nothing back to me for such a long time – whether you have heard anything from our elders or about . . . in which unit he is; and greet him from me in my words and Virilis

---

* Both Solemnis and Paris are believed to be slaves in a cohort of Batavians, one of the two principal units at Vindolanda in the period AD 85–130. The other was the Tungrian cohort.

the veterinary doctor. Ask him [Virilis] whether you may send me through one of our friends the pair of shears which he promised me in exchange for money. And I ask you, brother Virilis, to greet from me our [?] sister Thuttena. Write back to us [?] how Velbutena is [?]. It is my wish that you enjoy the best of fortune. Farewell. [The back of the letter carried instructions to deliver it to London.]*

The letters at Vindolanda – so valuable to us now – were not written with an eye on posterity, and no one handling them in, say, AD 105, would have thought for a moment about their future value. Their brevity, immediacy and mundanity may appear to us closer to mobile phone texts or tweets than full letters. And no one would claim they were beautiful pieces of writing, or instructive beyond their specific historical details. They are often charming, but they rarely convey anything of a philosophical nature. For that we need to go back to other excavations, to letters written on papyrus and rediscovered in the last three centuries, and to the undisputed first masters of the form.

---

* The number of question marks in this passage exposes the translator's dilemma. But the word 'translator' is in itself inadequate: a phalanx of historians, palaeographers and linguistic experts have pored over these texts in the past decades, analysing the smallest curvature on the faintest letterform, cross-referencing indistinct names and locations, and piecing together logical textual and physical combinations – the ultimate lexicologist's jigsaw. And then there is the problem of wider contextual interpretation, a task akin to reconstructing a forest from scattered bracken. It is scholarship for which the inexpert modern enthusiast can only be inestimably grateful.

Chapter Three

The Consolations of Cicero, Seneca and Pliny the Younger

Perhaps we should begin with the oldest letter that we have, fictional as it is. Homer's *Iliad*, probably written in the eighth century BC, contains a stirring passage in the sixth book in which a letter almost kills its bearer. King Proteus has been entertaining a new visitor, the handsome and virile warrior Bellerophon, and it is the fatal nature of these things that the king's wife Anteia falls in love with him. Bellerophon, however, is less than keen, and his virtue leads almost to his downfall. Anteia, livid at his rejection, informs her husband Proteus that he has tried to rape her, and Proteus leaps into action immediately by deciding that rather than killing Bellerophon himself, he should get Anteia's father to do it. So he writes bad things about Bellephron in a letter written on sealed tablets ('things that would destroy a man's soul', according to Homer), and commands Bellerophon to deliver the tablets to Anteia's father himself, the original turkey voting for Christmas.

Mythological madness follows, in which Anteia's father Iobates, king of Lycia, decides not to kill Bellerophon, but to send him a seemingly impossible mission to kill the fire-snorting Chimera, which he does with the aid of winged Pegasus, after which he must defeat two armies singlehandedly. He lives to tell the tale to Poseidon, who sends a flood. The story goes on.

In the real world, Greek letters were generally of less

consequence. Often, we find a simple thing: that many letters adopt a formality and mode of expression that we find instantly recognisable. Papyrus fragments and scrolls from 350 BC unearthed at a Herculaneum villa in 1752, at Arsinoe from 1877 and from rubbish mounds at Oxyrhynchus from 1897 (and at least 20 other locations close to the Nile) point to the sort of uniformity of style that we have come to expect from PowerPoint presentations. There is the regular opening – 'From A to B, greetings' – that we have seen employed by the Romans at Vindolanda, frequently extended according to circumstance. When writing to a person of seniority, perhaps a king, a writer would respectfully reverse the order to 'Demetrius the Fair, King of Cyrene, from Hippopapos, greetings.' There may be further information to aid identification and location: 'Antogonus, brother of Capedonus, horse breeder in Olympia, to Leodonus, teacher at Delphi, greetings.' The sign-off would usually be simple: 'Farewell' (usually abbreviated from 'I trust/pray that you fare well) or, too modern though it sounds, 'Best wishes'. (Although it is now used only informally, 'Best wishes' was primarily reserved for business letters.) Only those in the highest positions tended to ignore these pleasantries, a public declaration that they had more important things on their mind. Alexander the Great, for example, purposely only used them for his most trusted generals and statesmen, including Antipater and Phocion.

Where did the 'greetings' element come from? One explanation suggests it became popular in Athens after 425 BC, when the statesman Cleon used the word at the start of his account of an unexpected victory against the Spartans in the Peloponnesian War. The report was an official council document, but its celebratory tone was soon deemed suitable for the common letter, initially perhaps as a reminder of the victory. Before this – and this is the case of the earliest Greek letter that survives, an indistinct fifth-century inscription on lead from the Black Sea – there was no greeting at all, as if a piece of papyrus that had been delivered by fleet-footed messenger after a journey of many days was somehow part of an ongoing and open conversation, like an email.* But once it was established, the hello-goodbye template would barely alter in style through the centuries (though it wouldn't be until the sixteenth century that the spacious layout of a modern letter took shape; certainly papyrus was far too precious to experiment with attractive blank space).

The contents of the letters, composed in black carbon ink with reed pen, are also familiar. There are enquiries about the recipient's health, usually optimistic, followed with news of the sender's health, which is almost always buoyant. The ancient history scholar John Muir observes that when this practice was later adopted by letter-writers in Latin it was so commonplace that it was sometimes abbreviated as SVBEEQV: *si vales bene est, ego quidem valeo.*** The receipt of previous letters was then acknowledged, or perhaps a rebuke for the lack of them. Good wishes were sent to all members of the family, each by name, and often including pets.

The practice of letter-writing was itself the subject of study as early as the fourth century BC, or at least the subject of criticism. Theophrastus, categorising the character traits of the 'arrogant man', observes that 'when sending instructions by letter, he does not write "you would oblige me" but "I want this to happen" . . . and "make sure it is exactly as I said".' In the third century, the philosopher Ariston found another definition: 'When he has bought a slave, he does not bother to ask his name but just addresses him as "slave" . . . and writing a letter, he neither writes "Greetings" nor "Farewell" at the end.'

---

* If a letter was particularly urgent, the folded and sealed papyrus would sometimes be addressed 'To Antogonus – now'.
** 'If you're well, that's good – all's well with me.'

The Greek letters that survive – some 2,000 examples scattered around the world's great museums – have value beyond their immediate content. They shed some light on the prominent role played by educated women, and certainly refute the notion that all were invisible in public debate. (The literacy rate in Greek cities is believed to have been less than 50 per cent, and the figure was lower for women, but the illiterate often hired scribes to communicate for them.) The letters have also enabled scholars to track developments in Greek language and grammar.

Predictably, the letters we find most intriguing are not the commonplace (the majority) but the quirky, the ones that make us gasp at their audacity or absurdity. In the first century BC a letter from a man working away from his wife (whom he calls sister, a common convention), is both caring and nonchalantly heartless.

> Hilarion to his sister Alis, very many greetings – and to my respected Berous and Appolonarion. Know that we are still at this moment in Alexandria . . . I ask you and urge you, look after the child, and as soon as I receive my pay I will send it up to you. If by any chance you give birth and it is male, let it live; if it is female, get rid of it. You said to Aphrodisias, 'Don't forget me'. How can I forget you? I ask you therefore not to be anxious.

A letter from older to younger sisters carries a hectoring air:

> Apollonia and Eupous to their sisters Rasion and Demarion, greetings. If you are in good health, that is well. We ourselves are in good health too. You would do us a favour by lighting the lamp in the shrine and shaking out the cushions. Keep studying and do not worry about mother. For she is already enjoying good health. Expect our arrival. Farewell. And don't play in the courtyard but behave yourselves inside. Take care of Titoas and Shairos.

A testy letter from the third century AD, from an eager son at school to an unresponsive father, smothers its frustrations as best it can:

> To my respected father Arion, Thonis sends greetings. Most of all I say a prayer every day, praying to the ancestral gods of this land in which I am staying that I find you and all our family flourishing. Look, this is the fifth letter I have written and, except for one, you have not written to me, even about your being well, nor have you come to see me. Having promised me, 'I am coming', you didn't come so that you could find out whether the teacher was attending me or not . . . So make the effort to come to me quickly so he can teach me – as he is keen to do . . . Come quickly to me before he leaves for the upper territories. I send many greetings to all our family by name and to my friends. Goodbye my respected father, and I pray that you may fare well for many years along with my brothers (safe from the evil eye).
>
> Remember my pigeons.

But for all their attractions, and for all their familiar templates, most Greek letters fall short of the key attribute we expect from letters in the modern world: they do not greatly enrich the personal experience. They may be fascinating, but the personal letters are rarely of consequence. Public letters – many purposely artificial, using the letter form as a new way of performing elaborate flights of philosophy and reaching a wider audience – are often just unperformed speeches, the equivalent of the 'open letter' in our modern media; many New Testament epistles would clearly model themselves on this practice.

The Greeks loved the *idea* of the letter and its high ambitions; they loved its *epistolarity*. But what of its private role as a conveyance of intimacy? Almost all letters were written to be read aloud; even private letters were primarily dictated to a scribe, and read in a low voice when received. There are rare snippets of private idiosyncrasy in Socrates and Plato, but the majority of correspondences are free of private emotion, and their oratorical heritage lends them a showy formality.

So what is lacking that we might expect to find? The historian John Muir notes that of the 2,000 or so papyrus letters we have, there are very few – he counts twelve or thirteen – that concern themselves with bereavement. Of these only six have sympathy as their main purpose, and a disproportionate three were written by women. Thus one of the few reliable mainstays of letter-writing in an age of email – the condolence letter – is almost entirely absent, and there is no logical explanation. And why were there no love letters? One possibility is that almost all were destroyed by the parties involved. Another, more plausible, is that letters were not yet regarded as the proper medium for such things. Because so many Greek letters were those of effect (or carried violent or dramatic instruction, such as that brought by Bellerophon), they may not have been considered appropriate for authentic outpourings from the heart. Muir also sounds a word of caution – their world was not as much like ours as we might imagine. The greetings and farewells were one thing, but 'there may be a salutary warning against assuming that the many undoubtedly recognisable feelings and situations in the letters imply that we are meeting people . . . who had notions of individuality very like our own. The "otherness" of the ancient world is sometimes easy to forget.'

Individuality and authenticity – a letter that was both personal and informative – begin properly with the Romans, the first true letter-writers, and the first to establish the tradition of letters both as biographical source material and a literature to be gathered and enjoyed in its own right. The classical scholar Betty Radice has compared the ancient history of letters to a trip round a marble-floored museum, 'the

Greek statue stands aloof with his stylized enigmatic smile, while the Roman portrait bust is recognisably someone like ourselves, and its regular features speak for a single individual at a point of time'. To the modern reader, Latin letters tend to have another beneficial attribute over their Greek counterparts – their straightforwardness. They are intelligent without being flashy, direct rather than imaginative, unpretentious rather than conceited. If Greek letters are rooted in the theatre, Roman ones are rooted in the tavern.

The trail begins in the second half of the first century BC with more than 900 letters from Marcus Tullius Cicero. Cicero was the consummate statesman on a world stage at a time when the Roman Republic was in significant decline. His oratory – as a lawyer in court and in the senate – was allegedly stupendous, but it is his surviving letters that confirm his talents. His

Cicero at work: pompous perhaps, but never dull.

lifelong correspondence with his friend Atticus is boastful, playful and varied like no other correspondence before it, and its prolific and sequential nature enables us to build an unusually intimate biographical picture of a politician. In other letters he is compelling particularly because he is spontaneous, vulnerable and prone to hyperbolic excitement, and because his political success is fuelled by ambition, vanity and weakness. Cicero does not emerge as a particularly likeable character, but his letters have made him a valuable one: there were few figures with whom he did not communicate as Rome suffered paroxysms of decline in the decades before 45 BC, and no other collection of writing so illuminates this world. But Cicero performs another trick too, a grand epistolary deflection. His is the oldest substantive collection to show how the consummate politician flatters to deceive; his apparent confidences invariably advance his own ends and enhance his reputation.

The survival and popularity of Cicero's correspondence is due largely to the discovery of a long-lost collection by Petrarch in the cathedral in Verona in 1345, while a second haul almost 50 years later at Vercelli boosted the supply. Together, the letters made an immeasurable literary contribution to the formative years of the Renaissance; Cicero had laid bare the values of classical antiquity with enough detail to inspire its artistic and cultural reconstruction.

We empathise with his domestic travails (two divorces, the untimely death of his daughter Tullia), almost enough to forgive his pomposity. Virginia Woolf once noted that 'there is a bareness about an age that has neither letter-writers nor biographers', and it is Cicero who proves the point first. There is no doubt that Cicero knew the value of his correspondence: it was carefully edited before being copied, with an aim to present a man in firm control of grand public events; Tiro, his secretary, played at least some role in this. The worth of his letters to subsequent centuries has changed over time, but as a late-Victorian translator of Cicero's writing claims in an introduction to his letters, 'In every one of them he will doubtless rouse different feelings in different minds. But though he will still, as he did in his lifetime, excite vehement disapproval as well as strong admiration, he will never, I think, appear to anyone dull or uninteresting.'

In 2011, the Princeton classics professor Denis Feeney noted that while Cicero has always been popular, the last decade and a half has seen an even greater scholarly interest in his letters, 'as if our own scurrying e-communications have created a nostalgia for a time when busy people could write pages of well-turned prose as part of their regular intercourse'.*

Two examples provide vivid snapshots of his times and a glimpse of his mischievous style (Cicero claimed he was no more able to keep a witticism in his mouth than a hot coal). The first, to his friend M. Marius at Cumae, a city near Naples, was written in 55 BC from Rome. His friend had missed the opening of the new theatre named after the leader Pompey, and with it a nice display of animal-baiting and other revelry.

> If some bodily pain or weakness of health has prevented your coming to the games, I put it down to fortune rather than your own wisdom: but if you have made up your mind that these things which the rest of the world admires are only worthy of contempt, and, though your health would have allowed of it, you yet were unwilling to come, then I rejoice at both facts – that you were free from bodily pain, and that you had the sound sense to disdain what others causelessly admire.
>
> . . . On the whole, if you care to know, the games were most splendid, but not to your taste. I judge from my own . . . For what is the pleasure of a train of six hundred mules in the 'Clytem-

* 'Caesar's Body Shook', *London Review of Books*, 22 September 2011.

nestra', or three thousand bowls in the 'Trojan Horse', or gay-coloured armour of infantry and cavalry in some battle? These things roused the admiration of the vulgar; to you they would have brought no delight ... Why, again, should I suppose you to care about missing the athletes, since you disdained the gladiators? in which even Pompey himself confesses that he lost his trouble and his pains. There remain the two wild-beast hunts, lasting five days, magnificent – nobody denies it – and yet, what pleasure can it be to a man of refinement, when either a weak man is torn by an extremely powerful animal, or a splendid animal is transfixed by a hunting spear? ... The last day was that of the elephants, on which there was a great deal of astonish-

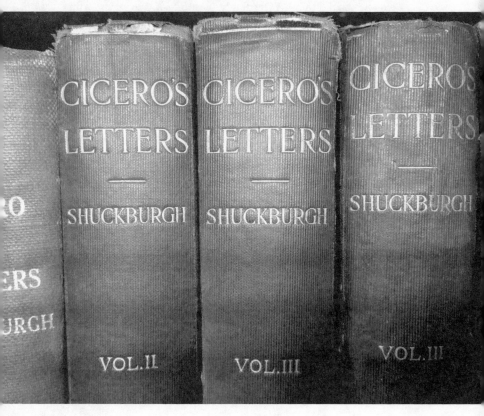

ment on the part of the vulgar crowd, but no pleasure whatever. Nay, there was even a certain feeling of compassion aroused by it, and a kind of belief created that that animal has something in common with mankind.

At the same theatre, just over a decade later, in 44 BC, the murder of Julius Caesar would take place by its entrance. But shortly before that, Caesar came to dinner at Cicero's house in the Bay of Naples, and Cicero wrote of the experience to Atticus in Rome in much the same way we might refer to overpowering visitors today.

> Well, I have no reason after all to repent my formidable guest! For he made himself exceedingly pleasant . . . He stayed with Philippus on the third day of the Saturnalia till one o'clock, without admitting anyone. He was engaged on his accounts, I think, with Balbus. Then he took a walk on the beach. After two he went to the bath . . . He was anointed: took his place at the table. He was under a course of emetics, and so ate and drank without scruple and as suited his taste. It was a very good dinner, and well served, and not only so, but 'Well-cooked, well-seasoned food, with rare discourse: A banquet in a word to cheer the heart.'
>
> Besides this, the staff were entertained in three rooms in a very liberal style. The freedmen of lower rank and the slaves had everything they could want. But the upper sort had a really recherché dinner. In fact, I showed that I was somebody. However, he is not a guest to whom one would say, 'Pray look me up again on your way back.' Once is enough.

A century later the Stoic philosopher, poet and dramatist Lucius Annaeus Seneca (Seneca the Younger) offered a different take on the Latin letter. Where Cicero was personal and scheming, Seneca was instructional and disarming, composing 124 letters telling us how to conduct our lives.* All written towards the end of his life to his writer friend Lucilius, they are a combination of philosophical treatise and spiritual guide, with the letter judged a suitable vehicle for the provision of robust and serious advice delivered in a digestible way.

The letters may be seen as the world's first correspondence course in self-improvement, or indeed – considered as a collection – the first self-help book. As would be expected, the complexity of his arguments increases as the course progresses. But the letters are also conversational, and it is largely assumed that the dialogue went both ways, though the contribution from Lucilius does not survive. They contain much modern thinking, and their range is vast: from musings on the respective merits of brawn and brains to old age and senility; from the value of travel to the despairs of drunkenness; from the futility of half-done deeds to the virtues of self-control; from specific ethical issues to broad matters of physics. They are never less than absorbing. Scholars have argued that Seneca is often playing *the role* of the philosopher, as concerned with the structure of his argument as he is with the treatise itself. But there is no doubt that he adores the challenges of the letter form, and his accessible, bite-sized approach has contributed to the continued popularity and influence of his work.

On travel, for example, Seneca advises against the hope of returning from a journey in a better frame of mind than the one we had on departure. He is evidently replying directly to a complaint of Lucilius:

---

* There were probably more; this is what survives. Seneca's letters were rather longer than the norm, ranging from 149 to 4,134 words, with an average of 955, or some 10 papyrus sheets joined on a roll. Philological scholars with time on their hands have calculated that a sheet of papyrus of approximately 9 x 11 inches contained an average of 87 words, and that a letter rarely exceeded 200 words. Cicero's letters ran from 22 to 2530 words, with an average of 295.

Do you suppose that you alone have had this experience? Are you surprised, as if it were a novelty, that after such long travel and so many changes of scene you have not been able to shake off the gloom and heaviness of your mind? You need a change of soul rather than a change of climate . . .

What pleasure is there in seeing new lands? Or in surveying cities and spots of interest? All your bustle is useless. Do you ask why such flight does not help you? It is because you flee along with yourself. You must lay aside the burdens of the mind; until you do this, no place will satisfy you.

It was one of the cornerstones of the Stoic tradition that an individual's well-being could be improved by clarity of being as well as clarity of thought, a distant forerunner of the unclutter movement. In 'Some Arguments in Favour of the Simple Life', Seneca considers 'how much we possess that is superfluous; and how easily we can make up our minds to do away with things whose loss, whenever it is necessary to part with them, we do not feel.'

There are a great many musings on aging and death, and several on suicide. In 'On the Proper Time to Slip the Cable' there can be no doubting Seneca's view of aging as a natural process to be welcomed, or his careful advocacy of euthanasia when the process is no longer bearable.

We have sailed past life, Lucilius, as if we were on a voyage . . . On this journey where time flies with the greatest speed, we put below the horizon first our boyhood and then our youth, and then the space which lies between young

Seneca, radical self-improver.

manhood and middle age and borders on both, and next, the best years of old age itself. Last of all, we begin to sight the general bourne of the race of man. Fools that we are, we believe this bourne to be a dangerous reef; but it is the harbour, where we must some day put in . . .

Every man ought to make his life acceptable to others besides himself, but his death to himself alone.

Dramatically, Seneca took his own advice. Implicated in the assassination plot against Nero, he was ordered to kill himself (which he did, although his bloodletting took slightly longer than expected, and his friends were encouraged to carry him into a warm bath to complete the ordeal).

His passing cleared the way for one more great letter-writer of the age. Pliny the Younger, born four years after Seneca's death, did more than anyone to establish the letter in its modern form, and to rescue it from the byways of inconsequence, pomposity, rhetoric and philosophical instruction. His letters from the turn of the first century, arguably the most buoyant period in the life of the Roman Empire, continue to entertain and inform the reader more than 2,000 years later.

Before the form is put back in the box by an early Christian world more interested in religious stricture and instruction, Pliny's letters serve as a beacon for what secular letters will become as they emerge in the twelfth century and beyond into the early Renaissance: commonplace, personal and indispensible.

We have 247 personal and professional letters from Pliny collected in nine books that were published in his lifetime, and 121 further official letters to and from the Emperor Trajan published posthumously. The letters were written when Pliny held some of the highest offices in the Treasury and legal profession, and many of his correspondents are also influential lawyers, philosophers and literary men, the majority of them in Rome, some also in his home town of Como (known then as Comum; Pliny owned several houses overlooking the lake). He writes generously and maintains consistent friendships, and his letters reflect wide cultural interests. His main value for us is historical, as a documenter of the times; that this is conveyed not through rhetoric, but through a natural, easy and expressive style renders it not only more accessible but also more authentic. The fact that he is often a vividly descriptive and aesthetic writer is a rare attribute for any Roman man of letters, and may explain why his correspondence has weathered so well.

Here are four letters. Written several decades apart, all are descriptive; the first (to a friend at Lake Como) is nostalgic and instructive, the second (about a failed dinner party) is woeful and comic, and the last two (about the eruption of Vesuvius) are famous and vital. All of them – in these translations from 1909 and the 1960s – could have been written yesterday, were it not for the fact that Lake Como is now a European fixture for the Hollywood A-list, and Pompeii a magnet for the international flip-flop brigade.

To Caninius Rufus (a former school friend and neighbour):

I wonder how our darling Comum is looking, and your lovely house outside the town, with its colonnade where it is always springtime, and the shady plane trees, the stream with its sparkling greenish water flowing into the lake below, and the drive over the smooth firm turf. Your baths which are full of sunshine all day, the dining rooms large and small, the bedrooms for night or the day's siesta – are you there and enjoying them all in turn, or are you as usual for ever being called away to look after your affairs? If you are there, you are a lucky man to be so happy; if not, you do no better than the rest of us.

But isn't it really time you handed over those tiresome petty duties to someone else and shut yourself up with your books in the peace and comfort of your retreat? This is what should be both business and pleasure, work and recreation, and should occupy your thoughts awake and asleep! Create something, perfect it to be yours for all time; for everything else you possess will fall to one or another master after you are dead, but this will never cease to be yours once it has come into being. I know the spirit and ability I am addressing, but you must try now to have the high opinion of yourself which the world will come to share if you do.

The following, to his friend Septicius Clarus (a leader of the Praetorian Guard at the beginning of the second century), carries a rebuke as delicious as the food it describes.

Oh you are a pretty fellow! You make an engagement to come to supper and then never appear. Justice shall be exacted: you shall reimburse me to the very last penny the expense I went to on your account; no small sum, let me tell you. I had prepared, you must know, a lettuce apiece, three snails, two eggs, and a barley cake, with some sweet wine [chilled with] snow (the snow most certainly I shall charge to your account, as a rarity that will not keep). Olives, beetroot, gourds, onions, and a thousand other dainties equally sumptuous. You should likewise have been entertained either with an interlude, the rehearsal of a poem, or a piece of music, whichever you preferred; or (such was my liberality) with all three. But the oysters, sows'-bellies, sea-urchins, and dancers from Cadiz of a certain _____ I know not who, were, it seems, more to your taste. You shall give satisfaction; how, shall at present be a secret.

And finally this, to the historian Tacitus, written some 20 years after the eruption of Vesuvius and the destruction of

Pompeii and Herculaneum in AD 79. Pliny was 17 at the time, and his eye-witness account (described in two letters, here slightly edited) carries its loaded portent and scorching intensity to the present day. Tacitus had requested a description of the death of Pliny's uncle, the writer, philosopher and naval commander who had been Pliny's mentor.

My uncle was stationed at Misenum, in active command of the fleet. On 24 August, in the early afternoon, my mother drew his attention to a cloud of unusual size and appearance. He had been out in the sun, had taken a cold bath, and lunched while lying down, and was then working at his books. He called for his shoes and climbed up to a place which would give him the best view of the phenomenon. It was not clear at that distance from which mountain the cloud was rising (it was afterwards known to be Vesuvius); its general appearance can be best expressed as being like an umbrella pine, for it rose to a great height on a sort of trunk and then split off into branches, I imagine because it was thrust upwards by the first blast and then left unsupported as the pressure subsided, or else it was borne down by its own weight so that it spread out and gradually dispersed. Sometimes it looked white, sometimes blotched and dirty, according to the amount of soil and ashes it carried with it. My uncle's scholarly acumen saw at once that it was important enough for a closer inspection, and he ordered a boat to be made ready, telling me I could come with him if I wished. I replied that I preferred to go on with my studies, and as it happened he had himself given me some writing to do.

As he was leaving the house, he was handed a message from Rectina, wife of Tascius whose house was at the foot of the mountain, so that escape was impossible except by boat. She was terrified by the danger threatening her and implored him to rescue her from her fate. He changed his plans, and what he had begun in a spirit of inquiry he completed as a hero. He gave orders for the warships (5) to be launched and went on board himself with the intention of bringing help to many more people besides Rectina, for this lovely stretch of coast was thickly populated. He hurried to the place which everyone else was hastily leaving, steering his course straight for the danger zone. He was entirely fearless, describing each new movement and phase of the portent to be noted down exactly as he observed them. Ashes were already falling, hotter and thicker as the ships drew near, followed by bits of pumice and blackened stones, charred and cracked by the flames: then suddenly they were in shallow water, and the shore was blocked by the debris from the mountain. For a moment my uncle wondered whether to turn back, but when the helmsman advised this he refused, telling him that Fortune favoured the brave. [The] wind was of course full in my uncle's favour, and he was able to bring his ship in.

Meanwhile on Mount Vesuvius broad sheets of fire and leaping flames blazed at several points, their bright glare emphasized by the darkness of night. My uncle tried to allay the fears of his companions by repeatedly declaring that these were nothing but bonfires left by the peasants in their terror, or else empty houses on fire in the districts they had abandoned. Then he went to rest and certainly slept, for as he was a stout man his breathing was rather loud and heavy and could be heard by people coming and going outside his door. By this time the courtyard giving access to his room was full of ashes mixed with pumice-stones, so that its level had risen, and if he had stayed in the room any longer he would never have got out. He was wakened, came out and joined Pomponianus and the rest of the household who had sat up all night. They debated whether to stay indoors or take their chance in the open, for the buildings were now shaking with violent shocks, and seemed to be swaying to and fro, as if they were torn from their foundations. Outside on the other hand, there was the danger of falling pumice-stones, even though these were light and porous; however, after comparing the risks they chose the latter ... As a protection against falling objects they put pillows on their heads tied down with cloths.

Elsewhere there was daylight by this time, but they were still in darkness, blacker and denser than any ordinary night, which they relieved by lighting torches and various kinds of lamp. My uncle decided to go down to the shore and investigate on the spot the possibility of any escape by sea, but he found the waves still wild and dangerous. A sheet was spread on the ground for him to lie down, and he repeatedly asked for cold water to drink. Then the flames and smell of sulphur which gave warning of the approaching fire drove the others to take flight and roused him to stand up. He stood leaning on two slaves and then suddenly collapsed, I imagine because the dense fumes choked his breathing by blocking his windpipe which was constitutionally weak and narrow and often inflamed. When daylight returned on the 26th – two days after the last day he had seen – his body was found intact and uninjured, still fully clothed and looking more like sleep than death.

A few days later, Pliny wrote to Tacitus again, amplifying his account. He expected the historian 'to select what best suits your purpose, for there is a great difference between a letter to a friend and history written for all to read.' But it is only the letter to a friend that survives.

After my uncle's departure I spent the rest of the day with my books, as this was my reason for staying behind. Then I took a bath, dined, and then dozed fitfully for a while. For several days past there had been earth tremors which were not particularly alarming because they are frequent in Campania: but that night the shocks were so violent that everything felt as if it were not only shaken but overturned. My mother hurried into my room and found me already getting up to wake her if she were still

'Sometimes it looked white, sometimes blotched and dirty':
Abraham Pether reinterprets Pliny.

asleep. We sat down in the forecourt of the house, between the buildings and the sea close by. I don't know whether I should call this courage or folly on my part (I was only seventeen at the time) but I called for a volume of Livy and went on reading as if I had nothing else to do . . .

By now it was dawn, but the light was still dim and faint. The buildings round us were already tottering, and the open space we were in was too small for us not to be in real and imminent danger if the house collapsed. This finally decided us to leave the town. We were followed by a panic-stricken mob of people wanting to act on someone else's decision in preference to their own (a point in which fear looks like prudence), who hurried us on our way by pressing hard behind in a dense crowd. Once beyond the buildings we stopped, and there we had some extraordinary experiences which thoroughly alarmed us. The carriages we had ordered to be brought out began to run in different directions though the ground was quite level, and would not remain stationary even when wedged with stones. We also saw the sea sucked away and apparently forced back by the earth-quake: at any rate it receded from the shore so that quantities of sea creatures were left stranded on dry sand. On the landward side a fearful black cloud was rent by forked and quivering bursts of flame, and parted to reveal great tongues of fire, like flashes of lightning magnified in size ...

Soon afterwards the cloud sank down to earth and covered the sea; it had already blotted out Capri and hidden the promontory of Misenum from sight. Then my mother implored, entreated and commanded me to escape the best I could – a young man might escape, whereas she was old and slow and could die in peace as long as she had not been the cause of my death too. I refused to save myself without her, and grasping her hand forced her to quicken her pace. She gave in reluctantly, blam-ing herself for delaying me. Ashes were already falling, not as yet very thickly. I looked round: a dense black cloud was coming up behind us, spreading over the earth like a flood. Let us leave the road while we can still see, I said, 'or we shall be knocked down and trampled underfoot in the dark by the crowd behind.' We had scarcely sat down to rest when darkness fell, not the dark of a moonless or cloudy night, but as if the lamp had been put out in a closed room. You could hear the shrieks of women, the wailing of infants, and the shouting of men; some were calling their parents, others their children or their wives, trying to rec-ognize them by their voices. People bewailed their own fate or that of their relatives, and there were some who prayed for death in their terror of dying. Many besought the aid of the gods, but still more imagined there were no gods left, and that the universe was plunged into eternal darkness for evermore ... I could boast that not a groan or cry of fear escaped me in these perils, had I not derived some poor consolation in my mortal lot from the belief that the whole world was dying with me and I with it.

At last the darkness thinned and dispersed into smoke or cloud; then there was genuine daylight, and the sun actually shone out, but yellowish as it is during an eclipse. We were terrified to see everything changed, buried deep in ashes like snowdrifts. We returned to Misenum where we attended to our physical needs as best we could, and then spent an anxious night alternating between hope and fear. Fear predominated, for the earthquakes went on, and several hysterical individuals made their own and other people's calamities seem ludicrous in comparison with their frightful predictions. But even then, in spite of the dangers we had been through, and were still expecting, my mother and I had still no intention of leaving until we had news of my uncle.

Of course these details are not important enough for history, and you will read them without any idea of recording them; if they seem scarcely worth putting in a letter, you have only yourself to blame for asking them.

'Of course these details are not important enough for history,' he wrote. In fact, Pliny's accounts are the only contemporary document of the eruption, preserving in words what the volcano preserved beneath ash. Pliny thought the memorial was to his brave uncle – who snored as Vesuvius roared – but history had grander intentions. He considered the details of his letters superfluous, the way letter-writers often do at the time of writing, but we now may argue against this.

Letters from Abroad

14232134 SIGNALMAN CHRIS BARKER
H.C., BASE DEPOT, ROYAL SIGNALS,
MIDDLE EAST FORCES

Somewhere in North Africa
5th September 1943

Dear Bessie,

Since Auld Acquaintance should not be forgot, and I have had
a letter to Nick and yourself on my conscience for some time,
I now commence some slight account of my movements since
arrival here some five months ago, and one or two other comments which will edify, amuse or annoy you according to the
Britishers' war-time diet or whatever you had for breakfast.

The 'security' advice of a Signals officer that in our travels we
should keep our bowels open and our mouths shut seemed
not to have been heard by the populace en route for our port
of disembarkation. The behaviour of the troops on board ship
was bad. They shouted, shoved, swore and stole to their black
hearts' content. I lost about a dozen items of kit, and was able
to replace most of it from the odds left about on the disembarkation date by chaps who had first pinched for the fine fun
of it. I cannot include my razor in this lot. That was removed
from the ledge I had placed it on, as I turned to get a towel to
wipe it.

A letter to Signalman Barker tries to get through.

Chris Barker, 29, was born and grew up in Holloway, north London. He left school at 14 to join the Post Office, working initially as a messenger boy and then a counter clerk, becoming an active trade union member. His training as a teleprinter operator, a 'reserved' occupation, kept him out of the war until the end of 1942, and after army training in Yorkshire he enlisted as a keyboard operator with Middle East Command. After a long sea voyage via the Cape, he arrived in Cairo in May 1943.

Four months later, serving with the Royal Corps of Signals in Tobruk, on the Libyan coast, he was looking after communications for the RAF in the southern Mediterranean. With time on his hands, he began writing to friends he missed back home.

His letter to Bessie Moore and her boyfriend Nick was just one amongst many (Chris had worked with Bessie at the Post Office). She was now working at the Foreign Office, where her training in Morse code was employed to translate intercepted German radio messages. She was 30 when their correspondence began. She remained in London throughout the war.

Our disembarkation arrangements were perfect and after a not uncomfortable rail journey we were brought to the above address. I had expected to be parked on a pile of sand, and told it was 'home', but the Depot is a very pleasant place, surrounded by pine and eucalyptus trees. The water comes from a tap, and one sits down to meals. There is a Church Hut, quiet and fly-free, an Army Educational Corps hut, where are excellent books, a good NAAFI and a Cinema. A little further away is a tent, run by voluntary labour, where refreshments are served (not thrown at one) at reasonable prices, and there is a lounge, library, writing room, games-room, and Open Air Theatre, where a free film show takes place weekly, also a Concert. There is a lecture one night, bridge and whist another, and a more 'highbrow' musical evening another night.

Directly I arrived, my brother applied for my posting to his units, and after two months of base life I started on the wearying but interesting journey to him. I met him after a separation of 26 months, and had a fine time talking of home and all that had happened there – the rows and the rejoicing – and in the evening walked through the sandy vineyard to swim in the blue waters.

Since leaving the [Post Office] Counter School and joining the Army, a period of twelve years, I had little real rest. I was either actually on the counter or doing some Union work. If I did relax, it was not for long and I was conscious of being 'guilty'. Since joining (or being joined to) H.M. Forces, I have had a great deal of leisure, and I have spent most of it reading and writing.

Since I have decided to make this my last sheet I had better drop a few remarks on the people here. The Egyptians, nominally neutral, are hostile, as are most people without 'independence'. The Arabs, poor, unhealthy, ignorant, need to be seen to be believed. Metropolitan life turns them into pests, but away from town they are not bad people. They work 12 hours for the shilling; only 25% of them can read and write, 170,000 have only one eye and they die about 40.

Oh, the Pyramids; yes, I have seen them, sat on them, and thought what a gigantic case for Trade Unionism they present. How many unwilling slaves died in the colossal toil involved in erecting these edifices. And how insignificant the erection compared with Nature's own hills and mountains?

I visited the Cairo Zoo, happily in the company of two young Egyptians who were being educated at the American mission. They made the day a success. The cruelty of having a polar bear (noble creature) in this climate, and the effort to console him with a 10 second cold water dip!

Excuse the writing, and confusion of this effort. But it's me, alright. I hope you are O.K. Nick, it's a long way from our Lantern Lecture on Sunny Spain at Kingsway Hall!

All the best Bessie.

Chris

Chapter Four

Love in Its Earliest Forms

You will not believe what a longing for you possesses me.

Around AD 102, more than 20 years after Vesuvius, Pliny was writing to his third wife Calpurnia.

> The chief cause of this is my love; and then we have not grown used to be apart. So it comes to pass that I lie awake a great part of the night, thinking of you; and that by day, when the hours return at which I was wont to visit you, my feet take me, as it is so truly said, to your chamber, but not finding you there I return, sick and sad at heart, like an excluded lover.

Calpurnia had been unwell; Pliny had been away on legal business. In another letter he wrote:

> You say that you are feeling my absence very much, and your only comfort when I am not there is to hold my writings in your hand and often put them in my place by your side. I like to think that you miss me and find relief in this sort of consolation. I, too, am always reading your letters, and returning to them again and again as if they were new to me – but this only fans the fire of my longing for you. If your letters are so dear to me, you can imagine how I delight in your company; do write as often as you can, although you give me pleasure mingled with pain.

The letters were an addiction now, reinforcing the couple's devotion just as they confirmed their absence. 'Write to me every day, and even twice a day: I shall be more easy, at least while I am reading your letters, though when I have read them, I shall immediately feel my fears again.'

How can the modern reader not be stirred by these out-pourings? But Pliny's letters (alas we don't have Calpurnia's) are valuable for another reason beyond their intimacy. They're almost all we've got. Beyond them, as we've seen, there's little evidence that epistolary love existed at all in the ancient Roman world.

But there is one other exception, discovered by chance in the Ambrosian Library in Milan in the nineteenth century. Cardinal Angelo Mai was something of an expert in the palimpsest – a scroll or document that has been scrubbed clean of its original inscriptions to be used again. In 1815 he came across something exciting written beneath something boring: the Acts of the first Council of Chalcedon of 451 concealed the second-century correspondence between leading orator and teacher Marcus Cornelius Fronto and a youthful Marcus Aurelius written some twenty years before he would become Roman emperor.

Three years later, the cardinal discovered further letters beneath the same Council document, this time in the Vatican Library. Both finds created an air of expectation. Could this be an early nineteenth-century revelation of the formative years of one of ancient Rome's great emperors? Absolutely, but not in the way anyone expected. In fact, when Cardinal Mai published his new collection the response was one of widespread disappointment. The letters appeared to be primarily about Latin prose style. The first full English translation appeared only in 1919, and again the response was muted. But hidden in plain view were many expressions of love and physical inti-macy that may have struck even the most liberal of Georgian readers as a tad excessive; Mai had found a stash of something approaching imperial pornography, a rare documentary exam-ple of boy meets boy, or, more accurately, boys.

*Marcus Aurelius, lovelorn
and erotic.*

In recent years an even stronger theory of infatuation between Fronto and Marcus Aurelius has been advanced, culminating in 2006 with the publication of *Marcus Aurelius in Love*, edited and translated by Amy Richlin. Richlin is in no doubt about their deep mutual affection, and wonders how deep this went. She suggests that the 'disappointed' Victorian reaction to the letters may suggest that their intimacies were judged to be in bad taste, and that it upset the traditional view of Marcus Aurelius as a saintly hero. But she finds it intriguing that even in the later periods, the letters were seldom analysed for their erotic qualities, nor regularly examined by students of gay history as a fine epistolary exemplar of homosexual love.

The letters between Marcus Aurelius and Fronto track the rise and fall of a courtship from about AD 139, when Aurelius was in his late teens and his teacher in his late thirties, until about AD 148. The heart of their correspondence is ablaze with passion. 'I am dying so for love of you,' Aurelius writes, eliciting the response from his tutor, 'You have made me dazed and thunderstruck by your burning love.'

We do not know how often they met for tutelage, although it is clear that the intervals were, for both of them, rather too long. Perhaps it was merely their minds that coalesced so fruitfully and willingly – Aurelius enraptured by his master's grasp on rhetoric, Fronto ensnared by his pupil's sparkling potential – but their letters speak of more than just deep intellectual mingling: the mind of the solitary writer wanders to other, sometimes unattainable, possibilities. It could also be that the letters were a form of erotic rhetorical art in themselves, a seductive bit of homework:

> How can I suffer when you're in pain, especially when you're in pain on account of me? Shouldn't I want to beat myself up and subject myself to all kinds of unpleasant experiences? After all, who else gave you that pain in your knee, which you write got worse last night . . . So what am I supposed to do, when I don't see you and I'm tormented by such anguish?

This kissing and thunderstriking aside, letters of longing are not much to be found in late antiquity, nor in the origins of the Christian or Byzantine worlds, nor indeed during the whole of the European Dark Ages, something we may blame on a collapse in literacy and the rise of the Church with more doctrinal and domineering affairs on its mind. The heart could freeze in such a period. There is devotion in Paul's letters in the New Testament, of course, and personal messages scattered through 1,000 years of official communications, but a search for intimacy and passion will not be fruitful until one reaches what can only be described as the reinvention of romantic love in the twelfth century, when we encounter the epistolary delights of one of the greatest true-love romances of any age.

That the desperate story of Abelard and Heloise still smoulders more than 800 years after its enactment is due entirely to the existence of letters and the interpretation one places upon them – be it celebratory humanist or condemnatory moralist. The saga provides the fullest and earliest example of what happens when unbridled sexual desire meets

Chaste as angels: Abelard and Heloise keep their secrets at Père Lachaise.

a suffocating religious society not altogether keen on such things, a raw and rare combination of doctrinal pedagoguery and cassock-ripping salaciousness.

The story begins around 1132, when Pierre Abelard, early fifties, a philosopher-monk in exile in Brittany, writes the story of his life. Abelard's autobiography is in the form of a letter to an unnamed friend, and takes on what will become a familiar form, a consolation letter – *Historia Calamitatum* – designed to make the recipient feel better about his own plight by learning of the far worse fate of another. Within it, as part of a full and grander Latin narrative about his life's travails, we learn of his involvement with a highly literate and intellectually attractive woman he once used to tutor, another weighted master-pupil relationship that, for all its pledges of lifelong devotion, has embedded within it the seeds of its own demise.

Abelard was one of medieval Europe's great iconoclasts. Famous for his originality of thought and quick-witted argument, and never doubting his own abilities or convictions, he was as sure of his appeal to women as he was of his skills as a commentator on Ezekiel ('I had youth and exceptional good looks as well as my great reputation to recommend me').* His optimism was well placed. Having seen a young woman (believed to be at least 17, probably older) living in Paris, possessed of an outstanding education and looks 'that did not rank lowest', he set upon seducing her by impressing her uncle and guardian Fulbert (a canon at Notre Dame Cathedral), and successfully enrolling her as his protégé. 'Need I say more?' Abelard asks his unnamed correspondent. 'With our lessons as our pretext we abandoned ourselves entirely to love.' There followed 'more kissing than teaching' and hands that 'strayed oftener to her bosom than the pages'. Indeed, Heloise seemed to receive very little formal teaching at all, as 'our desires left no stage of love-making untried, and if love could devise something new, we welcomed it'.

As their nocturnal passion endured, so Abelard found his teaching beginning to suffer. He became bored with his other duties, and his lectures became uninspired. And he never failed to be amazed at how everyone apart from Heloise's uncle had a fairly good idea of what was going on. Abelard quoted St Jerome in his letter to Sabinian: 'We are always the last to learn of evil in our own home, and the faults of our wife and children may be the talk of the town but do not reach our ears.'

But when he did find out, Fulbert, not an entirely indulgent guardian (he had previously told Abelard that he was permitted to hit Heloise with force if she didn't apply herself), was not wholly happy at the way Heloise *had* applied herself. The lovers flee his anger, Heloise finds she is pregnant,

---

* The translations of his autobiography and the subsequent letters are by Betty Radice, Penguin Classics, 1974.

and the two agree on a secret marriage, which initially seems to please Fulbert. A son is born named Astrolabe. But when Fulbert decides to make the marriage common knowledge, it is Abelard – shamed by his actions – who breaks off their relationship, sends Heloise to a convent and Astrolabe to his sister. And that should have been that, were it not for a fuming Fulbert, who sees his niece abandoned and her life ruined. So Fulbert and his friends hatch a plan.

As Abelard describes it, 'one night as I slept peacefully in an inner room in my lodgings, they bribed one of my servants to admit them and there took cruel vengeance on me of such appalling barbarity as to shock the whole world; they cut off the parts of my body whereby I had committed the wrong of which they complained.'

Thus mutilated, Abelard takes up holy orders and devotes himself to the love of God and the scriptures. But he was a questioning soul, and he did not endear himself to his peers by exposing what he saw as the many inconsistencies in Christian teaching. He wrote much in favour of rational understanding, and publicly – by anatomical necessity – he renounced the pleasures of the flesh. But when, nine years after his castration, his epistolary confession fell into the hands of Heloise in her convent at St Argenteuil (how, we don't know – it could be that Abelard sent her a copy), he again became ensnared with his former lover.*

Heloise disagreed with some of the details in Abelard's account to his friend, and was wholly dismayed at his previous silence, but it was clear she was still devoted to him. More to him than God, indeed:

* There has been some academic discussion that the unnamed correspondent to whom Abelard sends his confession was a creation of Abelard's making, a device to focus his attention and garner some sympathy. There is also a theory that suggests that all the correspondence between the lovers was consciously manufactured between the two, or even later invented by another writer, but the authenticity of the early letters at least is generally accepted.

Even during the celebration of the Mass, when our prayers should be purest, lewd visions of the pleasures we shared take such a hold upon my unhappy soul that my thoughts are on their wantonness instead of on my own prayers. Everything we did, and also the times and places, are stamped on my heart along with your image, so that I live through it all again with you. Even in sleep I have no respite. Sometimes my thoughts are betrayed in the movement of my body, or they break out in an unguarded word.

Heloise is convinced that her life has been wrecked, and is certain she has suffered more than Abelard. He has found redemption in faith; she feels only shame at her failure to do so.

Where God may seem to you an adversary he has himself proved himself kind: like an honest doctor who does not shrink from giving pain if it will bring about a cure. But for me, youth and passion and experience of pleasures which were so delightful intensify the torments of the flesh and longings of desire, and the assault is the more overwhelming as the nature they attack is the weaker.

Abelard's rational response to her outpouring is subdued, and far more measured than she was asking for. He offers spiritual and religious assistance, and trusts that she will run her convent well. But he has abandoned all sexual desire for her, and it is not just his castration that has made this switch for him. He now regards libido as degrading, and views his nights with her as offering only 'wretched, obscene pleasures'. He believes he often forced his lust upon her unwillingly, and is now grateful for his reduced state, regarding it as 'wholly just and merciful'.

for me to be reduced in that part of my body which was the seat of lust and sole reason for those desires ... in order that this member justly be punished for all its wrongdoing in us, expiate the sins committed for its amusement, and cut me off from the slough of filth in which I had been wholly immersed in mind as in body. Only thus could I become more fit to approach the holy altars.

Heloise reluctantly appears to accept these arguments, or is at least defeated by their force. The couple's letters end on philosophical rather than intimate concerns, the so-called 'Letters of Direction', although the chiming of their minds appears still to form an irrevocable bond.

But the story does not end there. In the early 1970s, a German ecclesiastical scholar named Ewald Koensgen published a thesis in Bonn describing a series of love letters written on wax tablets that had originally been published in an anthology compiled by the fifteenth-century monk Johannes de Vepria. The writers of the letters were unknown, but Koensgen had a hunch – little more – that they might be the original letters of Abelard and Heloise written to each other in Paris before things went wrong. His hunch had become a little stronger by 1974 when he published *Epistolae duorum amantium. Briefe Abaelards und Heloises?*, but the slim book created little noise. There was more of a controversy in 1999, when Constant J. Mews, a professor at Monash University in Melbourne, published the letters under the unequivocal title *The Lost Love Letters of Heloise and Abelard*, and there was yet more commotion when the Latin letters appeared in a French translation in 2005. The debate still enflames medieval scholarly debate: are the letters genuine? If so, are they the genuine letters of Abelard and Heloise?*

Certainly there were letters between the two at the height of their passions. In his autobiography, Abelard reasoned that in their earliest days together, even when separated, 'we could

---

* Forged letters were not unknown at this time, the most famous being a letter purportedly from Prester John in 1165 in which he positioned himself as a mythical king and detailed fantastical creatures in Central Asia. But the motivation behind the possibly fake letters of Abelard and Heloise remains unclear, beyond mere titillation or a desire to re-expose hypocrisy and scandal within the Church.

enjoy each other's presence by exchange of written messages in which we could speak more openly than in person'. The more Professor Mews studied and translated the letters, the more he had become convinced of the similarities in grammar and language between the established letters and the later discoveries. When he examined their context within the mores and other manuscripts of twelfth-century France he found only further confirmations. The 113 letters range considerably in length from three or four lines to more than 600 words, and from incomplete snippets of prose to strictly metered long passages of verse. They speak of a constancy of love found in faithfulness, and there is a repeated mingling of human love, spiritual love and the love of God. Many seem to exist quite independently of any others, as if written into the wind with no expectation of consequential reply.

> WOMAN: To one loved thus far and always to be loved: with all her being and feeling, good health, joy, and growth in all that is beneficial and honourable ... Farewell, farewell, and fare well for as long as the kingdom of God is seen to endure.

> MAN: To his most precious jewel, ever radiant with its natural splendour, he purest gold: may he surround and fittingly set that same jewel in a joyful embrace ... Farewell, you who make me fare well.*

The lapidary cloying never lets up even in longer examples, and remains rather infuriatingly vague. (She: 'Farewell, sweetest. I am wholly with you, or to speak more truly I am wholly within you.' He: 'To the inexhaustible vessel of all his sweetness ...' She: 'Since you are the son of true sweetness ...') But the physicality of their relationship does emerge gradually,

---

* Mews and his colleague Neville Chiavaroli uphold Ewald Koensgen's tradition of crediting the correspondents merely with male/female monikers rather than definite names.

albeit in a more muted form than we are used to from the fantasy-in-the-pews of the later letters (Man: 'My spirit itself is shaken by joyful trembling, and my body is transformed into a new manner and posture.') And then, by Letter 26, off they go into a language of feverish floridness, an ardour we surely recognise from our famous lovers:

> MAN: How fertile with delight is your breast, how you shine with untouched beauty, body so full of moisture, indescribable scent of yours! Reveal what is hidden, uncover what you keep concealed, let that whole fountain of your most abundant sweetness bubble forth ... Hour by hour I am bound closer to you, just like fire devouring wood.

The 'new' letters, genuine or not, share one more thing with their established counterparts: nothing runs them close for forthright entertainment.

The Fathers of the Church did not shirk from letter-writing in the long period between Pliny the Younger and Heloise, but neither did they sparkle with the possibilities of the form. Yet for about a thousand years, theological letters are all we have. Literacy was not encouraged among the populace, and in the shadow of the Church their views were deemed inconsequential. An oral tradition largely took the place of a textual one. Only the wealthy could employ messengers, and writing ability and materials were almost exclusively the domain of scribes and their ecclesiastical employers. Moreover, what else of worth could occupy a lay person's thoughts beyond strict doctrine?

The letters that we do have constitute an uninspiring selection. Their saintly authors were duty bound; they were literate; their letters were more likely than others to be preserved (we are not very aware of royal correspondence until much later). The ecclesiastical choice of greetings and farewells relied much on the practices of late antiquity, but there the comparison ended; they were not concerned with worldly philosophy or self-improvement, and not for them the barefaced political manoeuvrings of Cicero or the advice on travel or modesty from Seneca. They were concerned predominantly with ecclesiastical matters, as one would expect, a righteous path with few diversions.

We have rather a lot of them to prove the case: about 240 letters survive from Gregory of Nazianzus spanning much of the fourth century, 360 letters of St Basil in the same period, some 2,000 brief notes from Isidore of Pelusium, and more than 200 from Theodoret of Cyrus from the fifth century. You may prefer death to the lingering torture of reading them.

So it is not surprising that the physical candour and the life-as-she-is-suffered quality of Abelard and Heloise still burns. Nor that their letters have entered our culture, one far removed from whispering cloisters. There is a grand poetic memorial by Alexander Pope, whose *Eloisa to Abelard* (1717) made our heroine long for what she calls the 'Eternal sunshine of the spotless mind!' (But all in vain, for 'Soon as thy letters trembling I unclose / That well-known name awakens all my woes.') This later faced lyrical competition from the opening of Cole Porter's 'Just One of Those Things': 'As Abelard said to Heloise / Don't forget to drop a line to me please.'

Always ripe for oils, the saga is depicted in many forms in many galleries, most plaintively perhaps in 'Lady Reading the Letters of Heloise and Abelard' by Auguste Bernard d'Agesci (c. 1780) at the Art Institute, Chicago (the Lady in question appearing so affected by what she has just read that her dress

Just too much: a state of undress brought on by reading Abelard and Heloise in this late-18th century portrait by Auguste Bernard d'Agesci.

has slid revealingly from her shoulders). At the cinema the couple feature as puppets in the Charlie Kaufman scripted *Being John Malkovich. Eternal Sunshine of the Spotless Mind* also became a Kaufman screenplay for Jim Carrey and Kate Winslet. Many television viewers first heard of the letters when they featured in an episode of *The Sopranos.*

When the story is retold for the modern audience it often comes with a certain amount of studied guesswork written as enlivening narrative, as in James Burge's *Heloise & Abelard* (2003), which envisages the heroine writing her first reply to Abelard's autobiography before 'the bell sounds for Vespers. The abbess must once again take her love, her emotions and the story that led her to this moment, close them up inside herself and assume her role as leader of a convent. She folds the letter, ties it up and seals it. Perhaps she slips it inside her habit.'

But the earliest and biggest crush on the affair came in the fourteenth century from Petrarch, whose admiration for Heloise ('Totally charming and most elegant!') ignited a new fascination with the lovers in much the same way he managed

John Cusack and A&H puppets in Being John Malkovich.

to reinforce Greek philosophy with Cicero. There could be no greater champion: more than anyone in the early Renaissance, Petrarch (Francesco Petrarca) was the man who rediscovered what letters could be. One of his own letters even defines the history of the word.

He was born in Arezzo in 1304, but his life as a perpetual traveller accounts for the many letters (almost 500 survive) to so many friends and acquaintances as he moved from near Florence to Pisa to Montpellier to Bologna before settling for an extended stay at Vaucluse in Provence and then Milan. A scholar and poet, Petrarch seemed uncertain as to the lasting value of his best work in his prodigious output, but the modern reader will find much of worth in his essays, biographies and religious treaties, as well as his most famous lyrical poems enflamed by his muse Laura, assured by him of immortality after she died of plague in 1348.

But certainly we should also remember him for something else: Petrarch's letters are intriguing and significant documents. Inspired by Cicero, Epicurus and Seneca, he wrote almost every day in personal terms, and his two large collections (one, *Epistolae familiares*, is a general gathering from his travels, the other, *Epistolae Seniles*, more specifically concerned with old age) lay good claim to be the first modern letters by the first modern mind at the dawn of our modern European civilisation.

As if to emphasise the richness of the letters to history, he writes an unfinished biography of his life not in poetry or standard chronological form, but in the shape of a letter 'To Posterity'. We may regard his opening modesty as a little false ('Greeting. It is possible that some word of me may have come to you . . .') and he is downright wrong when he claims such an 'insignificant and obscure' name such as his 'will scarcely penetrate far in either time or space'. History has been kind to him, and to us.

At the beginning of his first collection he writes to his life-long friend Ludovico (whom he nicknames Socrates) of how his letters almost didn't make it even to their first collected publication (in the 1360s), most being eaten by mice or 'the insatiable bookworm', and some deliberately destroyed by him on the fire. He writes of being in one of those gloomy moods where he doubted the worth of all his work, but a dreamlike vision of Ludovico (who had previously expressed an affection for his letters) changed his mind. So now he looked back on his work with some satisfaction, and an ability to offer some observations on letter-writing he hadn't expressed before.

> The first care indeed in writing is to consider to whom the letter is to be sent; then we may judge what to say and how to say it. We address a strong man in one way and a weak one in another. The inexperienced youth and the old man who has fulfilled the duties of life, he who is puffed up with prosperity and he who is stricken with adversity, the scholar distinguished in literature and the man incapable of grasping anything beyond common-place – each must be treated according to his character or position.

Writing to Boccaccio in 1365, shortly after his collected letters were evidently being freely copied by numerous scribes, he writes of one overriding wish for his work – that it be legible. Not for him 'ill-defined though sumptuous penmanship', nor writing which 'delights us at a distance but . . . strains and tires the eyes when we look at it intently'. It all comes down to etymology, he writes, for after all 'the word letter comes from legere, to read'.

The modern reader may have further hopes: that his letters are not only readable but still worth reading. Many are. They are wide-ranging in content, contradictory, sure of themselves, elitist and erudite, which generally guarantees a good read in any language. He wrote to many friends and also some imagi-

The first man of letters? Petrarch clasps his legacy in this 19th-century painting.

nary ones, such as Cicero and Homer. Subject matter ranges from politics, biography, classical poetry and contemporary literature, but one of the essential things that sets them apart is his writing about travel. Petrarch lays a strong claim to being the world's first tourist.

His letters to his friends are nothing if not parchment postcards home, and he writes not as one who has observed novel native customs as he flits through Europe conducting important business, but as a pleasure seeker, a holidaymaker, a *flaneur*. He travels to Paris, the Low Countries and the Rhine, he climbs mountains, he reports back. The only thing that prevents him travelling further – to Jerusalem, for example – is his terrible sea-sickness. 'Would that you could know,' he writes to one friend, 'with what delight I wander, free and alone, among the mountains, forests, and streams.' His letters become travel guides, itineraries and mental maps, and an early form of anthropology.

'I then proceeded to Cologne,' he writes to Cardinal Giovanni Colonna in the summer of 1333,

> which lies on the left bank of the Rhine, and is noted for its situation, its river, and its inhabitants. I was astonished to find such a degree of culture in a barbarous land. The appearance of the city, the dignity of the men, the attractiveness of the women, all surprised me.
>
> The day of my arrival happened to be the feast of St John the Baptist. It was nearly sunset when I reached the city ... I allowed myself to be led immediately from the inn to the river, to witness a curious sight. And I was not disappointed, for I found the riverbank lined with a multitude of remarkably comely women. Ye gods, what faces and forms! And how well attired! One whose heart was not already occupied might well have met his fate here.
>
> I took my stand upon a little rise of ground where I could easily follow what was going on. There was a dense mass of people, but no disorder of any kind. They knelt down in quick succession on the bank, half hidden by the fragrant grass, and turning up their sleeves above the elbow they bathed their hands and white arms in the eddying stream.
>
> ... When anything was to be heard or said I had to rely upon my companions to furnish both ears and tongue. Not understanding

the scene, and being deeply interested in it, I asked an explanation from one of my friends . . . He told me that this was an old custom among the people, and that the lower classes, especially the women, have the greatest confidence that the threatening calamities of the coming year can be washed away by bathing on this day in the river, and a happier fate be so assured. Consequently this annual ablution has always been conscientiously performed, and always will be.

In whatever high regard we may hold Petrarch's letters, it would be hard to match the regard in which he held them himself. He desired that his readers, whom he thought of as predominantly male,

should think of me alone, not of his daughter's wedding, his mistress's embraces, the wiles of his enemy, his engagements, house, lands or money. I want him to pay attention to me. If his affairs are pressing, let him postpone reading the letter, but when he does read, let him throw aside the burden of business and family cares, and fix his mind upon the matter before him . . . I will not have him gain without any exertion what has not been produced without labour on my part.

His letters usually run to well over a thousand words. The well-hashed line 'Sorry this letter is so long, I didn't have time to write a short one', has been attributed in various forms to Blaise Pascal (1657), John Locke (1690), William Cowper (1704) and Benjamin Franklin (1750), but the thought may have originated – in a naturally elongated form – with Petrarch. Writing again to Boccaccio towards the end of his writing life, aware that his time was now limited, he resolved to keep his letters tight, and to 'write to be understood and not to please'. Yet he remembered making that promise before: 'But I have not been able to keep this engagement. It seems to me much easier to remain silent altogether with one's friends than to be brief, for when one has once begun, the desire to continue the conversation is so great that it were easier not to begin than to check the flow.'

He encountered other difficulties too. Too often he would write letters and they would not make it to their inattentive readers at all, their carrier having been intercepted by anxious agents of the state or random Italian highwaymen, or even an early incarnation of the autograph hunter. Not long before his death, Petrarch wrote to Boccaccio that a combination of old age and the perennial unreliability of the messenger system had resigned him to a regretful fate: he would write letters no more.

> I know now that neither of two long letters that I wrote to you have reached you. But what can we do? Nothing but submit. We may wax indignant, but we cannot avenge ourselves. A most insupportable set of fellows has appeared in northern Italy, who nominally guard the passes, but are really the bane of messengers.
>
> They not only glance over the letters that they open, but they read them with the utmost curiosity. They may, perhaps, have for an excuse the orders of their masters, who, conscious of being subject to every reproach in their restless careers of insolence, imagine that everyone must be writing about and against them; hence their anxiety to know everything. But it is certainly inexcusable, when they find something in the letters that tickles their asinine ears, that instead of detaining the messengers while they take time to copy the contents, as they used to do, they should now, with ever increasing audacity, spare their fingers the fatigue, and order the messengers off without their letters. And, to make this procedure the more disgusting, those who carry on this trade are complete ignoramuses . . . I find nothing more irritating and vexatious than the interference of these scoundrels. It has often kept me from writing, and often caused me to repent after I had

written. There is nothing more to be done against these letter thieves, for everything is upside down, and the liberty of the state is entirely destroyed.

The liberty of the state destroyed by an uncertain postal service? Even allowing for the odd flourish of Italian melodrama, it did appear that the value of letters – their role in cultural discourse as much as their importance in official affairs – was now something a civilised world at the dawn of the Renaissance could not do without. And this was just the beginning: the worth of letters to historical record, the danger of letters to a nervous monarchy, the importance of a reliable delivery network for the passionate expression of love – all these were just starting to be assessed. Clearly, a growth in literacy was going to be both a blessing and a curse.

How to Build a Pyramid

14232134 SIGMN. BARKER H.C., 3 30 WING,
1 COY., 9 A.F.S., M.E.F.

17th December 1943

Dear Bessie,

I received yesterday your surface letter of 20th October. I read it avidly as from an old pal – noting that though time has chattanooga'ed along, your style remains pretty much as it was in the days when we had that terrifically intense and wonderfully sincere correspondence about Socialism and the Rest Of It – unlike the present time, when, hornswoggling old hypocrite that I am, the Rest Of It seems infinitely more attractive. Thanks for the letter, old-timer, I am sending this by Air Mail because it will have enough dull stuff in it to sink a Merchant ship.

Yes, I remember our discussions over 'Acquaintance' and my views are still as much for as yours remain against. I have, perhaps, one hundred acquaintances (I write to fifty) yet I could number my friends on one hand. The dictionary:

Acquaintance: a person known.

Friend: one attached to another by affection and esteem.

You are 'known' to me, and while I have 'affection' for you it does not amount to an attachment. You hung on to my coat tails 'in friendship', you say?

I am sorry that Nick and you are 'no longer', as you put it, and that you should have wasted so much time because of his lack of courage. You must have had a rotten time of it, and I do sympathise with you – but are you writing to the right bloke? I'll say you are! Joan gave me my 'cards' a couple of months back, though I had seen them coming since April, when I got my first letters.

I think you had better write some more on your view of emotions. You say that if they could be ruled out it would make New-Order-building easier. I deny that. We only feel like that when our emotions are tinkered and played about with.

I can quite believe your estimate of the way the London-leave soldier improves the shining-hour. You can understand chaps who get three or four days leave before a campaign opens, 'painting the town red', but unfortunately quite a large number who are in comfortable Base jobs have their regular unpleasant habits. When I was at Base our evening passes bore the injunction 'Brothels Out of Bounds. Consorting with Prostitutes Forbidden.' Where we collected the passes there was a large painted sign, 'Don't Take a Chance, Ask the Medical Orderly for a – doodah'. The whole emphasis of Army Propaganda is 'Be Careful', even the wretched Padre at Thirsk, when he said a few words of farewell, said merely that most foreign women were diseased, and we should be careful.

[At the pyramids] when I found a preventative on the place I had chosen to sit down on, I thought it was a nice combination of Ancient and Modern! Whoever told you Pyramids told the time was pulling your leg. No iron or steel was used, cranes or pulleys. Ropes and Levers only. Their erection was due to Superb Organisation, Flesh and Blood, Ho Heave Ho, and all the other paraphernalia of human effort.

I am afraid this letter is not what it set out to be, but I have little doubt you find it acceptable. What paper do you read nowadays?

I luckily secured a bed, a great help when one remembers the many crawly things. Flies are nauseatingly numerous, and fleas annoyingly active. (I got two from my left leg while writing this, earlier. It's not often you can kill them.) Washing is a difficulty, petrol tins are our bath tubs. Squeeze a rag at the shoulder, and the water trickles interestedly down for re-use. Mice are a nuisance, scratching around. The ubiquitous, utilitarian petrol tin is here made into a trap, properly baited and it gets three or four a day for a time. They go in the tin which is on its side, then a lid comes down and they are trapped. Killing them afterwards is a nasty business, stunning, drowning, then burying. I have avoided it so far. Much rain lately has made an ornamental lake of the wide flatness; but we have now got grass and some tiny flowers where before was merely sand. I have transplanted some of the flowers into a special patch we have made into a garden. Bert and I play chess most of our spare-time, on a set we made with wire and [a] broom-handle. There are some dogs about the camp which is far from anywhere. No civilians. We have two pigs fattening for Xmas, poor blighters, though I believe the uxorious male has given the sow hope of temporary reprieve.

I hope you hear regularly from your brother and that your Dad and yourself are in good health.

Good wishes,

Chris

Chapter Five

How to Write the
Perfect Letter, Part 1

There is a new pope. Hooray for his holiness. But how, in 1216, should you write to him about the management of your church? Or about a terrible miscarriage of justice? How best to address your student son about the dangers of excessive study? Or give warning regarding the unhappy events that befall students at the outset of their courses?

All these problems may be solved with the purchase of the *Boncompagnonus* (also available as the *Boncompagnus*) a six-volume manual featuring all of the real-life examples above. There are others: how to write a grant application and a letter of recommendation, how to persuade people to go on pilgrimage and how to compose a letter to settle a matrimonial dispute. You could also learn how to write to jugglers about their fees. The guide was composed in 1215 by Boncompagno of Signa. A Bolognese professor of rhetoric and a master at chess, he had a reputation as a megalomaniac* and a bit of a prankster, but his letter guide is all business, particularly when it comes to money and the law, and how to write a letter of condolence following bereavement. The condolence templates, which formed the 25th section of the first book, were so diverse as to allow no room for error. There was consideration of the particular practices of the mourning habits of the

---

* He wrote, for example, of how he ruled 'the field of eloquence with exalted genius and a solemn style'.

95

Hungarians, the Sicilians, the Slavs, the Bohemians and the Germans, and the different ways to interpret the 'bliss of priests and clerics' and the customs of 'certain provincials'.

What was Boncompagno's motivation for writing such a guide? He hoped that the well-written letter might go some way to correcting society's ills, with the prime targets being injustice and jealousy. These ills, he believed, would plant the teeth of the hydra upon you, a beast that 'never rests, but surveys the world, tracking down any sort of good fortune, and always it tries to find any sort of excellence, which when it cannot harm, it is confused, grumbles, shrieks, rages, becomes delirious, swallows up, harasses, becomes livid, becomes pale, clamours, becomes nauseated, hides, barks, bites, raves, foams at the mouth, rages, seethes, snarls' and that kind of thing. But motivation and effect are different things.

The medieval epistolary expert Alain Boureau has observed that Boncompagno's manual was one of our earliest proofs of the complex and changing hierarchy of European society,

Aristotle, who believed one should write as one speaks.

with a classification that relied on a wide variety of positions and ranks rather than just divisions in the Church and nobility. Letter guides such as this bear witness to the emergence of a middle class, and the influence of the universities. They gave voice to a new grouping of people in villages and towns that had previously not been incorporated into either feudal or ecclesiastical worlds, many of them in the burgeoning legal professions. Soon merchants would demand letter-writing guidance of their own.

But the *Boncompagnonus* was not the first guide to the art of letter-writing. For that we should credit a man called Demetrius, date uncertain, background unknown. This Latin tract has been dated somewhere between the fourth century BC and the fourth century AD, and the Demetrius at the helm may be Demetrius of Phaleron or Demetrius of Tarsus, although most bamboozled scholars have found it easier to consider the author as anonymous.

What is clear is the certitude of the advice. The author's brief is far less specific than many of the manuals that followed it, but its generality should be useful to all. He begins by questioning the advice once given by Artemon, the editor of Aristotle's letters, that 'a letter should be written in the same manner as a dialogue', a letter being one of two sides of a conversation.* 'There is perhaps some truth in what he says, but not the whole truth,' Demetrius contends. 'The letter should be a little more formal than the dialogue, since the latter imitates improvised conversation, while the former is written and sent as a kind of gift.'

He remarks that the sort of sudden sentence breaks that are so common in dialogue do not translate well to letter-writing: 'abruptness in writing causes obscurity'. Letters can

---

* The letters of Aristotle that Demetrius refers to have not survived. The advice that one should 'write as one speaks' has become a classic doctrine, and was favoured by Jane Austen amongst innumerable others. We'll return to it in later chapters.

do some things much better than speech. 'The letter should be strong in characterization,' Demetrius observes. 'Everyone writes a letter in the virtual image of his own soul. In every other form of speech it is possible to see the writer's character, but in none so clearly as in the letter.'

With regards to length, a letter should be 'restricted'. 'Those that are too long, not to mention too inflated in style, are not in any true sense letters at all but treatises with the heading "Dear Sir".' It is also 'absurd to be so formal in letters, it is even contrary to friendship, which demands the proverbial calling of "a spade a spade".' And there were some topics for which a letter was just plain unsuitable, not least 'the problems of logic or natural philosophy'. Rather, 'A letter's aim is to express friendship briefly and set out a simple subject in simple terms . . . The man who utters sententious maxims and exhortations seems to be no longer chatting in a letter but preaching from the pulpit.' Demetrius allowed for one or two exceptions to this, such as letters addressed to 'cities or kings', which permitted a little more elaboration. 'In summary, the letter should combine two of the styles, the elegant or graceful and the plain, and this concludes my account of the letter.'

By the thirteenth century, when Boncompagno crafted his advice, the range of letter templates available had expanded greatly, and their abundance fulfilled a need: letter-writing was not an intuitive skill. The craft of letter-writing was only beginning to be taught in European schools, and although Cicero and Seneca would shortly be back in vogue, their antiquity was not always suited to contemporary challenges. So there were two choices: the professional paid scribe who set up a stall in the market as if he was selling root crops, or the *ars dictaminis*, the self-help manual. The *ars dictaminis*

would soon have a sibling, the *ars notariae*, which specialised in writing advice for legal and patent matters, but its main purpose was to provide a guide to writing 'familiar' or more personal and general letters, albeit ones that still bowed firmly to rhetorical tradition (and were usually designed to be read out loud to whoever was gathered when they arrived).

Italy and France led the way, with England following their trail, and there were soon so many that it was hard to distinguish between them, the faddy self-help books of their day. The earliest available inspiration came from a guide by the Benedictine monk, Alberic of Monte Cassino, published around 1075, while a short and anonymous manual published 60 years later in Bologna was one of the earliest to give detailed instruction on the correct forms of opening address, the *salutatio* that was to remain a standard entry in general etiquette guides, cleverly combining the *benevolentiae captatio*, the securing of goodwill by flattery (the best technique was to induce a sense of fatherly or brotherly feeling, or failing that a sense of 'fellowship'). A pupil may get his way with his master if he sticks to something like 'To [master's name here] By divine grace resplendent in Ciceronian charm, [your name here], inferior to his devoted learning, expresses the servitude of a sincere heart.' The next three categories of advice were not too far removed from something we might expect today: the *naratio* (the latest news), the *petitio* (the real reason for writing) and the *conclusio*.

One of the first such textbooks in English was compiled by an Italian, Giovanni di Bologna, specifically for use by the Archbishop of Canterbury, while Lawrence of Aquilegia wrote some of the first recognisable examples of the 'form letter', whereby a user fills in the blanks on a template by picking the relevant words from a list. The choice of recipients alone provides quite a range, from kings and archdeacons to heretics and 'falsos infidelos', the latter perhaps more deserving of a pub brawl than flawless correspondence.

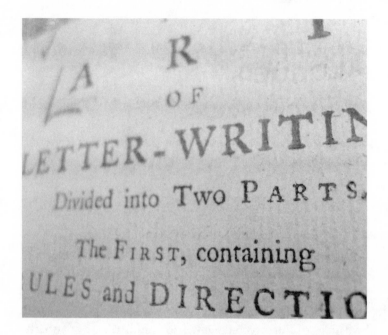

Soon the university cities of Bologna and Orleans were offering so many different professional guides that their authors, the master *épistoliers*, were called *dictatori*, a term which underlined their overbearing political influence. Many were members of the clergy, some also held teaching posts at universities. Their names were famous in their day: Geoffrey of Vinsauf, Arnulf of Orleans, Peter of Blois, Ludolf of Hildescheim and Conrad of Zurich.

As with the more refined reaches of academia, many *dictatori* seemed to be writing for the sole benefit and approval of fellow *dictatori*; many of their letter templates describe the masterful art of letter-writing, a hall of mirrors. A prime example is supplied by Hugh of Bologna in his *Rationes Dictandi* from the twelfth century. After a slow and suitably grovelling start ('To X, a very great scholar in the science of letters, a very eloquent man' etc), the letter considers its navel: 'The grace of God was not content, oh master and most revered lord, to make you a peerless scholar in the liberal arts; it has also provided you with a great gift in epistolary art. This is what is reported by an insistent rumour that fills the greater part of the world; this rumour could not persist were it not true.'

Portrayed thus, master letter-writers of late medieval Europe bestrode society as an enviable combination of healer of the sick and rock god.

> Indeed, through the operation of an incomparable grace, you have known how to teach to your disciples that which God has given to you to know, much more quickly than other masters. That is why so very many disciples forsake the other masters and hasten from all sides towards you, as fast as they are able. Under your instruction, the uneducated are immediately cultivated, the stutterers are immediately eloquent, the dull-witted are immediately enlightened, the twisted are immediately made straight.*

The letter-writing manual changed significantly during the Renaissance as humanism embraced Petrarch's influence and, by default, Cicero's. By the beginning of the sixteenth century we had certainly arrived at the modern sort of guidebook we would have still acknowledged as useful 20 years ago, the *methodus conscribendi epistolis*. The latest champion of the art was Desiderius Erasmus, the masterful Dutch humanist and perhaps the foremost scholar of his day; he not only ushered in the Protestant Reformation, but also found time to write thousands of tracts and letters on non-theological themes. His

---

* As quoted in Alain Boureau, 'The Letter-Writing Norm, a Medieval Invention' in *Correspondence: Models of Letter-Writing from the Middle Ages to the Nineteenth Century* by Roger Chartier, Alain Boureau and Cecile Dauphin, translated by Christopher Woodall, Polity Press, 1997.

tracts confronted head on the Seneca-toned concerns of how best one should live one's life (and not waste it: one of his most famous treatises was about folly). And his letters, of which about 1,600 have survived (he claimed to have spent about half of his life writing them) range from his rational defence of his stance against new Catholic doctrines, through his translations of classical literature, to far more personal matters such as the disappointing vintage of the local wines to his poor finances and health (he had debilitating arthritis, and in later years had to pass on writing duties to an assistant). And of course several of the letters contained the one recurring topic we've seen before and may see again: Erasmus chiding his friends and family for not writing sooner and more often.

Writing in about 1487 from a monastery near Gouda to his older brother Pieter, a monk based near Delft, Erasmus pushed the guilt button from the start:

> Have you so completely rid yourself of all brotherly feeling, or has all thought of your Erasmus wholly fled your heart? I write letters and send them repeatedly, I demand news again and again, I keep asking your friends when they come from your direction, but they never have a hint of a letter or any message: they merely say that you are well. Of course this is the most welcome news I could hear, but you are no more dutiful thereby. As I perceive how obstinate you are, I believe it would be easier to get blood from a stone than coax a letter out of you!

Erasmus's letters were strewn all over Europe: he wrote to correspondents in London, Cambridge, Dover, Amsterdam, Cologne, Strasbourg, Bologna, Turin, Brussels and Lubeck. He believed there was 'almost no kind of theme which a letter may not treat', but he was largely a traditionalist, believing it preferable to have a studied letter than a spontaneous one: 'rather . . . a letter should smell of the lamp than of liquor, of the ointment box, and of the goat'. Above all he liked the

Half his life writing letters: Erasmus in furs by Holbein.

idea of the letter, the material artefact, the letter as the great discursive template for the modern world. If you write a letter well (which you could do if you took his strict advice), then you would surely declare yourself a man of that world.

His letter-writing guide, compiled while he was a teacher in Paris in the early 1500s, covered some familiar ground (the clarity and aptness of expression), and he wrote particularly well about how the writer should above all be versatile: a letter should be 'as closely suited as possible to the argument, place, time, addressee; which when dealing with weighty matters is serious, which with mediocre matters is neat; with humble matters elegant and witty; which is ardent and spirited in exhortation, soothing and friendly in consolation.'

But perhaps the most noteworthy element of both the manual and the collections of his own letters that Erasmus supervised towards the end of his life was that they were formulated not for the scribe but for the printing press, initially in Cambridge in 1521, and then widely disseminated through several other printing houses in Italy and Germany. However ironic it seemed, the art of letter-writing had found its greatest ally in moveable type. Far from inhibiting the art, machines only amplified its significance to history and ideas.

Letters could now be collected and bound; printing ensured archiving, and a greater shot at survival; the unique letter cache, the rare fair manuscript copies – these would still be posterity's wonderful and invaluable things. But now, for the great public thinkers whose collected letters were regarded as both history and currency, their discovery and safe-keeping may not be so necessary; libraries would take care of that from here on. The printing press brought with it the collected letters and the man of letters (and, within two centuries, women of letters too). Erasmus claimed that his letters were not history but literature, and now both arts would have their day, and it would be a lasting one.

Two English publishers produced manuals that swiftly became vernacular classics, and to turn the pages of the first of these at the Bodleian Library in Oxford is to experience an early tang of Machiavellian intrigue notably absent from previous guides. The new letter specimens continued to be predominantly concerned with respect – the correct form, the ever-humble approach – but now there were new considerations: technique, mild manipulation, clever compromise, advice on the use of letters to get one's way. Cicero had employed letters to his political ends, and now there was guidance on how we could all do it.

William Fulwood's *The Enimie of Idlenesse* (1568) was the first bestselling guide published in English, enjoying ten editions in the next 50 years.* One reads it with a clear sense of the growing importance of letters in Elizabethan society, not least their use in bonding a society; largely through trade and other economic necessities, families were beginning to disperse. Fulwood's work was translated from a successful French guide, but the author was careful to adapt as much of the local colour and situations as possible to his English readers, although he kept most of the addresses in his examples as either Lyons or Paris. Fulwood's main appeal lies in his acknowledgement that most letters are replies to others, and the fact that the hypothetical situations he presents are not only practical but highly engaging. In one, he ponders the scenario of a merchant father suspecting his son of selling their silk goods at far below their market value. In the first letter, the father writeth unto the sonne.**

> Verily my sonne, though wilt be the occasion through thy evill behavior, to haste me sooner than I thought unto my grave: for one of these dayes in this Towne of Lyons many gentlemen

---

* The title may have derived from *The Image of Idleness* (1555), a fictional account of letters between a bachelor and a married man written by 'Olyver Oldwanton and dedicated to the Lady Lust'.

** The old English grammar and spelling are retained here for flavour, although the 'v' has been replaced with our now-familiar 'u', and the letter 'j' has been substituted for 'i' when the occasion merits it. As quoted in *The Art of Letter Writing: An Essay on the Handbooks Published in England During the Sixteenth and Seventeenth Centuries* by Jean Robertson, University Press of Liverpool, 1942.

and marchants confirmed unto me that all the clothes of scarlet which thou didst cary with thee are lost. Also I am advertised by my trusty frends, that sundry dames in Lyons go sumptuously arayed with our clothes of Silke, and thou of them hast none other payment, but that thou takest accompt secretly in ye night.

This is not the fayth which thou didst promise me at thy departure: therefore thy mother continually weepeth, and thy two virtuous and honest Sisters lament without ceassing. But tell me, with what knyves thinckest thou that thou doest wounde the most secrete partes of our heartes: therefore be redy to amend thy errour, or else veryly cease to call me Father, and holde thy selfe assured (except thou amend) that neither of my goods nor money thou shalt ever have any parte hereafter.

Thy Carefuull Father

The Sonne Maketh Answere Unto His Father

My dearly beloved Father, I have ben advertised by your sorowful letter of evill adventure of our merchandise: but bicause you are my Father & a prudent Father, it is lawfull for you without occasion, to reprehende and threaten me: howbeit he that who committeth not the fault, is always accompanied with sweete hope. Those that have tolde you that I give your clothes of Silke unto the dames of Lyons, peradventure have taken it in evill part, that I have not given some peece of silk unto their wives, & would peradventure have taken no care to have asked them from when ye garments have come, so that they spare theyr pens.

I praye you therefore my deare father, be content & glad: for I consume not your goods, but I sell them aswel unto women as unto men. I send you by our Factour two thousand pounds for clothes of scarlet, & six hundreth poundes for clothes of silke: I will tary to finish the rest, & the cursed envie languishing shall fall unto the ground: and you shal finde me (God to frend) a good, just & faithfull Sonne &c.

The other highly success-ful manual (nine editions in 50 years) was Angel Day's *The English Secretorie* (1586). This contained more original material than Fulwood, not least when it came to guid-ance over love letters. And the specimens were convincing creations, often involving the resolution of conflicts between

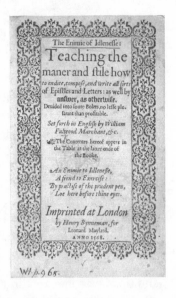

lovers or fathers and sons, a basis perhaps for the earliest epis-tolary novels. In English Elizabethan schools the most popu-lar Latin manual, taught consistently alongside letters from Cicero and Erasmus, was Georgius Macropedius's *Methodus de Conscribendis Epistolis*. The theory holds that it was this guide, more than any other, that influenced the style of letters in the works of Shakespeare.

✝   ✝   ✝

But not everyone subscribed to the wisdom of these guides. Writing in the 1570s, the progressive French essayist Mon-taigne claimed he was 'a sworn enemy to all manner of falsi-fication,' (by which he meant inauthenticity), and in an essay entitled 'A Consideration upon Cicero' he took sceptical issue with Erasmus when it came to the formality of a letter. Mon-taigne rejected studiousness in favour of expressive spontane-ity, and he believed his own style suited only 'familiar' letters rather than business ones. He thought his language 'too compact, irregular, abrupt, and singular' to suit formal composition, and he mistrusted letters that 'have no other substance than a fine contexture of courteous words'. He said that he always wrote personally rather than employ a scribe, even though his handwriting was 'intolerably ill'. And the less he thought about things in advance, the better the letter.

> I have accustomed the great ones who know me to endure my blots and dashes, and upon paper without fold or margin. Those that cost me the most pains, are the worst; when I once begin to draw it in by head and shoulders, 'tis a sign that I am not there. I fall too without premeditation or design; the first word begets the second, and so to the end.

And there was another thing Montaigne didn't like about the manuals with their ideal specimens: the beginnings and the endings. 'The letters of this age consist more in fine edges and prefaces than in matter,' he argued. He said he had deliberately avoided writing to 'men of the long robe and finance' for fear of making mistakes in addressing them. And for the closing niceties, 'I would with all my heart transfer it to another hand to add those long harangues, offers, and prayers that we place at the bottom, and should be glad that some new custom would discharge us of that trouble'.

Montaigne's views would have received solid support from the satirists of the day. Almost as soon as it was born, the letter-writing manual was down on its knees begging for parody, and the only surprise was that it took until 1602 for the first hit to appear, *A Poste with a Packet of Madde Letters* by Nicholas Breton. Breton was an English pamphleteer and publishing opportunist, author of what we would today call toilet books. And he was very good at them. His *Madde Letters* was written with the intention 'to pleasure many', and he achieved this aim through many editions, an acknowledgment that his readers clearly regarded his targets as fair game. Because his letters were fiction, his work could also claim to be the first epistolary novel.

He took aim against the begging letter, the letter dissuading a friend from marriage, and what is probably the earliest example of the Dear John letter. In this, a naive country bumpkin-type won't quite admit defeat:

> The cause of my writing to you at this time is, that Ellen, I do hear since coming from Wakefield, when you knowe, that talk we had together at the sign of the blue cuckoe, and how you did give mee you hand, and swear that you would not forsake me for all the worlde, and how you made me buy a Ring and a Hart, that cost me eighteen pence, which I left with you, and you gave me a Napkin to weare in my Hat, I thanke you, which I will weare til my dying daye: and I mervaile if it be true as I heare, that you have altered your minde, and are made sure to me neighbour Hoblins younger sonne, truly Ellen you do not wel in so doing, and God will plague you for it, and I hope I shall live and if I never have you: for there are more maides than Maulkin, and I count myself worth the whistling.*

Breton inspired further parodies. *Conceyted Letters, Newley Layde Open* was followed by *Hobson's Horse-Loade of Letters, A Speedie Poste* and then *A President for Young Pen-Men, or the Letter-Writer*, the latter thought to be the first to include 'letter-writer' in a title. One of the best was the anonymous *Cupids Messenger* of 1629, and as its title suggested it was concerned primarily with love letters. But it is love in all its disarray, a comedy of cruelty, such as this *cri de coeur* from a man in prison to his former intended. He feels she was more than happy to take his money when he lavished it on her, but is less loving now that it's gone, and the bile spits up a recipe

---

* A maulkin was a harlot.

for revenge that appears to draw directly from the cauldron of Macbeth's Three Witches.

> If my paper were made of the skins of croking Toades, or speck-led Adders, my inke of the blood of Scorpions, my penne pluckt from the Screech-owles wings, they were but fit instruments to write unto thee, thou art more venomous, more poisonous, more ominous than the worst of these: for do but descend into the depth of thy guilty conscience, and see how manie vows, promises, and deepe protestations, nay millions of oaths hast thou sworne thy fidelitie unto mee, which one day will witnesse against thee.

The end of the page would surely bring a little respite, perhaps even a redemptive finale. Or not:

> Leprosie compared to thee is all health, and all manner of infec-tion but a flea-biting, and all manner of diseases, though they were fetcht from twentie Hospitals, were but like the fit of an ague: for thou art all Leprosie, all diseases for neither thy bodie nor thy soule are free from the disease of shame and disgrace of the world . . . God amend and pardon thee.

> Once thy friend,

> I.P.

The serious art of epistolary courtship received a boost in the seventeenth century from – where else? – France and the French. *Le Secretaire à la Mode* by Jean Puget de la Serre billed itself as a 'refined way of expression in all manners of letters', and indeed set a standard for the century to come. By 1640, when the book was translated into English by John Massinger, letters had attained both an elevated and popular status they hadn't enjoyed since the days of Pliny the Younger: a status of widely practised and wholly indispensible daily traffic in words. The letter had moved from something written solely by the Church and the state, the fearsome and powerful, to the realm of middle-class art. And despite much scattered evidence that letter-writers chose to ignore the wisdom proffered in these guides, the how-to genre was clearly here to stay: in 1789, an inventory of a printer and bookseller in Troyes, north-central France, revealed 1,848 copies of a late edition of *Le Secretaire à la Mode*, and some 4,000 copies of similar manuals. The more the world wrote, the more it required guidance.

Once you knew what to write, how should you display your new knowledge on paper? How should a letter be laid out?

That largely depended on how wealthy you were, or what status you held. The specimen guides were rather strict in their presentations, suggesting that anyone should be able to glance at a letter and, without reading a word, be able to tell if it was addressed to a recipient inferior or a superior to the sender. In the opinion of Fulwood's *Enimie of Idlenesse*, the opening of a letter should be designed 'according to the estate of the writer, and the qualitie of the person to whom wee write'. 'For to our superiors wee must write at the right side in the neither end of the paper, saying: By your most humble and obedient sonne, or servant . . . And to our equals we must write towards the middest of the paper, saying: By your faithful friend for ever . . . To our inferiours wee may write on high at the left hand.'

Angel Day's and de la Serre's manuals also emphasised the minutiae – precisely how big a gap to leave between the name of the addressee and the main body of the text, and also how much to indent the first paragraph, the white space again depending on the level of submission and deference one intended to convey, referred to as 'the honorary margin'. The historian James Daybell suggests that there is evidence from thousands of letters that what he calls 'the social politics of manuscript space' was widely adhered to. When John Donne wrote with great humility to his estranged father-in-law, he signed his name at the extreme bottom right-hand corner of the letter, thus stressing his insignificance, a tiny reverential afterthought. This practice was particularly visible in the letters sent by subjects to monarchs. Women writing to men in the seventeenth century almost always signed their name in the uttermost bottom right-hand corner, another miserable sign of flattened social standing.

And the opposite was also apparent. When the second earl of Essex dashed off a note to his cousin Edward Seymour in 1598, he consciously chose the top of the letter to sign his name. The short six-line instruction left a huge amount of blank space beneath it on a large uncut sheet. It wasn't a design statement, it was a statement of wealth; paper was costly, and the message surely was, 'I've got reams of the stuff.'

Paper size in early modern England was something we might regard as fairly standard for official correspondence today, if a little squarer. A 'folio' sheet was commonly either 30 by 35cm or 42 by 45cm, depending on the local mill. The sheet would then usually be folded in half, and the writing would cover one or two sides. The other two blank sides would be used to conceal the contents by folding and tucking, with one of them being used for the address and the other for the seal.

Smaller Elizabethan letters often betrayed poverty, but in the middle of the seventeenth century the letter size shrunk from the folio size to the 'folded half-sheet quarto', significantly smaller and more rectangular at about 20 by 30cm. The smaller sheets left less blank space, but sometimes no blank space at all was desirable: it was common for writers to cross-hatch around their words to ensure that no one tried to add any further sentiments to the ones they had originally composed.

But what happened then? You could write to almost anyone about almost anything, and you could lay it out according to the respectful customs of the day. But how on earth – before letterboxes, stamps and a regular delivery network – would a letter reach its intended recipient? And why did we ever assume that a personal letter containing important information would ever remain private as it battled gamely towards its destination?

Trying to Impress

21st and 27th February 1944

Dear Bessie,

I received your letter of 1st January on 7.2.44, since when I have been busting to send you a 'smashing' reply, yet feeling clumsy as a ballerina in Army boots, who knows that her faithful followers will applaud, however she pirouettes. I could hug you till you dropped! The un-ashamed flattery that you ladled out was very acceptable – I lapped it up gladly and can do with more! Yes, I could hug you – an action unconnected with the acute shortage of women in these parts, and mostly symbolic of my pleasure at your appreciation of qualities so very few others see, and which really I do not possess. I must confess that your outrageous enthusiasm banishes 'acquaintance' from my mind, and that I recognise the coming of a new-kind-of-atmosphere into our interchanges, and one which you will need to watch.

To be honest, rather than discreet: Letters from home sometimes contain curious statements. 'Paddling' one of my own, I had told them of my first letter from you. Back came a weather forecast: 'Perhaps she will catch you on the rebound.' I, of course, have no such wish, yet I certainly haven't told anyone of your latest letter, and was glad I was able to conceal it from my brother. I find myself engaged on the secretive, denying dodge that has marked the opening stages of all my little affairés since the first Girl Probationer crossed my path. I can see that willy-nilly I am having a quiet philander, and I want to warn you it'll end in a noisy flounder unless you watch out. I haven't a 'aporth of 'rebound' in me. I warm to you as a friend and I hope that remains our mutual rendezvous, although I feel that the more I write you, the less content you will be.

I hope you will not think I regarded your letter as purely a back-pat for me. As I read yours I wha-rooped too. You'll find this effort somewhat 'forced'. I believe it is true that when you want to be natural, you aren't. If you understand me, you have made me a bit 'conscious'. I'm blowed if I am not trying to impress you. You say your mind is a rambling rubbish box, and your youthful desires for improvement remain unfulfilled. I don't remember having many youthful desires (except that I do recall Madeline Carroll featuring in one of them). I am glad you accept my view on others not being informed of the contents of our letters. It will be much more satisfactory, we shall know each other much better through an 'in confidence' understanding.

I do not share your views about the 'waste of time' involved in a crashed courtship.

You say it is odd that I can be so ignorant about women, but apart from the important omission of never having slept with one, I regard myself as capable of detecting a wile when I see one, and I do not think women are so very different from men in any important aspect. If I were really plonking down what I did know, I should have to admit that I am puzzled very often by the behaviour of many of my own sex, and not a little quizzical about my own at times.

I am sorry you felt the least bit 'weepy' at my chess, garden, pigs. The things your tears are best reserved for are beetles this size [small sketch], and fleas whose size is much less horribly impressive, but whose powers of annoyance are far greater. I exult in the possession of a sleeping sheet, which is very nice to have next to the skin compared with the rough Army blankets. At night, if the fleas are active and I cannot subdue them with my fevered curses, I take my sheet and my naked body into the open, and turn and shake the sheet in the very cold night air. Then I get back into bed and hold the ends of the sheet tight around my neck, to keep out my nuisance raiders. The last few months have been very pleasant as regards heat, and fleas have been few. I am not looking forward to the summer.

So on to our pigs – yesterday came the day for the male (boar) to be sent away for slaughter. Half a dozen of us were detailed to hold various parts of the massive, dirty, unfortunate creature, while the man who knows all about pigs got a bucket firmly wedged over the poor thing's head and snout. I was originally deputed to take hold of the right ear, but in the opening melee found myself grasping the right leg, which I held on to firmly as it lumbered out of the sty, and heaved on heavily as, somehow, despite a terrific struggle and the most heartrending screams, we got it on the lorry, which was to be its hearse. Directly it got up there, it went very quiet and then started snuffling around for something to eat. In the afternoon it met its man-determined fate, and this morning as I came away from dinner, I saw its tongue, its heart, liver and a leg, hanging from the cookhouse roof. I had my doubts about eating it in the days when it was half the eighteen stone it weighed at death. But now I have none. I certainly can't help eat the poor old bloke. The sow lives on, she has a large and sore looking undercarriage, and will be a Mother in three weeks. I suppose we shall eat her progeny in due course.

Here am I, nominally a soldier, feeling tender hearted about a pig. And there, a couple of weeks ago, were four of our chaps deputed to shoot three of the camp dogs, no more than puppies, laughing, bright, happy, who had somehow got canker of the ear necessitating their destruction. The stomachs of these chaps were really affected, and they were thoroughly miserable.

My eye on post-war arguments when I shall be accused of disloyalty and lack of patriotism because of my desire for changes, I recently made application for 'The Africa Star', which most chaps here are wearing. I have first heard that I am to get it.

When you know that I arrived out on April 16th and the hostilities ceased May 12th, you can see how very easily medals are gained. It is the same very often with awards supposedly for gallantry.

My Dad, a thorough going old imperialist, will be delighted that he can talk about two sons with the medal, and mentally they will be dangling with his – EIGHT altogether, though his nearest point to danger was really the Siege of Ladysmith (in a war maybe you would have condemned?). Since the war, my Dad has had medal ribbons fitted on most of his jackets and waistcoats, and goes shopping with them all a'showing! My Mother comes in bemoaning the fact that there is no suet to be had. Dad comes in with a valuable half-a-pound he extracted from a medal-conscious shopkeeper. Once, my Mother was not able to get any soda, and my Dad went out and ordered 56lbs, which actually arrived the same afternoon, to my Mother's mixed joy and regret! I can tell you plenty about my Dad, who has many faults and the one redeeming virtue that he is all for his family, right or wrong.

I have just seen a Penguin, 'Living in Cities', very attractively setting forth some principles of post-war building. I always think how well off we suburban dwellers* are compared with

---

* Chris Barker lived in Tottenham; Bessie Moore in Blackheath.

the people who live in places like Roseberry Avenue or Beth-nal Green Road, and die there, too, quite happily since they never knew what they missed.

I saw a suggestion for a new house to have a built-in bookcase, or place for it, and thought this a rather good idea, especially as my three or four hundred nondescripts are shoved, wedged, packed tight at the top of a cupboard at the moment. I carry with me now only an atlas, a dictionary, Thoreau's 'Walden' (ever glanced at it – a philosophy), selected passages from R.L. Stevenson, and 'The Shropshire Lad', by Housman.

We all try to carry on as though we were at home, and where we act differently we are doing things we would have liked to have done at home, if the chance had arisen. The Army turns very few saints into devils, though it may be easier than the reverse process. A Sergeant Major is usually a curt, barking, more-in-anger-than-in-sorrow, kind of chap. Yet the one we have here couldn't treat us better if he was our Father. He does more fatigues than anyone else in the Camp, asks you to do things, never orders. When he came here three months ago, we had one dirty old tent to eat our meals in, and that was all. Since then, we have added several more tents; plenty of forms and tables; a rest tent with a concrete floor; dozens of games, a regular weekly whist drive, a small library. Once we could only bathe in our tent, petrol tin fashion. Now, we use the showers in town, doing some forty miles in the process. If this is the Army – well, it's not bad.

We get a Film Show every Saturday; whatever the weather, it is held in the open air, the audience (stalls) sitting on petrol tins, while those in the gallery sit on top of the vehicles, many of which come several miles for what is usually the only event of the week. I have sat in the pouring rain with a ground-sheet over me. I have sat with a gale bowling me over literally while Barbara Stanwyck (in 'The Great Man's Lady' – she was a brunette) bowled me over figuratively. Only occasionally does a weakling leave the huddled concourse. We take our fun seriously, and when we can get it, though I always think of the Open Air Theatre at Regent's Park, seeing 'Midsummer Night's Dream' on a brilliantly lit sward, with a pre-war searchlight dancing in the sky above us.

George Formby has done a lot of talking since his trip here, but not a word (publicly) about losing ten bottles of beer from the back of his charabanc. Some chaps I was with at the time did the pinching and subsequent drinking, so I know!

Best wishes, Friend (The Lord Forgive Me),

Chris

Chapter Six

Neither Snow nor Rain nor the Flatness of Norfolk

In 1633, *The Prompters Packet of Letters*, yet another popular how-to manual for an increasingly literate Europe, displayed a woodcut on its title page of two galloping horsemen. The first carried the mail in his saddlebag, the second, an aristocratic type with a whip, was probably there to protect the first. The mail carrier sounds a bugle as he rides, and the sound he emits appears in a speech bubble that says simply 'Post Hast'. The phrase had already been in use for at least 60 years, a regular instruction for speedy delivery written on the outer letter as 'haste, post, haste'.

But how typical was this galloping sight through the English countryside? How did the post work?

For the beginning of the answer we need to briefly revisit England in the fifteenth century, and a wealthy extended family called Paston, named after the seemingly idyllic coastal Norfolk village where they lived (seemingly idyllic until letters reveal local anarchy, executions, civil wars, domestic shortages and bitter cold). For the Pastons, letters were the glue that held the family together. Their correspondence consisted of frequent (usually weekly, sometimes on consecutive days) communication through several generations and the reigns of Henry VI, Edward IV and Richard III. The many hundreds of letters that survive make up the most illuminating concentration of letters of fifteenth-century England. After a prolonged period of obscurity (the Paston line ended in 1732), the letters were redis-covered by local historians at the end of the eighteenth century and were acquired by the British Museum in the 1930s.

What can we learn from them now? Most are what we may call personal business letters – matters of property and legal affairs conducted colloquially through family members. A fair number are about love and marriage, several are about family decorum, and many are requests for supplies, not least heavy gowns and worsted cloth to ward off the winters. A modern reader may feel closest to Margaret Paston, wife of John Paston I (and mother to John Paston II and John Paston III), as she writes to her scattered family in London. Over the course of about 70 letters she acts as maternal moral advisor and estate manager, and despite her relatively comfortable domestic situation she must frequently ask for extra supplies of food and clothing. But these things are merely daily blips in the face of the grander issues, such as the threat of being over-run by charging armies. The bloody pageant of the Wars of the Roses unfurls in the background as she writes, and her days appear frantic (the majority of her letters are written 'in haste' as she regrets that 'want of leisure' prevents her writing more).

Unlike most of the male members of her family, Margaret Paston dictated her letters to a local scribe. On 7 January 1462 she began a letter to her husband in her usual way ('Right worshipful husband, I recommend me to you'), and continued with news composed straight for the history books:

> People of this country beginneth to wax wild, and it said here that my Lord of Clarence and the Duke of Suffolk and certain judges with them should come down and sit on such people as be noised rioutous in this country . . . In good faith men fear sore here of a common rising . . . God for his holy mercy give grace that there may be set a good rule . . . in this country in haste, for I heard never say of so much robbery and manslaught in this country as is now within a little time.*

Taken as a whole, the lexicographer and grammarian may also learn much from the Paston correspondence about the state of fifteenth-century English. The letters are packed with simple but well-formed sentences, and a high level of literacy and learning. We learn, as above, that the polite method of greeting is no longer 'greetings'; family and friends, male and female almost all open their post to read a derivation of 'Name of Recipient, I recommend me to you'. There are many early sightings of proverbs and other epithets: 'I eat like a horse', one Paston brother writes to another in May 1469, a metaphor not recorded again until the eighteenth century, and in a letter to the youngest Paston brother in 1477, a cousin advises him not to be discouraged by his prolonged pursuit of a wife, 'for . . . it is but a simple oak that is cut down at the first stroke'.

But we also learn about one other great thing: the workings of the post. By the 1460s, the smooth running of the economy demanded an efficient mail system, but it was not always

---

* Country in this context means county. A few months later, Margaret of Anjou, wife of Henry VI, led the Lancastrian faction in the invasion of Northumberland.

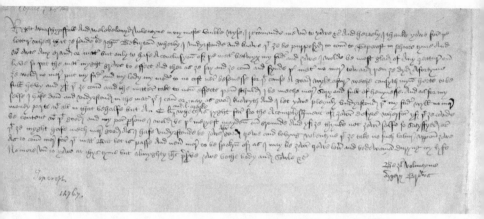

'If you love me . . . you will not leave me': Margery Brews sends one of the earliest Valentine greetings to her fiancé John Paston III in February 1477.

forthcoming. The Pastons were well connected (with strong links to the legal profession and parliament), but so many of their letters concern the fate of other letters – letters received, letters gone astray – that one can easily imagine the additional stress placed upon their lives by such a significant but unreliable service. They wrote at a time before the establishment of any official postal network, trusting their letters to friends or professional carriers. The system was thus little changed from the service at Vindolanda about 1,350 years before, a process of write, entrust and hope.

The Pastons occasionally write of finding 'the first speedy carrier' to rush information through, and they frequently called on a man called Juddy to journey back and forth on horseback to London (because of their status, the Pastons may have relied on Juddy almost as a private chauffeur). But the letters tell their own story of uncertainty; undelivered letters may mean unreliable carriers, or they may mean worse. At the start of her letter to her husband regarding Norfolk's lawlessness, Margaret Paston wrote:

Please it you to weet [know] that I sent you a letter by [my cousin] Berney's man of Witchingham which was written on St Thomas' Day in Christmas; and I had no tidings or letter of you sin the week before Christmas, wherof I marvel sore. I fear me it is not well with you because you came not home or sent ere this time ... I pray you heartly that ye will vouchsafe to send me word how ye do as hastely as ye may, for my heart shall never be in ease till I have tidings from you.

A hundred and forty years later, in the last years of Queen Elizabeth I, one may reasonably have hoped for improvement. In an intriguing bit of postal sleuthing, the historian James Daybell has forensically tracked one letter from 1601 as it travelled in vain from London to Dover and back again without ever reaching its intended reader. The letter, which now resides at Hatfield House in Hertfordshire, was written by Sir Robert Cecil, the secretary of state. Its recipient should have been the MP Sir Francis Darcy, but Darcy is still waiting for it.

The letter was slight, merely a cover note informing Darcy that he was to receive other letters from court and an unnamed French book. Sir Robert left a large amount of blank space around his 57-word note written on a sizeable sheet, denoting power and profligacy. It was written by a scribe but signed by Sir Cecil. Addressed 'To my verie loving friend Sir Francys Darcye knight at Dover,' this wasn't quite as optimistic as it would be if we sent such a letter today. It wasn't the vagueness of the location that stumped the post – being a Sir, he probably would have been tracked down to some or other courthouse, coffeehouse, alehouse, or house of ill-repute – so much as the fact that Sir Francis had already fled Dover for elsewhere. The instructions on the outside of the letter – 'post

hast hast hast for life life life lyfe' – was not only in vain, but evidence (for such a perfunctory message) of a sort of desperate madness.

The letter was carried along the Dover Road on horseback, presumably (as was the custom) by a number of riders working as a relay. The letter was endorsed with the words 'For he Mats affayres', which permitted it to travel free of charge by an early version of the royal mail, rather than by private carrier. The regally endorsed riders would be stationed at a series of established stops, either inns or signposts, a similar system to the one established within the Roman Empire. These 'post-stage' landmarks, which were usually towns dotted from eight to twenty miles apart, can also be thought of as the earliest forms of pillar boxes; before such a practical thing was invented centuries later, a regular series of deliveries and collections would be made along a set road, with letters being either dropped off as a final destination or handed on to the next rider like a baton. The Dover Road was one of England's very few established routes, so the Robert Cecil letter arrived within a day, and, failing to find Darcy, finished its journey in the hands of Sir Thomas Fane, Lieutenant of Dover Castle.

The markings on the envelope provide yet more details, the Elizabethan equivalent of UPS tracking. The first endorsement was 'London this 23 of September at 8 in the morninge', possibly written, James Daybell suggests, by Rowland White, the Post of the Court responsible for gathering official correspondence from several quarters to the main depot in central London. The next endorsement, 'London at past eight in the morning', was followed by 'Dartford at 11 in the fornone', and then Rochester 'at 2 in the afternon'. We also know it got to Sittingbourne at 7 and then Canterbury after 9, reaching Dover at some point the following morning. Sir Thomas Fane woke up to learn that Darcy had scarpered, and tried to locate him in the Kentish Downs, another failed mission.

Sir Thomas then sent the whole thing back to Sir Robert in a covering packet, which stopped off at all the places it had stopped off on its way down (reaching Dartford at almost 4 a.m.). In addition, the new packet was endorsed with an illustration of a gallows, presumably donating urgency, or the fate a trembling postmaster would meet if the letter wasn't delivered.

Beyond all the clear absurdities of this frantic toing and froing through night and day across the pastures of England for nought, the example did at least point to one unmistakable truth: the post – even the fate of a single transaction – was important. The post may not have been particularly private (Sir Robert's tired letter was opened before he got it back, perhaps by his secretary but conceivably by others too, and it may have passed through a dozen hands before it didn't reach where it was intended) but there was no doubting the investment in trying to get it through. If you wrote it, many people would try to deliver it. The fact the post-stages existed at all, and the bureaucratic feat of tracking the letter at every calling station, meant there had indeed been slender improvement in at least one primitive branch of the postal service compared with the preceding centuries.

But this was a court letter travelling with all the haste and urgency that royal command could throw at it, a system for the chosen. What hope for the commoner? And what hope even for the landed commoner such as a latter-day Paston?

⊗   ⊗   ⊗

The stirrings of what we would now recognise as a modern regular postal service did slowly emerge in the sixteenth century, and for this we should be grateful to a *cause célèbre* – the passions and paranoia of Henry VIII. It helped everyone concerned with the transmission of letters that Henry VIII had reason to write letters of his own beyond the usual tally of courtly housekeeping. His letters to Anne Boleyn, some of the very few he wrote by hand, are amongst the purest examples we have of a smitten monarch from any era. The tone of the correspondence is vulnerable and lavishly purple, and, if we didn't know how the story turned out, would have been a classic romance for the history books. The letters form a rare sequence, a wooing that stretches over 18 months of their early courtship from around May 1527 to October 1528. Presumably there were more; his divorce from Catherine of Aragon and the separation from Rome that accompanied it would take five more years. Through the letters we are able to track how a proud and ambitious courtship by the king meets an initially non-committal response from his intended, and how his love life entwines his plague-ridden, hunt-struck daily one. Because they are undated, there is disagreement among historians as to the correct ordering of the letters, although there are enough clues to provide at least a rough framework.

'On turning over in my mind the contents of your last letters,' he begins,

'Wishing myself in my sweetheart's arms': Henry promises all to Anne Boleyn.

I have put myself into great agony, not knowing how to interpret them, whether to my disadvantage, as you show in some
places, or to my advantage, as I understand them in some others,
beseeching you earnestly to let me know expressly your whole
mind as to the love between us two. It is absolutely necessary
for me to obtain this answer, having been for above a whole year
stricken with the dart of love, and not yet sure whether I shall fail
of finding a place in your heart and affection, which last point
has prevented me for some time past from calling you my mistress . . . But if you please to do the office of a true loyal mistress
and friend, and to give up yourself body and heart to me . . . I will
take you for my only mistress, casting off all others besides you
out of my thoughts and affections, and serve you only.

Two others follow with similarly hesitant tone, one with news
of 'a buck killed late last night with my own hand' which the
king hoped would cause Anne to 'think of the hunter' when
she ate it. Court and public gossip then appear to cause Anne
to be banished to her childhood home of Hever Castle in
Kent, where, regretting her absence, Henry sends her 'a picture set in a bracelet, with the whole of the device, which you

already know, wishing myself in their place'. Even by the sixth letter her affection remains cool, although he is sure 'that I have since never done any thing to offend you, and it seems a very poor return for the great love which I bear you to keep me at a distance both from the speech and the person of the woman that I esteem most in the world'.

By the ninth letter, a few weeks later, he expresses concern at her recent illness, perhaps the plague, and promises to send his physician as fast as he can, and subsequent letters carry further news of illness, more advice on keeping well, and another slain hart to aid her recovery. By the twelfth letter, Henry's usual letter carrier Suche is also 'fallen sick of the sweat', and so he sends a new man. By the fifteenth letter, addressed to 'Mine own SWEETHEART' he is again openly lovestruck, reporting both grieving and pain at her absence. The letter is brief (he has a headache), but he closes 'wishing myself (especially an evening) in my sweetheart's arms, whose pretty dukkys* I trust shortly to kiss.'

The final letters touched upon hopes for the divorce, the attainment of a lodging for Anne for improved mistress proximity, and further news of hunting. The seventeenth letter was, perhaps unsurprisingly, 'Written after the killing of a hart, at eleven of the clock, minding, with God's grace, to-morrow, mightily timely, to kill another, by the hand which, I trust, shortly shall be yours.'

By the last letter we appear to have reached some sort of resolution. The legate from Paris with crucial news of his possible divorce is sick, but otherwise 'all my pains and labour' seem to be at an end, and 'thereby shall come, both to you and me, the greatest quietness that may be in this world.' Anne is installed in dwellings near the king, and the need for letters has diminished. But their marriage is still more than four

* Breasts.

for whose sake I am now as I am, whose name I could some
good while since have pointed unto, your grace being not
ignorant of my suspicion therein.

But if you have already determined of mee and that not only
my death but an infamous slander must bring you the enjoying
of your desired happiness. Then I desire of god that he will pardon
your greate sinne herein and likewise myne enemye es the
Instruments thereof And that he will not call you to a straight
account for your unprincely and cruell usage of mee at his
generall judgment seate where both you and my self must
shortly appeare And in whose iust iudgment I doubt not
whatsoever the world may thinke of mee my innocency shall
be openly knowne and sufficiently cleared.

My last and only request shall be that my selfe may onely beare the
burthen of your graces displeasure And that it may not
touch the Innocent soules of those poore gentlemen whome as
I understand are likewise in straight imprisonment for my
sake. If ever I have founde favour in your sight if ever the name
of Anne Bullen hath been pleasinge in your eares lett mee
obtayne this last request And I will soe leave to trouble your
grace any further with my earnest prayers to the Trinitye
to have you in his good keepinge And to directe you in
all your actions.

From my dolefull prison
in the Tower 6th May

your most loyall and
ever faithfull wife

Anne Bullen

Anne Boleyn writes to Henry from the Tower in 1536. Apparently.

years distant, and the 'quietness' of which he writes, ushering in the English Reformation, would sound its effects through the constitutional halls for centuries.

The letters are now in the Vatican Library, glued into a book and tempered with a Vatican seal. They may have been stolen not long after Boleyn's execution and brought to Rome as a spoil of war while the excommunication furore raged. We do not have Anne's responses to his longings, and the only extant relevant letter by her during this period was written to Cardinal Wolsey, thanking him for his support in these months and hoping that the legate will soon bring positive news of a divorce.

But there is another letter from Anne that has become famous – her last to Henry in 1536, sent from the Tower where she was accused of adultery and treason. It is remarkable as much for its beauty, restraint and composure as its plaintive contents, and it is a letter that, in its heartbreaking simplicity, does more to seal an innocent, golden reputation than any other letter in the English language. The culture of Anne Boleyn that has spawned the novels and films and devotional websites, largely draws from this:

> Sir,
>
> Your Grace's displeasure, and my imprisonment are things so strange unto me, as what to write, or what to excuse, I am altogether ignorant ...
>
> But let not your Grace ever imagine, that your poor wife will ever be brought to acknowledge a fault, where not so much as a thought thereof preceded. And to speak a truth, never prince had wife more loyal in all duty, and in all true affection, than you have ever found in Anne Boleyn: with which name and place I could willingly have contented myself, if God and your Grace's pleasure had been so pleased. Neither did I at any time so far forget

myself in my exaltation or received Queenship, but that I always looked for such an alteration as I now find; for the ground of my preferment being on no surer foundation than your Grace's fancy, the least alteration I knew was fit and sufficient to draw that fancy to some other object. You have chosen me, from a low estate, to be your Queen and companion, far beyond my desert or desire. If then you found me worthy of such honour, good your Grace let not any light fancy, or bad council of mine enemies, withdraw your princely favour from me; neither let that stain, that unworthy stain, of a disloyal heart toward your good grace, ever cast so foul a blot on your most dutiful wife, and the infant-princess your daughter. Try me, good king, but let me have a lawful trial, and let not my sworn enemies sit as my accusers and judges; yea let me receive an open trial, for my truth shall fear no open flame; then shall you see either my innocence cleared, your suspicion and conscience satisfied, the ignominy and slander of the world stopped, or my guilt openly declared.

... But if you have already determined of me, and that not only my death, but an infamous slander must bring you the enjoying of your desired happiness; then I desire of God, that he will pardon your great sin therein, and likewise mine enemies, the instruments thereof, and that he will not call you to a strict account of your unprincely and cruel usage of me, at his general judgment-seat, where both you and myself must shortly appear, and in whose judgment I doubt not (whatsoever the world may think of me) mine innocence shall be openly known, and sufficiently cleared ... If ever I found favour in your sight, if ever the name of Anne Boleyn hath been pleasing in your ears, then let me obtain this request, and I will so leave to trouble your Grace any further, with mine earnest prayers to the Trinity to have your Grace in his good keeping, and to direct you in all your actions. From my doleful prison in the Tower, this sixth of May;

Your most loyal and ever faithful wife,

Probably not a real letter though. Or rather, it was a real letter, purportedly found among Thomas Cromwell's papers after his death and then frequently copied, but it was not a real letter written by Anne Boleyn in the Tower. Too many inconsistencies – the way she spelt her name 'Bullen' (which she hadn't done for many years), her judgement of herself as 'from low estate' – suggest inauthenticity to the great majority of modern historians. The reason for its forgery may be religious, political or just mischief-making, and its compelling attractiveness, its ability to charm just as it deceives, may derive from the multitude of caustic samples in the letter-writing manuals.

That Henry VIII feared frauds and spies there can be no doubt, and it was his attempt to control these (the combined effort we would now call Intelligence) that led to the formation of the first Royal Mail to ensure the safe passage of correspondence from the court. In the early part of his reign, Henry created a new role for the treasurer of the king's chamber: the master of posts. Brian Tuke, who was also Cardinal Wolsey's secretary, was entrusted with improving the haphazard network of posts along key roads, with a particular emphasis on a northern route through York to Edinburgh and the roads to the Cinque Ports, particularly Dover for the crossing to Calais. His responsibilities are best described in a letter he wrote to Thomas Cromwell in August 1533, observing that 'The king's pleasure is that posts be better appointed, and laid in all places most expedient; with the commandment to all townships in all places, on pain of life, to be in such readiness, and to make such provision of horses at all times, as no tract or loss of time be had in that behalf.'

London was the obvious centre for this activity, with a team of 'King's hackneymen' on permanent standby in the city at Lombard Street.

The new urgency urged by Tuke did improve the system marginally, and it encouraged private operators to use the extended network and improve their own carrier systems as much as royal pardon would allow. For the Royal Mail now imposed a monopoly on letters and other post, a control that soon extended beyond domestic packets towards the 'strangers' post' across the Channel, and Tuke ensured that his master of posts was entrusted with another new task: he held an official warrant to enable all mail on royal business both in and out of the court to be opened, read and redirected. On the surface this could be passed off as a grand secretarial role; but beneath it lay a darker vision.

The darker vision was 'The Great Snooping'. A paranoia of plotting that descended over the Tudors would extend into Elizabethan England, and successive postmasters after Tuke increasingly controlled not just a postal monopoly but played a leading role in suppressing anything deemed anti-monarchist or papist, or anything, indeed, that might threaten national security. Yet it wasn't until the 1650s that the secretive and disruptive role of the Letter Office was confirmed.

When, in 1655, John Thurloe became postmaster general (as the job was now called), the burgeoning postal service was in the process of opening up its networks to commoners' letters not on royal business. Merchants had petitioned for this reform in earlier decades, and successive state secretaries had savoured the prospect of large postal revenues, but it was only with Oliver Cromwell's 'Act for the Setting of the Postage of England, Scotland and Ireland' of 1657 that the first General Post Office established an enshrined framework for both domestic and foreign mail. The first London penny post followed a few years later, setting a uniform rate within the capital, allowing letters to be sent back and forth several times in a day. It heralded the beginning of an efficient concept: at the

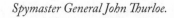

Spymaster General John Thurloe.

turn of the century Daniel Defoe remarked how 'Letters are delivered at the remotest Corners of the Town almost as soon as they can be sent by a Messenger, and that Four, Five, Six or Eight Times a Day. We see nothing of this at Paris, at Amsterdam, at Hamburgh or any other City.'

'Eight times a day' was overplaying it a bit, but his international comparisons were well grounded. The need for an established postal service for a country with grand visions of empire was long overdue. Britain didn't quite lead the pack – that credit should perhaps go to the Dutch Taxis dynasty given Church approval in 1600 to charge a postage fee for private letters – but Britain set an enviable example to a shrinking world. The intellectual and cultural discourse that had been unleashed by the Renaissance had been mirrored in the expansion of trade and global ambitions; oceans were newly navigable, and the very earliest stirrings of globalisation were taking shape. Letters would carry news of these developments, and increasingly reflect people's needs as they expanded their philosophical and geographical horizons.

For the time being, letter-writing in Britain remained predominantly a pursuit of courtiers, churchmen and merchants; the penny post introduced by William Dockwra in 1680 shouldn't be confused with the great equalities afforded by the universal penny postage promoted by Rowland Hill in 1840, but it was the beginning of something long overdue.

In the late seventeenth century the cost of letters was borne by the recipient not the sender (which caused some writers to ask permission before commencing a correspondence), and outside London rates varied widely: a single sheet sent less than eight miles cost 2d, while two sheets cost double; the cost of longer journeys cost up to 4d per sheet, but there were many reports of letters costing the recipient 8d or more; a letter from London to Scotland was considered tardy if it took more than five days. But there was no doubting the improvement of this service over the haphazard network of carriers, nor the encouragement it gave to letter-writers. In 1698 the penny post carried more than 790,000 letters and packets within the capital, and 77,500 outside it; five years later the number topped one million.*

We'll return to the peculiarities and shortcomings of the system when we consider letters from the eighteenth and early nineteenth centuries, but for now we should note that John Thurloe also had another role in Cromwell's nervous government beyond postmaster general; he was spymaster general too.

A full account of Thurloe's vocation only came to light in 1898 with a new examination of the papers of the privy council and other state offices of Charles II. One document, by a certain Major John Wildman, revealed that, because all the letters to be distributed to all parts of the kingdom came through a central London office, the task of 'sorting' them through the night took on an entirely new meaning. The document relates that Cromwell employed a certain Isaac Dorislaus

> to reside constantly at the [Letter Office], who had a private roome allotted him adjoining to the forreigne Office, and every post night about 11 a clock he went into that roome privately, and had all the letter[s] brought and layd before him, to open any

---

* Not that the carrier system didn't continue to compete against the state monopoly. In 1637, just after the then-postmaster Thomas Witherings and the king's principal secretary of state John Coke laid down the first principles of the post office and new post roads, *The Carriers Cosmographie* by John Taylor listed many hundreds of unofficial routes and schedules.

as he should see good, and close them up again, and there he remained in that room, usually till about 3 or 4 in the morning, which was the usuall time of shutting up the male, and in the processe of time the said Dorislaus had got such a knowledge of all hands and seals, that scarcely could a letter be brought him but he knew the hand that wrote it; and when there was any extraordinary occasion, as when any rising was neare or the like, then S. Morland [a secretary of Thurloe's] went from Whitehall between 11 and 12, and was privately conveighed into that roome, and there assisted Mr Dorislaus, and such letters as they found dangerous he brought back with him to Whitehall in the morning.

Wildman's account is backed up by Thurloe's own state papers, where there are many instances of 'interrupted' and 'intercepted' letters, and several letters from his henchman Dorislaus. 'Sir, I Have been up all night,' states one letter of June 1653. 'The inclosed are my last night's worke . . .'

The merchants here doe generally write, that the king of Spayne hath deceaved them, lest them to shift for themselves, and that hee and this state are agreed for the coyning and disposing of the silver by this state. I will goe this morning to Whitehall, and tell Bishop, that I am now layd aside, have nothing more to doe with the post letters. I will manage that businesse for you with that secrecy and dexteritie to your owne heart's desire; and am resolved henceforward not to impart one sillable of any thinge I know to any living soule but yourselfe, who am now wholy engaged to you; and you shall finde me reall, faythfull, and true in every particular trust or word you shall impose upon me. I am very sleepy, and will tell you more of my minde at Whitehall.

Your most faythful and humble servant, Dorislaus.

Some form of officially sanctioned clandestine censorship remained in place in London until 1844. So how best to avoid this furtive small-hours surveillance? With counter-espionage creativity. Letter-writers had to learn not only the craft of composition but the art of concealment too, and soon there were manuals for sale alongside *The Enimie of Idlenesse* that taught ciphers and code-breaking. The state of the art was considered in 1605 in *The Advancement of Learning* by Francis Bacon, itself a letter (to James I). The attributes required of a good code were threefold: 'That they be not laborious to write and reade; that they bee impossible to discypher; and in some cases, that they be without suspition.' To illustrate the last requisite, Bacon developed what he called a 'biliteral cipher', a process wherein a letter would appear normal on the surface but only reveal its true meaning to the recipient. This involved the use of two parallel alphabets, one forming a decoy, the other the intended secret text. To befuddle further, five times as many letters would be used than were necessary in a single word, a process he called 'infolding'. It appeared to be an early form of binary or genetic coding: words such as 'aababaab-baabbaaabaa' would not be uncommon in Bacon's ciphers, though it is unclear why this seeming gibberish wouldn't at once be rightly regarded as fishy.

Ciphers were an essential piece of the ambassador's tool kit, often involving prearranged numerical and alphabetical cryptographies known only to the recipient. They were popular too among merchants eager to conceal new markets, for which they also developed their own form of shorthand. These mathematical and linguistical tricks soon moved from the writing desk to the parlour and a magician's cabinet of illusions: Johann Wecker's *Eighteen Books of the Secrets of Art and Nature*, published in 1660, included instruction on 'The way to write in an Egge' and 'How to make Letters that lye hid appear, and to hide those that are visible' (hint: use both 'vinegar and piss'). Code words were common too. Mary Queen of Scots employed a Scottish cipher secretary named Gilbert Curle, who used the sort of deflections we have become familiar with from the great wars: the queen of England was referred to as 'the merchant of London'; the queen of Scotland was 'the merchant of Newscastle [sic]'.

And then there was that other confounding schoolboy favourite: invisible ink. Again, one perhaps imagines this as originating with early spy novels, but the rough science gained full momentum in the seventeenth century. And here again vinegar and urine were found to have their uses, alongside alum powder, milk, onion water and the juice of oranges and lemons. Its most notorious use was during the Gunpowder Plot of 1605, with a group of Jesuit priests conducting regular correspondence on what must have appeared to be partially blank paper.

One of them, John Gerard, later wrote of his activities from prison, confessing to using the juice of citrus fruit between lines of pencil: 'In the penciled letter I confined myself to spiritual topics, but in the white space between the lines I gave detailed instructions to different friends of mine outside.' And Gerard was particular about the type of juice he used. Lemon juice was valuable, becoming visible when exposed to water or heat; when it dries or is taken away from a flame the writing disappears again. 'But orange juice is different,' he wrote in his autobiography. 'It cannot be read with water . . . Heat brings it out but it stays out. So a letter in orange juice cannot be delivered without the recipient knowing whether or not it has been read.'

Increasingly aware of state intervention, writers – be they spies on intelligence missions or traders on mercantile ones – found new ways to secure their information. And increasingly too, they began to regard the secrecy of their letters as a sacrosanct right, a belief strengthened, ironically as we've seen, by the emergence of an official royal postal network opening its service to the public. When all else failed, the recipient had a simple instruction: burn after reading.

And what rich rewards should we expect from this century of great postal transformation? Surely Shakespeare's letters would be worth a look? Perhaps a note to his leading actors as they prepared to take the stage? Or a handful of love letters to Anne Hathaway, one with a lock of his hair? And perhaps a letter from Elizabeth in appreciation of his playes addressed to the Globe bye Thames? All these were on offer for the first time in 1795, and a man called Samuel Ireland was taking orders for a limited print edition at a charge of 4 guineas. The letters were the main attraction, but *Miscellaneous Papers and Legal Instruments under the hand and seal of William Shakspeare* also included deeds, a radical draft of *King Lear* and an entirely new play entitled *Vortigern and Rowena*. Understandably enough, the letters and their publication were the cause of some hysteria, at least until the leading Shakespearian scholar Edmond Malone delivered his critique of the documents in the spring of 1796. According to Malone, the letters contained so many discrepancies – grammatical, orthographical, phraseological, tragical-comical-historical-pastoral – that they couldn't possibly be genuine. And he was

'*Some have greatness thrust upon them . . .*' Stephen Fry's Malvolio misinterprets a letter in Twelfth Night.

right. The letters were written, as were the plays, by Samuel Ireland's son William Henry to please his father.*

In fact, nothing of Shakespeare's correspondence survives. We know of a carrier named William Greenway who ran mail horses between Stratford and London, but no searching beneath floorboards or local restorations has ever produced a line from the bard not written for profit or publication. But there is another plentiful supply of his letters in his plays, of course, and from these we may divine not only a sense of how the playwright regarded the common use of letters in his day, but an early glimpse of the sort of epistolary drama that would infect so much literary endeavour in the next two centuries.

The Shakespeare scholar Alan Stewart has found, 'at a conservative estimate' III letters that make an appearance on stage, and there are many more alluded to in an expository way. It is easier to list the plays where letters do not have a role – *The Comedy of Errors*, *A Midsummer Night's Dream*, *The Taming of the Shrew*, *Henry V* and *The Tempest* – the latter with a dreamy Gonzalo envisaging a land where 'Letters should not be known'. The onstage letters were all composed at a time before postal reform, where they were still reliant on private carriers, uncertain terrain and regular miscarriages. Letters are

---

* The play *Vortigern and Rowena* caused so much initial excitement that it even received a performance at Drury Lane. A long run it wasn't: in the manner of *The Producers*, the play seemed destined to close on page four, but it staggered on gamely, finally closing on the same night it opened. The actors left the stage to widespread laughter.

These days, a bit of forensic work on the ink would have consigned it to the dustbin before it hit the boards. Unlike the ink available in the late eighteenth century, which was made from squid, soot and turpentine, Shakespeare's fluid derived predominantly from ground 'gall nuts', the product of the gall fly on oak trees. These would then be soaked in red wine, and mixed with iron sulphate and gum Arabic while being dried in the sun. A cut-down goose quill was the favoured writing tool, and the ink would be dried on the parchment or rough paper by dusting with a fine powder of 'pounce', made from pumice stone or salt; a letter would thus be judged 'done and dusted'.

delivered from the battlefield in the nick of time, but more usually they arrive fatefully late. Letters in Shakespeare assert authority, conceal identity, and are forged to deceive. They are purposely intercepted or they accidentally fall into the wrong hands. They are not sent via the Royal Mail, but through the messier channels, a reliable fault line of the absent-minded or the inefficient.

The failed delivery of a letter to Romeo informing him of Juliet's fake death hastens his own real one; Malvolio's delusions of grandeur gather hilarious pace as he reads a fake love letter written by Maria in Olivia's hand; Goneril's letter to Edmund revealing their adultery and her desire to have her husband Albany killed is intercepted and delivered to Albany instead. But it is *Hamlet* that has it all: our protagonist writes to Ophelia, to Claudius the king, to his mother and to Horatio. Polonius reads and write letters; Claudius writes too. The play twists a plot we may recognise from Homer, something Alan Stewart rightly calls the oldest letter in the book. The *Iliad*'s account of Bellerophon's escape from death at his own command, discussed in Chapter Two, receives a reboot as Hamlet sails to England. It's the old switcheroo: Hamlet travels with Rosencrantz and Guildenstern to England, where a letter carried by the courtiers from Claudius contains instructions for his execution. Hamlet slits the seal, substitutes the letter for one of his own, skilfully folds and reseals it. At the end of the play we learn that Rosencrantz and Guildenstern are dead, as Claudius had seemingly instructed.

The use of letters in drama goes back to the ancients, to Euripides and Plautus. But under Shakespeare's direction they become something else, not merely a vehicle for news but practically characters in themselves, a constant prop as well as a function of the plot (and for many actors the prop has served as a thankful breather, something they could effectively read rather than learn). Shakespeare has turned what is essentially an anti-theatrical device – words on a page, seemingly private, sent from one person to be read only by another – into something communally witnessed and contested, something entirely necessary to the adornment of the human drama. And yet letters in Shakespeare are also more than dramatic: their insistent, constant presence help to preface a day where they are a normal part of the discourse, objects (rather than just texts) that move from person to person, as expected as the weekday post. If an audience wants to believe a drama, even an historical one, it is required to witness the interplay of letters as a regular part of the action. For letters were rapidly becoming a regular part of life.

Your New Lover

14232134 SIGMN. BARKER H.C., 30 WING, I COY.,
9 AIR FORMATION SIGNALS, M.E.F.

14th March 1944

Dear Bessie,

I had not expected that my Air Mail letter would travel so quickly, and am delighted that you should already have it, and have spent some time, probably, in reading it. At the moment, and for the present, there isn't a shadow of doubt that we are both in the same mutually approving mood, and that if we were within smiling distance of each other, we should soon be doing rather more than that. Of course, maybe the safety of our separate distances permits us to indulge in these happy advances. Perhaps we would beat hasty retreats into our shells if we knew that the seeds we are now sowing were due for early reaping. I might be on another planet for all the chance there is of hearing you say the good things you've written. But how much I enjoy you, how jolly fine it is to know that you really do understand what I write, when only a little while ago I was saying that I felt like Marconi would have done on the morrow of his invention, had all the world gone deaf.

If I had the chance, I might do a lot of things, or nothing. As it is I shall remain very polite and become as friendly as I dare without undertaking obligations I have no intention of fulfilling. I am safe from physical indiscretion for a long while, but I am also wanting you seriously to see that while we might have fun at a later date, it would not be so funny for you ultimately. I can't help being your 'hero' – and I breathe heavily and exultingly at your clear, bare admittance; but please don't let me make you break your heart in 1946 or 47, when I scurry off with 'one, two, three, or more'. If I was a wise guy I would not write you and thus encourage your racing thoughts. But I am selfish; at present I need your loyal support of my actions. I admit to a state of gleaming, dangerous excitement as I read again and again your written words. You fascinate and weaken me, and make me feel strong. Presumably you wrote the same in the old days (in an earlier letter I said I was hazy even about any 'letters'), have I become so much more susceptible to flattery, or is the change due to the fact that I have been away from home fourteen months, and haven't seen a woman (other than about four on a stage) in the last six?

You say that men concentrate on the job in hand and it fills their world completely. I would not say that 'active doers' are only men. I have seen many a blithering, dithering male who hadn't any idea of doing anything. I've known women who were very competent and energetic. Don't be a man-worshipper, or an anything-worshipper if you would be happy. The main difference, emotionally, between men and women, is said to be that a woman is loyal to one man always, but that a man's attention wanders more than a little. This sex item is the biggest there is, apart from the instinct to survive, because no-one is impervious to it and it controls us always. I think I have mentioned that one chap of 18 who I met in hospital told me he had 'had' 35 girls, several on the first day of meeting. This 'loyalty' of the woman has been blown sky-high during this war – one of the chaps here asked his girl why she hadn't written for six weeks, and she replied she had been busy, didn't he know there was a war on?

You want your old hero to be your new lover. What a pity that they have just given me my mosquito net for my second summer, and not a ticket for an air journey home. I am writing these particular words at midnight 13.3.44 – I could have breakfast with you on the 14th, if only one or two people would co-operate. It might be a little late, but what matter. Here am I, wondering when I last saw you and what you look like. I have an idea, I wish I could confirm by personal investigation. Do you still smoke? A bad habit.

Expectant, willing, and compliant as you are, I seem to have discovered you anew. I find you very warm and appetising. I rejoice at our intimacy for the present. I simply wallow in your friendly sentiments which I feel as keenly as if a couple of seas and a continent did not separate us. You have smashed my perimeter defences, I am all of a hub-bub, and as I write my cheeks are red and I am hot. When I finish one letter to you, I want to start again on another, as today. I hope that I shall often have something to comment on, rather than initiate my own discussions. I know this strange unity of expression and understanding cannot last, for I feel just as though I was sitting at your feet. This is bound to peter-out sooner or later. You say, 'here's to the beginning of a beautiful friendship.'*

You are a terrific love-maker by letter. I can but wonder what you are like at it in the soft, warm, yielding, panting flesh. Please pardon the rub-out, and the re-writing hereabouts. Truth is that with the morning I became timid and decided on deletion. Let me go back a few lines, say that I can but wonder, and warmly do.

I must avoid writing one whole letter slobbering, however pleasant it is for both of us, I must make a pretence of telling you all about our camp. Our picture on Saturday (luckily I was

* *Casablanca* had been released in London the previous year.

on duty) was as childish as the previous two I have described earlier. 'Stars Over Texas', Stage Coach hold-ups, and pistol duels. We are getting more than disgusted.

Having interposed that sentence I can return to our new thrilling relationship, to be fully enjoyed while it lasts, and unlamented when it is done. I am 'all for you, dear' and the prospect of soaking in you, luxuriously for a while, of touching you where you will let me, from here, is absorbingly, naturally, before us.

Chris

Chapter Seven

How to Write the Perfect Letter, Part 2

What does it take to become the greatest letter-writer of your age? To build up a reputation of such epistolary grandeur that whenever you were mentioned in centuries to come you would be remembered not by what you had achieved but how you had written about it? How would one ensure immortality as a writer not by grand artistic endeavours – not by the dramas created by your compatriots Molière, Corneille or Racine, nor the sweeping philosophies of Descartes, all of whom you knew – but by simply attending their plays and reading their works and passing opinion on them through the post? And how to establish an historical reputation not by the grand public gesture during a lifetime but by private intimacies and indiscretions revealed after death?

A tall order these days, but for Madame de Sévigné in the high-haired years of the everlasting reign of Louis XIV it was a different proposition. Precocious, hedonistic, gallant, witty, scathing, protective, bombastic, objectionable, daring and unforgiving: Madame de Sévigné wrote some 1,300 shining letters in a 50-year period. She stands with Voltaire as one of the most enduring epistolary companions. Her letters are not always pleasant to read – too hardened an attitude, too many truths perhaps – but they are consistently compelling.

There was little in the second half of the seventeenth century that didn't catch her eye. She was modern in her candour and independence of thought (and must have seemed shockingly and titillatingly so to her subsequent Victorian readers), and she was proud of what she saw as her grounded contribution to philosophical debate (she disputed Descartes' interpretation of the mechanistic theory of nature, for example, plumping instead for a view that was a forerunner of romanticism, seeking her pleasures of nature in God-given wonder and solitude).* On the big issues she remained fundamentally a traditionalist, seldom breaking with the values of the majority or the court; it was essential for the maintenance of her reputation that she did so. Her letters endure through their emotions: her bereavements, longings and familial worries still reach us because they are seldom very different from our own, although we may baulk at her frivolity and her dismissive attitude towards those in less fortunate positions than her own. But who was this woman, and how best to explain why leather-bound volumes of her letters are still buckling the shelves of the world's great libraries?

She was born Marie de Rabutin-Chantal in a Paris suburb, married the Marquis de Sévigné in 1644 at the age of 18, and gave birth to two children before being widowed in 1651 when her husband lost a duel over his mistress. She never remarried, devoting her time to managing various estates, bringing up her granddaughter, conducting literary salons and engaging in the brightly lit life of the Parisian *beau monde*. And then she wrote.

She appeared to write every day, and with increasing intensity on Wednesdays and Fridays when the regular post left Paris. Her letters may still be appreciated when read in sequence and in their entirety, a feat seldom recommended for most letter-writers; there is seldom a sense that she is writing

---

* In a letter to her daughter in September 1680 she implored, 'Speak . . . about your machines, the machines which love, the machines which make an election of someone, the machines which are jealous, the machines which fear. Now go on; you are mocking us. Descartes never should have tried to make us believe this.'

out of obligation, and even her business matters are conducted with verve. Her relationships with the principal recipients of her attention develop over time, as one would expect, and it is one of the rare pleasures of the collection that one may watch grudges fester and then fall away (not least with her cousin, the memoirist Roger de Bussy-Rabutin). That Madame de Sévigné possessed a unique talent was immediately acknowledged by those with whom she corresponded; her letters contained news and gossip dished up with gasps and relish, and they were anticipated and passed on with the ink still moist. The most famous letter of all – the most anthologised – appeals primarily today for its shrieking hyperbole (which she intended), and its ultimate inconsequence (which she did not). 'What I am about to communicate to you is the most astonishing thing,' she wrote to her cousin Philippe-Emmanuel de Coulanges in December 1670. But the thing wasn't just most astonishing, it was

> the most surprising, the most marvellous, the most miraculous, most triumphant, most baffling, most unheard of, most singular, most extraordinary, most unbelievable, most unforeseen, the greatest, the tiniest, the rarest, the most common, the most talked about, the most secret up to this day, the most brilliant, the most enviable, a thing without parallel in the present age, . . . a thing nobody can believe in Paris (so how could anyone believe it in Lyons?), a thing that makes everybody cry 'have mercy on us' . . . I can't make up my mind to say it. Guess – I'll give you three tries. Give up? Very well, I shall have to tell you. M de Lauzun is marrying on Sunday, in the Louvre – guess who? I give you four guesses, ten, a hundred . . .

This was obviously getting beyond annoying, and it went on. Monsieur Lauzun, a louche and controversial figure at court, was due to marry La Grande Mademoiselle, granddaughter of Henry IV. In the end it didn't happen. After some persuad-

*Pearls of wisdom at her fingertips: Madame de Sévigné
plucks out another* bon mot.

ing by the queen and his courtiers, Louis XIV put his foot down, judging Lauzun not quite the right sort. Lauzun married another and lived to 90. Mademoiselle stayed single and suffered an ignominious burial at which her entrails exploded. And Madame de Sévigné went on to write about other most astonishing things, such as the civil war and the fate of the imprisoned disgraced French finance minister Nicolas Fouquet.

These days the modern reader may enjoy one thing above all others – her correspondence with her daughter. This was a loving and caring relationship, but it was also an overwhelmingly possessive one. We do not have her daughter's replies, but we may suspect them to be less fussy, less suffocating and less insecure.

Her daughter, Francoise-Marguerite, married a military man of whom her mother approved, Francois comte de Grignan, famed both for his ugliness and elegance, a tricky *pas de deux*. Initially all was well, but things turned sour when Grignan was posted to Provence. For Madame de Grignan this was an opportunity, but for her mother it was a bereavement, and the grieving continued for a quarter of a century. 'I am dying to have news of you,' she wrote to her daughter in mid-February 1671, and many times thereafter. 'As soon as I get a letter I want another one at once, and only breathe again when one comes ... I feel I suffer at having lost you, and this separation pains my heart and soul like a bodily illness.'*

A few days later she wrote again, her usual mix of local

---

* Understandably, Madame de Sévigné's moods revolved to a great extent around the performance of the postal service. Occasionally she would complain about tardiness, particular regarding mail from Italy. But she could also praise, and, because it wasn't her most common attribute, her approval strikes one as a memorable thing. Elsewhere in France (as in England), one read mostly complaints. 'I cannot but wonder at the skill of those gentlemen – the postilions – who spend their lives racing back and forth carrying our mail,' she wrote to her daughter in June 1671. 'There is not one day in the week, nor a single hour in the day when they are not on the road. Those wonderful people! What a wonderful invention the postal service is!'

news and betrothal updates, amid reassurances that 'you are the delight of my life, that nobody has ever been loved as dearly as you'. And then there was news of a fire, described in a way only a personal letter may do, the sort of immediate account that guaranteed the writer's reputation. There is, indeed, a touch of the Vesuvius about it. 'At three in the morning I heard people shouting "Thieves!", "Fire!" and these shouts were so near me and so persistent that I was sure it was here in the house.'

> I even fancied I heard my granddaughter's name, and felt sure she had been burnt alive. I got up with this fear in the dark and trembled in such a manner that I could scarcely stand. I ran directly to her room, which is the room that was yours, and found everything quiet; but I saw Guitaut's house all in flames, and the fire spreading to Madame de Vauvineux's. The flames cast a light over our courtyard and that of Guitaut, that made them look shocking. All was outcry, hurry, and confusion, and the falling beams and joists made a dreadful noise. I immediately ordered our doors to be opened, and my servants to give assistance . . .

> As for our house, I knew it was safe as if it had been in an island, but I was greatly concerned for my poor neighbours. Madame Gueton and her brother gave some excellent directions, but we were all in consternation; the fire was so fierce that there was no approaching it, and no one supposed it would cease till it had burnt poor Guitaut's house entirely down. Guitaut himself was a melancholy object; he wanted to save his mother, who was in the midst of the flames in the upper part of the house; but his wife clung about him, and held him as tightly as she could. He was in the greatest distress between the grief of not being able to save his mother, and the fear of injuring his wife, who was nearly five months pregnant. At last he begged me to restrain his wife, which I did, and he went in search of his mother, whom he found had passed through the flames and was safe. He then

tried to save some papers, but found it impossible to get near the place where they were. At length he came back to the spot where he had left us, and where I had prevailed on his wife to sit down.

Some charitable Capuchins worked so well, and so skilfully, that they contained the spread of the fire. Water was thrown upon the rest that was burning ... but not till several of the best apartments were entirely consumed ...

You may be wondering how the fire started in that building; but that no one can tell. There was not a spark in the room where it first broke out. If anyone would have thought of diverting himself at so melancholy a time, what pictures could he have drawn of the state we were in! Guitaut was in his nightshirt and breeches. Mme de Guitaut was stockingless and had lost a slipper. Mme de Vauvineux was in a short petticoat with a nightgown. All the servants and neighbours were in nightcaps. The Ambassador was in nightgown and wig, and maintained perfect serenity, but his secretary was a wonderful sight – talk about the breast of Hercules, this was something else. Everything was exposed and we had a full view: white, fat, plump, the string to his shirt somehow lost in the escapade.

Almost two months later she wrote to her daughter again, this time with news of her son Charles. 'And now a word or two about your brother,' one paragraph began, revealing a comical case of sexual malfunction. That she would betray such a personal confidence only just told to her by one of her children is astonishing; she clearly couldn't help herself with such powerful stuff. And for all our qualms, it is still hard to look away. Her son had just broken off one relationship and begun another, this time with the actress Mademoiselle de Champmesle, a favourite of Racine.

Yesterday your brother came from the other end of Paris to tell me about the accident that had befallen him. He had found a favourable opportunity [with Miss De C], and yet, dare I say it? *His little gee-gee stopped short at Lérida.* It was an extraordinary thing; the poor damsel had never found herself so amused in her life. The unhappy knight beat a retreat, thinking himself bewitched. And what is better still is that he couldn't wait to tell me about his fiasco. We laughed heartily, and I told him I was very glad he had been punished in the place where he had sinned. He then turned it on me and said I had given him some of the ice in my composition, and that he could well do without that inheritance, which I would have done better to pass on to you . . . It was a scene worthy of Molière.

The first of Madame de Sévigné's letters appeared in print less than a year after she died of what may have been pneumonia in 1696. The collected correspondence of her cousin, the Count de Bussy, brought 100 letters between the two of them to a readership beyond the court, sparking what may be called, if not a mania for her letters, then at least a ravenous

appetite. It was as if a collective girdle had been untied; the gossip that was once only exchanged behind the flutter of patterned fans was now hooked up to a loudspeaker. The first short collection of de Sévigné's letters to her daughter appeared in 1725, and another selection was published the following year to meet demand. Many were expurgated, her granddaughter increasingly convinced that they reflected unflatteringly on her family. The collections kept on coming: eight volumes of 770 letters in 1754, ten volumes in 1801, 14 volumes in 1862, each with new translations and new discoveries. The most noteworthy find came in 1872, when a collection known as the 'Capmas manuscript' turned up, after auction, in the window of a shop in Dijon, and was subsequently hailed as a discovery as great as Pompeii and Herculaneum. This it wasn't, but it was an eye-opener. We had seen many of these letters before, but not in this form. The 319 letters newly discovered by Charles Capmas, a law professor at Dijon University, were a true copy of the originals de Sévigné had composed two centuries before – uncut and untampered with. It was as if the bride had raised her veil, the difference between an individual's true voice and that of an impersonator, something that would later inspire Virginia Woolf to claim that de Sévigné 'seems like a living person, inexhaustible'.

In 1868, an American edition of de Sévigné's letters published in Massachusetts suggested: 'We are a letter-writing people; and no better models for letters exist than Madame de Sévigné's. We are a practical and energetic people; and no better complement to such virtues can be found than the tender affection and delicate refinement of Madame de Sévigné.'

But surely there were other models? In 1686, a decade before de Sévigné died, a man called Philip, Second Earl of Chesterfield, wrote a book of instruction for Lady Mary Stanhope, his eldest daughter by his third wife. It was a one-off, handwritten publication of about 40 pages, and it resembled the sort of almanac popular as a Christmas present in the twentieth century before the Internet. There was guidance on mathematics, on syntax, on the parables of Aristotle and Cicero, a disquisition on astronomy, a sampling of Descartes and other modern luminaries, and the meaning of 175 words that every nimble lady should know, including Affinity and Ambrosia. There was even a skewed poetical treatise on love: 'Is a pleasant evill, a concealed poison, a frenzical feaver, an infirmity that is not easily cured, a pleasing death, and some times a great misfortune.'

When these instructions were privately printed in 1934, its editor, a certain W.S. Lewis, described its author as having pursued 'a career dedicated to wickedness', by which he meant debauchery and the possible murder of his second wife (by adulterated sacramental wine, presumably the 'concealed poison' he referred to in his considerations of love). Which would lead one to wonder precisely what this man could possibly teach his daughter, who was 22 at the time she received his manuscript. By far the largest element of his instruction concerned letters, and he took a particular approach ('Date your letters at the bottom of your paper . . . for it is much more respectful.') Elsewhere, his guidance relied much on the size of one's hand.

> If you write to a Queen . . . begin your first line within three fingers breadth of the bottom of the paper . . . If you write to a Dutches, begin your letter in the middle of the paper. If you write to one of your own quality, leave the space of three or four fingers breadth between Madam and the first line. And if you write to any mean body begin 'Mrs' and write in the same line or just beneath it.

Chesterfield was strict about sign-offs. Writing to a person 'of your own quality or above you' you should end with 'most obedient humble servant'; but when you write to any ordinary person 'your most affectionate friend' will suffice. As a general rule he advised his daughter to make at least two drafts: 'Write it at first foul, and blot out such words as are writ twise or thrise . . . mend thy spelling by a Dictionary, and consider that some words (tho the sense be good) doe not sound well coming after other words, and your eare must be judg.' And there was one parting shot: 'It is a very great incivilitie not to answer all the letters wee doe receive, except they come from our servants or very mean persons.'

The following century saw more moderate, less judgemental, more widely read guidance from so many sources that it was difficult to keep track. How to account for the mid-eighteenth-century wonders *The Complete Letter-Writer; Or, Polite English Secretary* and *A New Academy of Compliments; Or, The Lover's Secretary?* and *The Polite Lady; Or, A Course of Female Education, In a Series of Letters, from a Mother to her Daughter*, or even *Familiar Letters on Various Subjects of Business and Amusement, Written in a natural easy manner; and published principally for the Service of the Younger Part of Both Sexes?* Certainly growing literacy and a more reliable postal service had something to do with this, but so did the further establishment of the letter-writing manual as a literary genre in its own right; the London bookshops were heaving under the weight of new guides, and although many were anonymous it was deemed a branch of writing respectable enough for Daniel Defoe and Samuel Richardson to have a shot.

But they were more than the guides we have read before. Because there was only a limited number of times one could instruct a reader as to the correct opening or closing addresses and the correct application of spacing, it was crucial that the manuals entertained, amusing those who could already write well. But they were not parodies: they were hefty practical examples and templates for almost every conceivable situation. And they were, more often than not, directed at women.

One of the most varied and amusing, stretching to 275 pages, appeared in 1763. *The Ladies Complete Letter-Writer* clearly had its sights on a broad market; its subtitle promised the teaching of *The Art of Inditing Letters on every Subject that can call for their Attention, as Daughters, Wives, Mothers, Relations, Friends or Acquaintance, Being a Collection of Letters Written by Ladies, Not only on the more important Religious, Moral and Social Duties, but on Subjects of every other kind that usually interest the Fair Sex: the Whole Performing A Polite and Improving Manual for their Use, Instruction and Rational Entertainment, with many other Important Articles.* Brevity, one imagines, not being the consistent message.

THE

L A D I E S

Complete Letter - Writer ;

TEACHING

The Art of INDITING LETTERS

On every Subject that can call for their Attention, as

DAUGHTERS,   RELATIONS,
WIVES,   FRIENDS, or
MOTHERS,   ACQUAINTANCE.

BEING A

C O L L E C T I O N

OF

L E T T E R S,

WRITTEN BY LADIES,

Not only on the more important RELIGIOUS, MORAL, and SOCIAL DUTIES, but on Subjects of every other Kind that usually interest the FAIR SEX :

THE WHOLE FORMING

A Polite and Improving M A N U A L,

For their Use, Instruction, and Rational Entertainment.

With many other IMPORTANT ARTICLES.

What's Female Beauty, but an Air Divine,
Through which the Soul's unfully'd Graces shine ?
That, like a Sun, irradiates all between ;
The Body charms, because the Mind is seen.

The situations were indeed multiple, a greatest hits compilation gathered from many other letter-writing manuals and newly ordered into efficient themes. Among the most alluring were letters about the lasting impact of scandal, the dangers of over-flirtatious behaviour, a consolation to one who had lost her beauty to smallpox, and the plight 'of a lady who had gone home late after a visit'. But the most readable were surely those regarding infidelity. One letter in the middle of the volume was written from a woman to a man she suspected of misconduct the night before.

> Sir,
>
> The freedom and sincerity with which I have at all times laid open my heart to you ought to have some weight to my claim to a return of the same confidence. But I have reason to fear that the best men do not always act as they ought. I write to you what it would be impossible to speak; but before I see you I desire you will either explain your conduct last night or confess that you have used me not as I have deserved of you.
>
> It is in vain to deny that you took pains to recommend yourself to Miss Peacoc. Your earnestness of discourse also showed me that you were no stranger to her. I desire to know, Sir, what sort of acquaintance you can wish to have with another person of character, after making me believe that you wish to be married to me. I write very plainly to you because I expect a plain answer. I am not apt to be suspicious, but this was too particular, and I must be either blind or indifferent to overlook it. Sir, I am neither, though perhaps it would be better for me if I were one or the other. I am,
>
> Yours, & c.

And then the scenario was flipped: a woman, herself accused of dalliance, responds:

Sir,

Whatever may be the end of this dispute, for I do not think so lightly of lovers' quarrels as many do, I think it proper to inform you that I never have thought favourably of anyone but yourself. And I shall add that if the fault of your temper, which I once little suspected, should make me fear you too much to marry, you will not see me in that state with any other, nor courted by any man in the world.

I did not know that the gaiety of my temper gave you uneasiness; and you ought to have told me of it with less severity . . . I desire you will first look carefully over this letter, for my whole heart is in it, and then come to me.

Yours & c.*

One further letter is worthy of note. A woman writes to her mother upon discovering she should be compelled to marry a man she abhors named Andrugio:

Most dear and honoured Madam,

. . . I am emboldened once more to pour out the fullness of my soul before you, to beseech you to have compassion on my forlorn condition, . . . this terrible dilemma that, whichever way I turn, affords nothing but the prospect of eternal ruin.

My aunt has just now shown me a letter she received from my father, wherein he desires her to prepare our return to London. But, O heaven, to what end! To be the wretched bride, the victim of a man I can have no taste for as a husband, a man who, were my heart entirely free from all attachment to another, I never could be brought to love! How can I assume a tenderness it is not in my power to feel!

---

* This sign-off '&c' is an abbreviated and alternative form of 'etc'.

To be sincere in all my words and actions was the first precept of my early youth, I have ever since held it sacred ... But I am now told that reason ought to guide inclination, that the softer passions should give way to the confederations of interest and the world's esteem, and that these plead strongly in favour of *Andrugio*. Alas, how different are my thoughts!

... Punish me by any other means provoked authority can invent; condemn me to pass the whole remainder of my days in lonely solitude; shut me from all society, or banish me where only lions and tigers dwell. Fate cannot reach me in any shape so horrid as the embraces of *Andrugio*.

Pardon, I beseech you Madam, the wildness of these expressions, which nothing but the most poignant anguish of the last despair could have forced from me. And be assured that, though I have said much more than you think I ought to have done, I have said little in comparison to what is felt by, Madam,

Your unhappy but obedient daughter.

The author of these epistolary fictions is unknown. But could it be that it is here, in these 120 clear-headed and strong-willed letters, that we glimpse the early stirrings of eighteenth-century feminism?

Young men had their own behavioural templates. For one man in particular, early life was governed by a sequence of letters that set a moral compass so particular and refined that, almost three centuries later, the guidance may still be regarded as relevant; like letters, the manners they promote are also vanishing from modern life. As with the letters of Madame de Sévigné, it wasn't a textbook that raised the cultural bar, but a contemporary collection of genuine letters.

In 1774, the London bookseller James Dodsley offered a new two-volume publication in his Pall Mall shop. *Letters written by the Earl of Chesterfield to his son, Philip Stanhope* was widely and well reviewed, and, even at the price of one guinea per volume, proved popular with Dodsley's clientele. (We are already familiar with his grandfather, the Second Earl of Chesterfield, who had composed the letter-writing manual to his daughter.) The Fourth Earl's letters were never intended for a wide public. But in the weeks after he died, Stanhope's

Famous for his letters and his sofa: the Fourth Earl of Chesterfield by Thomas Gainsborough.

widow realised that his thoughtful words to his son would benefit all potentially wayward offspring; and she realised too that the hefty £1,500 she received for this foresight would come in handy.

The earl's letters were composed between 1739 and 1765. His son Philip was illegitimate, and, living apart from his father, stood the risk of pursuing a life of 'inexactitude' (which is to say, a life lived beneath the exacting standards of his father). Composed several times each month, his letters served as an educational correspondence course. Chesterfield was attempting a task not witnessed in scale since Seneca: the development of character and career by epistolary instruction. In May 1751 he wrote candidly to his son of how he considered him his 'work'. 'There is, I believe, room for farther improvement before you come to that perfection which I have set my heart upon seeing you arrive at; and till that moment I must continue filing and polishing.'

What qualified him for this role? The fourth earl was both more sagacious and more modern than his grandfather, and he had more diplomatic experience upon which to draw: he was a highly effective orator in the Lords, the British ambassador at the Hague, lord lieutenant of Ireland, and secretary of state under Prime Minister Newcastle. His most enduring legacy, alongside his letters, was that he was the chief political instigator of the British adoption of our Gregorian calendar,* and (although this is disputed) the first to commission the indestructible and uncomfortable dimpled leather sofa that bears his name. He was generous both with praise and financial assistance; when he learnt that his son had established a secret family, he swiftly offered to pay for his grandchild's entire upbringing. His literary talents were advanced; his letters were

---

* Which shaved eleven days off the prevailing Julian calendar, reduced the length of the year by 10 minutes and 48 seconds, and established a new system of February leap days.

sweetened with humour, which rendered them cajoling rather than hectoring, and he clearly had his son's interests at heart, even when administering firm guidance about looking after his teeth or cultivating his fashion sense. Beyond all this, he had postal form: the Fourth Earl of Chesterfield was descended from John Stanhope, the master of the king's posts in the sixteenth century; and he was the grandson of the Second Earl of Chesterfield, the suspected wife-murderer and purveyor of letter-writing advice to his daughter.

One of the earliest letters, written in July 1739 when his son was seven, set a tone from which he never wavered.

My Dear Boy,

One of the most important points in life is decency; which is to do what is proper and where it is proper; for many things are proper at one time, and in one place, that are extremely improper in another; for example, it is very proper and decent that you should play some part of the day; but you must see that it would be extremely improper and indecent if you ere fly your kite, or play at nine pins, while you are with Mr Maitaire [his tutor; the young Philip would shortly attend Westminster]. It is very proper and decent to dance well, but then you must dance only at balls and places of entertainment; for you would be reckoned a fool if you were to dance at church or at a funeral.

I hope, by these examples, you understand the meaning of the word Decency, which in French is *Bienseance*, in Latin *Decorum* ...

As young Philip entered his teens, his father concerned himself increasingly with public conduct, arming him with a set of social skills designed to gain him friends and influence. 'There is nothing that people bear more impatiently, or forgive less, than contempt,' he wrote in October 1746, and an injury is much sooner forgotten than an insult. If, therefore, you would rather please than offend, rather be well than ill spoken of, rather be loved than hated, remember to have that constant attention about you, which flatters every man's little vanity ... Most people (I might say all people) have their weaknesses; they have their aversions and their likings, to such and such things; so that, if you were to laugh at a man for his aversion to a cat, or cheese (which are common antipathies), or, by inattention and negligence, to let them come in his way where you could prevent it, he would, in the first case, think himself insulted, and, in the second, slighted, and would remember both. Whereas your care to procure for him what he likes, and to remove from him what he hates, shows him that he is at least an object of your attention; flatters his vanity, and makes him possibly more your friend.

Chesterfield wrote to his son about 400 times, but many more letters didn't get through. Regretting their inevitable non-delivery, he again used the imagery of kites: some of his letters were blown in the wrong direction by the wind while others were 'torn by the string'; he was content that at least a few soared, including this one, on how not to be boring:

October 1747

Dear Boy,

The art of pleasing is a very necessary one to possess, but a very difficult one to acquire. It can hardly be reduced to rules, and your own good sense and observation will teach you more of it than I can. Do as you would be done by is the surest method that I know ...

Take the tone of the company that you are in, and do not pretend to give it; be serious, gay, or even trifling, as you find the present humour of the company; this is an attention due from

Lord Chesterfield writes to Solomon Dayrolles in 1754.

every individual to the majority. Do not tell stories in company: there is nothing more tedious and disagreeable: if by chance you know a very short story, and exceedingly applicable to the present subject of conversation, tell it in as few words as possible; and even then throw out that you do not love to tell stories, but that the shortness of it tempted you. Of all things, banish the egotism out of your conversation, and never think of entertaining people with your own personal concerns or private affairs; though they are interesting to you, they are tedious and impertinent to every-body else: besides that, one cannot keep one's own private affairs too secret.

When his son turned 18, Chesterfield supplemented his letters by sponsoring a Grand Tour, the traditional traipse round the ruins of Europe. He kept on writing as Philip reached Paris, Rome and Leipzig, turning increasingly to matters of politics and commerce, switching his opening gambit from 'My Dear Boy' to 'My Dear Friend'. In February 1750, the subject was the cautious use of one's resources.

My Dear Friend,

Very few people are good economists of their Fortune, and still fewer of their Time; and yet, of the two, the latter is the most precious. I heartily wish you to be a good economist of both; and you are now of an age to begin to think seriously of these two important articles. Young people are apt to think they have so much time before them, that they may squander what they please of it, and yet have enough left; . . . Fatal mistakes, always repented of, but always too late . . .

For example; you are to be at such a place at twelve, by appoint-ment; you go out at eleven, to make two or three visits first; those persons are not at home: instead of sauntering away that inter-mediate time at a coffee-house, and possibly alone, return home, write a letter for the ensuing post . . .

Many people lose a great deal of time by reading; for they read frivolous and idle books, such as the absurd Romances of the two last centuries; where characters that never existed are insip-idly displayed, and sentiments that were never felt pompously described: the oriental ravings and extravagancies of the Arabian Nights, and Mogul Tales; and such sort of idle frivolous stuff, that nourishes and improves the mind just as much as whipped cream would the body. Stick to the best established books in every language; the celebrated Poets, Historians, Orators, or Philosophers.

Many people lose a great deal of their time by laziness; they loll and yawn in a great chair, tell themselves that they have not time to begin anything then, and that it will do as well another time. This is a most unfortunate disposition, and the greatest obstruction to both knowledge and business . . . Never put off till tomorrow what you can do today.

The letters were full of such epigrams and *bon mots*, many freshly minted, some recycled, a heady bag of Polonius-style windbaggery and inspiration. Kipling's 'If –' appeared to draw a lot from it. And within the thickets there was much good sense.

Fix one certain hour and day in the week for your [accounts] and keep them together in their proper order; by which means they will require very little time, and you can never be much cheated.

Never read History without having maps, and a chronological book or tables lying by you, and constantly recurred to; without which, History is only a confused heap of facts.

Rise early, and at the same hour every morning, how late-soever you may have sat up the night before. This secures you an hour or two at least of reading or reflection before the common interruptions of the morning begin; and it will save your constitution, by forcing you to go to bed early at least one night in three.

And sometimes there were even more fundamental problems to attend to. In November 1750 Chesterfield was disturbed to discover that his 18-year-old son still had a limited grasp on the fundamentals of English.

You spell induce 'enduce' and grandeur you spell 'grandure'; two faults of which few of my house-maids would have been guilty.

I must tell you that orthography, in the true sense of the word, is so absolutely necessary for a man of letters, or a gentleman, that one false spelling may fix a ridicule upon him for the rest of his life; and I know a man of quality who never recovered the ridicule of having spelled 'wholesome' without the 'w'.

To what advantage did Philip Stanhope put his father's all-encompassing advice? Did he become a courtly general or prime minister? He did not, and fairly failed to become prime anything. His father paid £2,000 to install him as MP for Liskeard and St Germans in Cornwall, but his shyness dulled his oratory and he spent much of his time at minor posts abroad, including a stint as the envoy extraordinary at the Perpetual Diet of Regensburg in Bavaria, the parliament concerned with the doomed maintenance of the Holy Roman Empire.

By December 1765, in the last letter to his son that survives, Chesterfield appears to have almost given up on him, reducing his message to some moderate thoughts on the American Revolution and a bit of good gossip.

My Dear Friend,

. . . One hears of nothing now in town but the separation of men and their wives. Will Finch the ex-vice-Chamberlain, Lord Warwick, and your friend Lord Bolingbroke. I wonder at none of them for parting; but I wonder at many for still living together; for in this country it is certain that marriage is not well understood.

I have this day sent Mr. Larpent two hundred pounds for your Christmas-box, which I suppose he will inform you of by this post. Make this Christmas as merry a one as you can . . . For the new years, God send you many and happy ones.

Adieu.

Chesterfield's son predeceased him by five years, dying, with a certain tragicomic inevitability, of dropsy, in 1768. His father never really recovered from the loss, spending his final years in failing health; not long before he died he claimed that he had already been effectively dead for two years. But his charming letters to his son are still in print, an unmatchable historical primer for manners and civility in the Age of Enlightenment. And his advice, ultimately, didn't go to waste: Lord Chesterfield used much of it again in the 262 letters he wrote to his godson, the fifth earl of Chesterfield, who was also called Philip Stanhope. He did rather better this time: his new protégé rose to become joint postmaster general.

Entirely Gone

14232134 SIGMN. BARKER H.C., 30 WING, 1 COY.
9 AIR FORMATION SIGNALS, M.E.F.

12 April 1944

Dear Bessie,

Yesterday I got your Letter Card dated the 3rd, the first I have had from you since your L.C. of 12th March, as your letter, unfortunately and unhappily has still to arrive.

I think we are so near to each other that our reactions to similar occurrences are very much, if not exactly, the same. So that you know the excitement I felt when I saw your handwriting on the L.C. my brother handed me. There was one from Deb [an old friend] and another from Mum; and, of course, I had to read these first. And I could read yours only once, and then had to put it in my pocket, while my poor old head tried to cope with its contents as far as I could remember. You have come at me with such a terrific rush of warmth, and I am so very much in need of you.

Well, I washed and made my bed (it was six o'clock before I received your letter) and fidgeted around. Then I thought, 'I must read it again before I sleep' – so I pushed off to the latrine (where the humblest may be sure of privacy) and read your words again. The comic expression 'It shakes me' is true in a serious sense about this deeply thrilling state of wellbeing that you have caused or created.

After I had re-read your letter, out came the chess-men, and we played one game (which I won!) before adjourning to the canteen to gather round the wireless for the 'news' (a rite in these surroundings). Then we were 'collared' for Bridge, which we played till ten o'clock. All the time, the only thing I wanted to do was read your words, this tiny part of you, again and again.

Back in the tent, and to bed. How impossible to sleep with thought and wonder of you hot within me. As I toss and turn and wriggle and writhe I think of you, probably doing the same. Isn't it blooming awful? I know that if I think of you, I will not sleep; yet I keep on thinking of you, and get hotter and hotter. Phew! I could do with a couple of ice-blocks around me.

Finally, to sleep. Up in the morning, my first thoughts, of your nearness and your distance from me, and the hope that I can race off this first six pages, to post this afternoon. Unfortunately there is no likelihood of my early return. I must be another year, I may be another three or four. Relax, my girl, or you'll be a physical wreck in no time. Regard me as what you will, but don't altogether forget circumstance, distance, environment. I do so joyfully, happily, eagerly, but you must have more sense.

In the film tonight there was a [joke] that the state of being in love was the happiest way of being miserable. So be miserable happily, don't look over your shoulder too much; enjoy what is, so far as you can, and remember the old, wise tag 'Today is the tomorrow we worried about yesterday.' I am a born worrier myself, but feel I could be all that you wanted me to be. Probably more important, I know that you are what I want, not in any limited sense, but in all. I want to confide in you. I want to creep into you. I want to protect you. That I am not capable is unimportant, what is significant is that you should think I am. My hands cannot caress you; my words strive hard to tell you all the things I dare. You spoke of yourself being 'guilty of slobbering' – it's no crime, I'm proud of it! If your incoherent babblings mean what mine do, it's jolly good. Don't worry about being bounced out of favour, and try to grow out of this 'engulfed – nothing belongs to oneself' feeling. Regard me as a promise rather than a threat, and 'pick holes' in me where you can – so that I seem less regal! Remember we are both in this together, and that it has somehow occurred undesignedly, unrehearsed, because we had it in us. Yes, I wish that I was with you. But life is hard – wishing won't make it so. My thoughts are with you far too often for my physical serenity and my mental equilibrium. During the day I simply lap you up and cause trouble at night. 'Engulfed' describes my state, too, a rather floundering, uncertain one.

I wonder what you look like (don't have a special photograph taken). I know you haven't a bus-back face but I have never looked at you as now I would. I wonder how many times I have seen you, and how many we have been alone. Now my foolish pulse races at the thought that you even have a figure. I want, very much, to touch you, to feel you, to see you as you naturally are, to hear you. I want to sleep and awaken with you. I want to live with you. I want to be strong and I want to be weak with you. I want you.

I want my letters to be of interest to you, so please let me know how and what you want me to write. On occasions, you'll understand, I may not be in a position to write.

Let me know if you think I'm mad. When my signature dries I am going to kiss it. If you do the same, that will be a complete (unhygienic) circuit!

Yours,

Chris

Chapter Eight

Letters for Sale

On 3 July 1973, Sotheby's offered a letter for sale in its London auction rooms, and on 3 July 2007, Christie's offered the same letter for sale again. In the intervening 34 years the letter had been in the hands of a man called Albin Schram, a plump legal historian from Prague.

Actually, not quite 34 years, since Schram had died a couple of years earlier. When his relatives started looking through his belongings in the months after his funeral they realised that this letter might be worth a fair amount, partly because it was a letter from Napoleon, and partly because it was a great and mad letter from Napoleon, written by hand following a quarrel he'd just had with his new lover. According to the letter, Bonaparte had been almost undone by the throes of love and lust. A few weeks before he was to embark on the long conquest of Europe he stood emotionally naked, almost fatally distracted by Josephine in the first flush of their relationship. The letter was beyond rare and unquestionably authentic: one of only three known letters addressed to her before their marriage, two pages of light blue-grey paper cut from a larger sheet at the upper edges, with four cancellations and corrections, encouragingly worn, torn and spotted. No one was terribly surprised when, as lot 387 at its sale in 1973, it fetched several thousand pounds. But how much would it be worth in 2007? The estimate stood between £30,000 and £50,000.

The letter was written at nine in the morning, but Napoleon gives no indication of the date or even the year; it is somewhere between the beginning of their romance in December 1795 and their marriage on 9 March 1796. It describes the powerful control Josephine holds over her lover, and it is down on its knees with apology; Napoleon is known to have enquired about her family wealth and property in the West Indies, but in the letter he assures her that he only loves her for herself. In a modern translation:

> So what is your strange power, incomparable Josephine? One of your thoughts is poisoning my life, tearing my soul apart . . . I well know if we argue, I should deny my heart, my conscience. You have seduced them, they are always yours.
>
> I went to bed really angry . . . So you thought I didn't love you for you? Whom then? Ah madame, have you really thought about it? How could such a low feeling be conceived from a soul so pure. I am still astonished, less so however than the feeling which since I woke up has led me without bitterness and effortlessly to your feet.
>
> I give you three kisses, one on your heart, one on your mouth and one on your eyes.
>
> NB

What is the strange power the letter holds over us? Napoleon's love letters resonate not so much for their universality as for their singularity – the particular French vocabulary, the constant echoes of weariness from the latest campaign – yet they can't but strike a common chord in anyone once consumed by the absence of another. Not everyone can lead a successful invasion of Austria, Italy, Egypt, Spain and Germany, but we can all fall in love with love, and we can all, as readers, revel in a doomed affair. History has additional claims. Josephine's brief hold on Napoleon amounted almost to a disease, and it is through his affliction, both its climax and decline,

Passion unbound: Napoleon writes to Josephine.

that we gain a permanently valuable record of his character and actions. Battles rage behind him as he writes, and we can almost smell the gunpowder.

Many of Napoleon's other love letters are less adulatory. They are accusatory, self-centred, mistrusting, self-immolating and usually composed from the depths of exhaustion. His love is not one of joy but of deprivation and melodrama; he demands sympathy but he risks contempt. 'My life is a perpetual nightmare,' he writes from Italy in June 1796, three months after their marriage. His wife had been unwell; he had been slaying Austrians and storming through Milan, Verona and Naples.

> A presentiment of ill oppresses me. I see you no longer. I have lost more than life, more than happiness, more than my rest. I am almost without hope. I hasten to send a courier to you. He will stay only four hours in Paris, and then bring me your reply. Write me ten pages. That alone can console me a little. You are ill, you love me, I have made you unhappy, you are in delicate health, and I do not see you! – that thought overwhelms me. I have done you so much wrong that I know not how to atone for it; I accuse you of staying in Paris, and you were ill there. Forgive me, my dear; the love with which you have inspired me has bereft me of reason. I shall never find it again. It is an ill for which there is no cure. My presentiments are so ominous that I would confine myself to merely seeing you, to pressing you for two hours to my heart – and then dying with you.

> . . . Josephine, how can you remain so long without writing to me; your last laconic letter is dated May 22. Moreover, it is a distressing one for me, but I always keep it in my pocket; your portrait and letters are perpetually before my eyes.

A month later, Bonaparte is stationed near Mantua, which he has just overrun. He had recently met Josephine in Milan 80 miles away, and their meeting had made him question whether she shared the heat of his passions. He wondered whether she wasn't already seeing others. On 19 July Napoleon's paranoia grew.

I have been without letters from you for two days. That is at least the thirtieth time today that I have made this observation to myself; you are thinking this particularly wearisome; yet you cannot doubt the tender and unique anxiety with which you inspire me.

We attacked Mantua yesterday. We warmed it up from two batteries with red-hot shot and from mortars. All night long that wretched town has been on fire. The sight was horrible and majestic. We have secured several of the outworks; we open the first parallel tonight. Tomorrow I start for Castiglione with the Staff, and I reckon on sleeping there. I have received a courier from Paris. There were two letters for you; I have read them. But though this action appears to me quite natural, and though you gave me permission to do so the other day, I fear you may be vexed, and that is a great trouble to me. I should have liked to have sealed them up again: fie! that would have been atrocious. If I am to blame, I beg your forgiveness. I swear that it is not because I am jealous; assuredly not. I have too high an opinion of my beloved for that. I should like you to give me full permission to read your letters, then there would be no longer either remorse or apprehension.

. . . I have summoned the courier; he tells me that he crossed over to your house, and that you told him you had no commands. Fie! naughty, undutiful, cruel, tyrannous, jolly little monster. You laugh at my threats, at my infatuation; ah, you well know that if I could shut you up in my breast, I would put you in prison there!

By February the following year, things are clearly going awry. 'Peace with Rome has just been signed,' he informed Josephine from Bologna, a monumental act which would see the capitulation of the pope. He had already entered Bologna, Ferrara and Romagna, and he was heading for Rimini and Ravenna. But his wife was either finding it hard to keep up, or didn't care. 'Not a word from you,' Napoleon complained,

> what on earth have I done? To think only of you, to love only Josephine, to live only for my wife, to enjoy happiness only with my dear one – does this deserve such harsh treatment from her? My dear, I beg you, think often of me, and write me every day.
>
> You are ill, or else you do not love me! Do you think, then, that I have a heart of stone? And do my sufferings concern you so little? You must know me very ill! I cannot believe it! You to whom nature has given intelligence, tenderness, and beauty, you who alone can rule my heart, you who doubtless know only too well the unlimited power you hold over me!
>
> Write to me, think of me, and love me.

He signed off 'Yours ever, for life,' a forecast which, by 1798, as Napoleon moved on Egypt, was already looking distinctly optimistic. News of an affair reached Napoleon while engaged on his Middle East expedition, and his letters cooled instantly; his infatuation and kisses were replaced by travel itineraries, financial instructions and weather bulletins. Napoleon began his own affairs, fathering illegitimate children en route, while maintaining the outward show of unity; he granted Josephine the title of empress in 1804.

> I start at once to outmanœuvre the English, [he wrote from Madrid in December 1808] who appear to have received rein-forcements and wish to look big.
>
> The weather is fine, my health perfect; don't be uneasy.
>
> I am despatching a page to bring you the good tidings of the

'L'empereur est parfait pour moi': Josephine addresses her son Eugene de Beauharnais in 1809.

victory of Enzersdorf, which I won on the 5th, and that of Wagram, which I won on the 6th [he wrote in July 1809].

The enemy's army flies in disorder, and all goes according to my prayers . . . Bessières has been shot through the fleshy part of his thigh; the wound is very slight. Lasalle was killed. My losses are full heavy, but the victory is decisive and complete. We have taken more than 100 pieces of cannon, 12 flags, many prisoners. I am sunburnt.

The couple divorced shortly before his marriage to Marie-Louise of Austria in 1810. His letter to her the following year carried a rather bold kiss-off:

I send to know how you are . . . I was annoyed with you about your debts. I do not wish you to have any; on the contrary, I wish you to put a million aside every year, to give to your grand-children when they get married. Nevertheless, never doubt my affection for you, and don't worry any more about the present embarrassment.

Adieu, dear. Send me word that you are well. They say that you are as fat as a good Normandy farmeress.

A few of these letters had come up for sale before. In July 1933, eight early examples were sold at Sotheby's as a single lot, with the London bookseller Ben Maggs spending £4,400 in order to see off several eager bids from what the *New York Times* described as 'manifestly disappointed' Frenchmen.* Maggs was evidently mad about Napoleon: in the same sale he had bought several of the emperor's less glamorous but more strategic letters, at what appear to us now to be knock-down prices: he paid between £37 and £72 per letter. And almost 20 years earlier, Maggs Brothers was the top bidder in an auction for Napoleon's penis, which Maggs staff proudly displayed in a velvet case at their Mayfair shop. (The article in question was variously described as 'a mummified tendon' and 'a shrivelled eel').

Men and women have been collecting letters since letters began. Unlike other collecting hobbies, philately say, or beautiful antique cars, the collecting of letters has always been a wholly natural endeavour. If you treasured what was said in a letter you kept it, and once you had three, you had a correspondence, and no one would accuse you of being a nerd or obsessive. But as the correspondence piled up over time you would have a decision to make: would you destroy the evidence? Or would you have the foresight/arrogance/grasp on social history to keep them for a future generation? The collecting of letters of the famous and influential had other motives: the archival connection with the sweep of history; and the belief that the archival connection with the sweep of history would one day go up in value.

* The figure, as with all sums mentioned here, includes buyer's premium.

Albin Schram was born in Czechoslovakia in 1926, schooled in Prague and Bavaria, and conscripted into the *Wehrmacht* in 1943. He became a Russian prisoner of war, escaped just before hostilities ceased, and developed a career in Austria and Germany as a civil servant in the justice ministry, and then as a banker and legal historian. He was living in Switzerland in the early 1970s when he received an unusual and unexpected gift from his family; unusual because Schram had never shown much interest in historical manuscripts before, and unexpected because the letter was written by Napoleon, with whom Schram had only a passing interest, perhaps no more than any other cultured man concerned with the great turning points in history.

The letter told of a quarrel and Napoleon's hope that three kisses would make it right. It set something off, and Schram became what the auction houses dream of – a hooked client with means. From nowhere, Schram, who was now in his late forties, became a letter collector. His motives were unknown, but they were probably similar to the norm: there is wonder to be had from handling a sheet of paper that was once inscribed by someone you admire, or someone who had a say in the world. And if you can own it, so much the better, for you then become a custodian of history rather than just an observer; through fate and fortune you hold an historical sliver of power. Money plays a big part in this custodianship, of course, but there is more: there is also judgement of worth and the thrill of the quest. Some collectors hire agents to do their bidding for them, or they buy from dealers. Schram primarily bought at auctions he attended himself. He did the annual rounds of Marburg, Paris and London, buying perhaps 10 choice items a year, the last purchase made just a fortnight before his death in 2005. And thus his collection became great and mouthwatering, and posthumously he achieved what all collectors secretly long for: a sale at a leading auction house devoted

The Albin Schram collection at Christie's.

entirely to one's passion, with your name on the catalogue and a photo inside, the final transition from dabbling enthusiast to connoisseur.

'Schram's guiding principle was his own insatiable intellectual curiosity,' Christie's manuscript specialist Thomas Venning writes in the introduction to the catalogue, noting that he was particularly interested in figures from his native Bohemia. 'But above all, it is a remarkably comprehensive collection, in all the principal fields: literature (from Donne and Defoe to Kleist, Pushkin, Rimbaud, Hemingway, Borges), the visual arts (Goya, Bernini, Vasari, Gauguin), history and politics (Napoleon, Calvin, Elizabeth I, Churchill, Cromwell, Gandhi), music (Telemann, Beethoven, Smetana, Tchaikovsky), and science and philosophy (Newton, Hobbes, Schopenhauer, Einstein, Hume, Kant, Locke).' There were women too: Madame de Sévigné of course, Charlotte Brontë, Elizabeth Barrett Browning, Catherine de Medici, George Eliot.

The Gandhi letter, written less than three weeks before he was assassinated, arguing for religious tolerance between Hindus and Muslims, was withdrawn and sold privately to the Indian government. But everything else was included and reached crazy prices. There were 570 lots in all, with many offering multiple letters, some from famous people that said little of note and were valuable primarily for their signatures. But the majority were remarkable, and a few of them merit brief attention.

In October 1624, the poet John Donne wrote what many consider to be his finest and most significant single letter. Addressed to his friend Bridget, Lady Kingsmill, it was a letter of consolation composed on the day of the death of her husband, and encapsulated the messages of his religious sermons, his metaphysical philosophy and his epistolary style. It was his 'God moves in mysterious ways' variation – a stained and browned letter for the ages.

In the letter, Donne is keen to distinguish between the things that God may destroy in one stroke (the universe at the Apocalypse) and 'those things w[hi]ch he takes in peeces, as he doth Man and wife', for they will eventually be reunited. And we shouldn't doubt God's purpose or methods: 'We would wonder, to see a Man, who in a wood, were left to hys liberty to fell what trees he would, take only the crooked, and leave the straytest trees; but that Man had perchance a ship to build, and not a house, and so hath use of that kinde of timber'. It was unwise to question God's actions, 'as though we could direct him to do them better'.

There were several letters in which authors reflected on the critical reaction to their work (Chekhov, for instance, expressing his delight in the praise heaped on *The Cherry Orchard*: 'I shan't hide it,' he wrote three months before he died). The most dissatisfied was Charlotte Brontë, unhappy at a snarling of *Shirley*, her follow-up to *Jane Eyre*, in the *Spectator* and *Athenaeum*. Writing to William Smith Williams, a literary adviser at her publishers Smith, Elder in November 1849, she observed that while the critics were 'acute men in their way', they were unsuitable to comment on her fiction. 'When called on to criticise works of imagination – they stand in the position of deaf men required to listen to music – or blind men to judge of painting. The Practical their minds can grasp – of the Ideal they know nothing.' The letter closes with a further regret – her inability to wrap books: 'I fear the unseemly bundles I produce must shock you much.'

Other writers provide tantalising glimpses of work in the works: T.S. Eliot writes to the art critic Clive Bell in 1941, thanking him for his kind words, 'all the more welcome at a time when one needs encouragement, if one is to persist in this odd occupation of making patterns with words. It will require only a little more such flattery, however (so exquisitely concentrated) to persuade me to complete work on my scheme of a set of four' [the *Four Quartets* were completed in 1942]. In 1949, J.R.R. Tolkien wrote from Oxford to the artist Pauline Baynes, thanking her for her illustrations for his 'rather slender squib' *Farmer Giles of Ham*, but regretting that her illustrations had been reduced in size. He hoped 'soon to get some larger works published, and in a more ample fashion.' and wondered whether she would consider illustrating these works too. 'One, a long romance in sequel to *The Hobbit*, is finished after some years of work, and is being typed.' It was *The Lord of the Rings*.

In Swansea in 1926 (so it is thought – the date is unconfirmed) Dylan Thomas wrote his first known letter. He was probably 12, and already keen on rhyme. His older sister Nancy had been unwell, and he wrote to cheer her up, quoting a popular American verse:

> *A drummer is a man we know who has to do with drums,*
> *But I've never met a plumber yet who has to do with plums.*
> *A cheerful man who sells you hats would be a cheerful hatter,*
> *But is a serious man who sells you mats a serious matter?*

Another copied poem considers the inconsequential concerns of daily local life, a theme he would echo in *Under Milk Wood*.

> *There's a worry in the morning because the coffee's cold,*
> *There's the worry of the postman & the 'paper' to unfold.*
> *It's a worry getting on your boots & going to the train,*
> *And you've got to put your hat on & take it off again.*
> *It's a wonder how I live with such a constant strain . . .*
> *Now comes the awful 'wowwy' of finishing this letter,*
> *One word before I end Dear – let's hope you're beastly better.*

The most brutal letter on sale on 3 July 2007 was by Ernest Hemingway. Written to Ezra Pound in July 1925, Hemingway was in Spain, on his way to the running of the bulls at Fiesta

Hemingway's cat skips over the correspondence on his bed.

de San Fermin de Pamplona, the great inspiration for *The Sun Also Rises*. He thanks Pound for a recent flattering profile of him and says he feels good for the first time in months, in fact 'so good there's nothing to write about'. But there is something: his distrust of Ford Madox Ford. The English novelist, aged 52 at this point, had just published the first of the *Parade's End* quartet, and had been a success since the appearance of *The Good Soldier* a decade before. He had evidently just delivered a talk about new writing, which Hemingway described as 'imaginary conversations between himself and Americans speaking an imaginary Yankee dialect . . . It gave his megalomania a gala night.' Hemingway then launches a tirade about the advantages bulls have over Ford and other things that don't appeal. Bulls are not political exiles, or print reviews, or expect to be invited to dinner; bulls do not tend to borrow cash or expect you to marry them. Bulls did not concern themselves with 'delicate studies' of American culture. Bulls, Hemingway attested, 'are not Jews'. He signed the letter 'Mother Eddy' after Mary Baker Eddy, the founder of Christian Science. And he closed it with the desire to have 'more and better fucking, fighting and bulls.'

And then, thankfully, there was something charming from Albert Einstein. Written in July 1936 from Old Lyme, Conneticut, to Paul Habicht, a friend from his youth, the letter is resonant in its innocence, and has attained greater poignancy with the passage of time. He reminisces in German about their former days together, 'working on the nice little electrostatic machines', while also pondering German political ambitions. Habicht had apparently defended Germany during the Great War, 'while I had already got to know extremely well the dangers involved in it. I did at least weigh anchor in time'. The US had many comforts for him. People are given more space, he wrote, and he could sit by a quiet bay and sail his boat.

The weight of the universe lives on in these letters, a fair array of Western genius, prejudice, arrogance and generosity. We catch Napoleon's infatuation, Tolkien's modesty, Einstein's measured nostalgia, and Hemingway's anti-Semitism. And we are shocked, entertained and educated as a result.

The Donne fetched £114,000. The Brontë went for £21,600, the Eliot £8,400, the Tolkien £7,800, the Dylan Thomas £6,600, the Hemingway £78,000 and the Einstein £15,600. And Napoleon's letter to Josephine (the one after the quarrel but before the steady conquest of Europe and the infidelity and the divorce) went for £276,000.*

But how would Napoleon fare against Nelson? The Albin Schram collection made up a venerated sale, but there are venerated sales of great letters every few months. In July 2005, for example, at an auction devoted to Horatio Nelson and the Royal Navy at Bonhams in New Bond Street, a letter set out something pivotal in British history: the position and ambitions of Nelson below decks on the *Victory* on 5 October 1805. It was 15 days before the Battle of Trafalgar, and the urgency of the admiral's letter to his superior Lord Barham, First Lord of the Admiralty, is unmistakable. Reading it now, even with its distant topography and unwieldy punctuation, one can still grasp the issues at stake and the anxieties at hand:

> On Monday the french and spanish Ships took their Troops on board which had been landed on their arrival and it is said that they mean to sail the first fresh Levant Wind and as the

* This was the highest price paid for a letter by Napoleon, but far from the highest price ever paid for a letter at auction. This honour attached itself to a letter written by George Washington in 1787 to his nephew Bushrod Washington, fetching $3,218,500 (£1,932,600) in December 2009 at Christie's, New York. The letter urges the ratification of the newly adopted constitution.

Carthegena Ships are ready and when seen a few days ago had their Topsail Yards hoisted up this looks like a Junction, the position I have taken for this Month is from 16 to 18 Leagues West of Cadiz for although it is most desirable that the fleet should be well up in Easterly Winds, Yet I must guard against being caught with a Westerly Wind near Cadiz for a fleet of Ships with so many three deckers would inevitably be forced into the Streights and then Cadiz would be perfectly free for them to come out with a Westerly Wind as they served Lord Keith in the Late War. I am most anxious for the arrival of frigates less than eight with the Brigs &c: as we settled I find are absolutely inadequate for this Service and to be with the fleet, and Spartel, Cape Cantin or Blanco, & the Salvages must be watched by fast Sailing Vessels in case any Squadron should escape. I have been Obliged to send Six Sail of the Line to Water & get Stores &c: at Tetuan & Gib.r for if I did not begin I should very soon be Obliged to take the whole fleet into the Streights. I have 23 Sail with Me and Should they come out I shall immediately bring them to battle but although I should not doubt of Spoiling any Voyage they may attempt Yet I hope for the arrival of the Ships from England that as an Enemys fleet they may be annihilated.

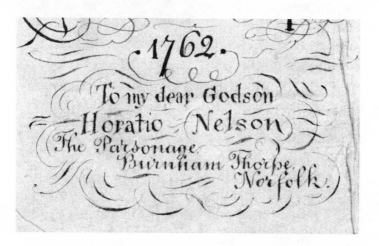

What would this fine specimen be worth (four pages, minor dust-staining and weakness at folds, modern archival restoration but overall in fine and attractive condition)? The Battle of Trafalgar – arguably Britain's greatest tactical victory at the height of its naval dominance, a battle at which the Franco-Spanish fleet lost 22 ships and Britain none (fulfilling Nelson's flagged missive that England expected every man to do his duty, a cause for which he gave his own life) – how, in the balance of history and celebrity, would one weigh such a thing against, say, the lustful hubris of Napoleon? Not entirely comfortably. In letters as everywhere else, sex sells: the Nelson went for £66,000, a fair sum but less than a quarter of a Bonaparte. *C'est magnifique, mais ce n'est pas la guerre.*

On 19 March 2013, Bonhams held another solid sale. This time there were letters from Lewis Carroll, Henry James and Marcel Proust, and a postcard from Sigmund Freud. But by far the most interesting item was a collection of letters from a writer that no one at the auction had heard of. James Lindsay Steven, progressively gunner, corporal and sergeant of 1st Troop, 1st Brigade of the Bengal Horse Artillery stationed at Peshawar and Umballa, wrote more than 20 letters home to his brother and mother in Edinburgh between 1852 and 1855. Described in the catalogue as a remarkably vivid and 'at times Kiplingesque' account of the life of a British soldier on the north-west frontier in

Writing left-handed: Horatio Nelson.

the years before the Mutiny, the letters work a different sort of charm from the others in the sale (and most sales), more valuable for their content than for their signature.

One letter, sent from Peshawar on 27 June 1852, captures the spirit of the rest: the easy manner and barrack-room prejudices may be attributed to the frank relationship Steven enjoyed with the letter's recipient, his brother, while its florid and boastful imagery foreshadowed *The Playboy of the Western World.*

An elopement took place the other day which astonished the whole lines. The bride belonged to parents in the 53rd Regiment, and had been the cause of great anxiety to a great many Sergeants and Corporals, all getting encouragement from her parents . . . One of our Troopers went down to see this far-famed wench (an ugly squinting-eyed thing), . . . when he told me he was determined to marry her . . . I spoke to the girl and proposed for her to make an elopement. The two got married, and I had a splendid night of it, they tell me I swore eternal love to a widow who had buried her sixth husband and she accepted me, putting a splendid gold ring on my hand. The day was fixed, and the old woman of sixty, with her hair as grey as a rat, actually thought I was going to marry her.

I was thunder struck, and when I assured her it was all gammon, and never had the least intention of anything of the sort, she got into a horrible passion, calling me everything that was uppermost, swearing she would take my life at the first opportunity . . . I had to run for my life. I was laughing over it when I got to the barracks, when I happened to look out at the door, when there was my poor woman, along with a file of the guard going to the guard-room . . . As I happened to pass her I asked her how she was getting on, and put my finger to my nose. She made one bounce at me, but I was too wide awake, I sprang to a side, and she fell all her length on her face, smashed her smeller that the claret run out and send two of her teeth . . . down her throat.

I had for to run again for my life, for she got up and got to a heap of stones, and began peppering me as hard as she was able.

J.L. Steven was killed, aged 27, during the retaking of Delhi in September 1857. His letters – unimportant in the broad scheme of things, but a zestful personal addition to official accounts – were accompanied in the Bonhams sale by the author's Indian Mutiny medal and his baptism certificate, from which we learn that his father was James Steven, a bookseller from

Thunder struck in Peshawar: a British soldier writes home.

Hope Park End by The Meadows in Edinburgh. The estimate for the lot was £1,000–£1,500, but it sold for £6,875.

But how was a potential buyer encouraged to buy these wares? The letters were described in the Bonham's catalogue by a man called Felix Pryor, a former manuscript specialist at Sotheby's who then set up as a freelance expert and anthologiser. 'Those India letters – terribly unusual,' he says. 'I had to restrain myself from making the entry four times as long.' And how does one value such a thing? 'My estimates are usually low. That's always been my thing. If you say £1,000 to £1,500 and it makes £1,800 then everybody's happy. But if you say £3,000–£4,000 and it makes £2,800 it's just all a bit flat. I basically price things according to what I'd want if I owned it myself and wasn't too pressed for money.'

We meet at the Academy Club, a stubbornly shabby members' bar in Soho, established (originally on a different site) by Auberon Waugh. 'I think the idea was that it would be mainly for journalists and authors,' Pryor says. 'Poets were discouraged.' He has photocopies of items he's been researching at the London Library, a letter from Felix Mendelssohn from 1944 ('He mentions a rehearsal, by which he means a concert'), and one from Victor Hugo, which brings back the story of the shortest letters ever written. Away from Paris and concerned about the success of *Les Misérables* in the early 1860s, Hugo wrote to his publisher with a single '?'. His publisher, delighted with sales, replied '!'.

'Letters like these are a finite resource,' Pryor acknowledges, 'and we'll never see their like again. The idea of collecting books leaves me completely cold. But letters and manuscripts, yes – you're connected.' Our conversation drifts to Sylvia Plath. 'I had her papers in my flat,' Pryor says. 'Well, all the *Ariel* poems. I was cataloguing them – they sold to Smith College, from Ted [Hughes] via Sotheby's. And I had her typewriter, a portable Corona. I had an American girlfriend at the time and she was deeply impressed that I typed letters to her on it. I imagine now that people are analysing Sylvia's typewriter ribbon and going "Hmmm . . . Dear Sal? And who's this Felix character?"'

He also had letters from Hughes. 'Occasionally I open a book and one falls out. I know I do this for a living, but the thought of [personally] selling something that someone's written? I'd rather starve.'

Pryor compiles the catalogue entries for three Bonhams sales a year, and he is both delighted and saddened at the items people bring into the saleroom. The most disappointing items are usually those that have already been framed or appear in what he calls 'shirt bags', those cellophane-fronted sleeves that bear the mark of a dealer's tired stock. 'What you want are fresh discoveries,' he says, discoveries after deaths or discoveries in attics. 'We recently got one from the Front in 1914 about the Christmas truce, and it does actually talk about playing football.'

He says that his work, requiring a large amount of rooting around the *Dictionary of National Biography* and increasingly the Internet, benefits from a broad approach – the advantages of a generalist over a specialist. 'I was recently in a court case, a forgery case where lots of Churchill had been faked, and the defence said, "Well Mr Pryor, what would you say if a Churchill specialist declared these to be true?" And I couldn't actually say – because it would have been rather rude – "Well they're the people most likely to get it wrong because they can't see the wood for the trees." But it's a general writing person who will spot the fakes.' Are there a lot of fake letters out there? 'A few. Almost all Raphael letters are faked. And in the nineteenth century they were mad about [Oliver] Goldsmith – a lot of those were fakes.'

In 1988 Pryor edited *The Faber Book of Letters*, a refreshingly concise collection (284 pages) containing much that is good, alarming and funny about the world. The range spreads from the Elizabethans to the Cold War, taking in Lord Byron, Abraham Lincoln, Captain Scott and Scott Fitzgerald.

The collection was compiled very much according to personal taste, and held fast to the promise Pryor made to himself that the letters should not be dull. He regrets that it is principally the letters of the famous that survive, and that among history's greatest casualties are the letters of ordinary people, who survive on paper only in legal documents. Some famous people, of course, are only famous *because* of their letters – Madame de Sévigné and Lord Chesterfield are in this band – and there are others whose reputations are immeasurably enhanced by their correspondence, among them Keats and Henry James. But some of the gems in Pryor's collection come from less well-known figures, among them Anthony Henley, MP for Southampton, owner of the estates of Northington and Swarraton in Hampshire (now the home of the Grange Opera and the grand Severals House), described by an acquaintance as 'a man noted for his impudence and immorality but a good estate and a beau'. Writing to his constituents in 1734 in response to the failed introduction of the Excise Bill in Sir Robert Walpole's government the previous year, Henley launched the sort of rant one would struggle to find in the files of today's more timid MPs.*

Gentlemen,

I have received yours and am surprised by your insolence in troubling me about the Excise. You know what I very well know, that I bought you. And I know what perhaps you think I don't know, you are now selling yourselves to Somebody Else; and I know what you do not know, that I am buying another borough. May God's curse light upon you all: may your houses be as open and

---

* The bill attempted to introduce a reduction in the land tax for the gentry, and an increase in salt tax; it was defeated as much by public opposition as parliamentary.

common to all Excise Officers as your wifes and daughters were to me when I stood for your scoundrel corporation.

Alas, the letter may have been a dare, a literary *esprit de l'escalier*. Henley did write it, but he may not have sent it. He did, however, send a disappointingly sober response more in keeping with parliamentary diplomacy.

Pryor told me that a few of his selections were determined by the lottery of copyright permissions. Pryor wanted to include a letter from T.E. Lawrence (Lawrence of Arabia), but had a choice to make. 'There was a critically important one about blowing up Arabs and their trains,' he told me, 'and then one about staying at a hotel in Bridlington with the sea coming up and down like a Lyons swiss roll. We got a letter back [from the copyright holder – his brother was still alive at the time] saying, "terribly sorry, you can't use the one about the Arabs, but the swiss roll one is fine". I went "hooray!" – that was the one I really wanted.

'I wanted to end with Einstein and the bomb, going out with a bang as it were.* And the University of Jerusalem, which owns the copyright, said we could do it if they got a cut of the royalties if the book sells. I said, "get stuffed" and they were quite nice – they said, "all right then, a copy of the book will do".'

In his introduction, Pryor notes that there were more letters being written at the end of the 1980s than at any other time in history, and that reports of letter-writing's demise were greatly exaggerated. But he also observes that letter-writing was not universally regarded as the elevated form we may imagine it to have been, either for the sender or the receiver. When the Jacobean playwright John Webster described a character on stage

---

* A letter from Einstein to Roosevelt from August 1939 in which he suspects that the element uranium may soon be turned into a 'new and important' source of energy.

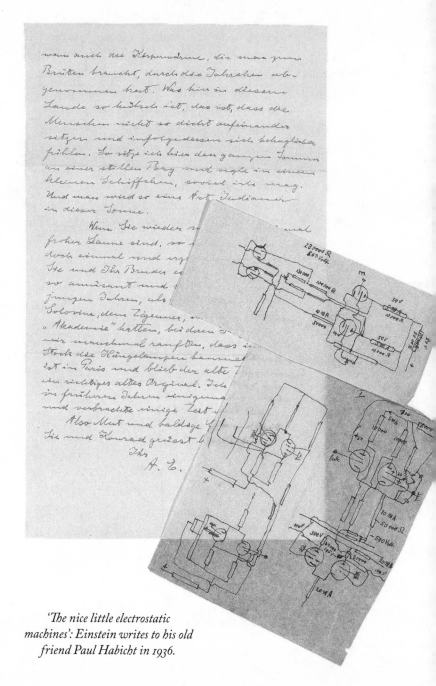

'The nice little electrostatic
machines': Einstein writes to his old
friend Paul Habicht in 1936.

being presented with some plot-churning letter, his immediate impression is one of gloom: he assumes it may be a complaint, or a bill, or a claim from a woman that he is the father of her child. Even before brown envelopes, in other words, letters were often considered doomy news, best avoided.

Taken as a whole, what can we learn from these excitingly random collections of letters at auction houses and the slightly more ordered gatherings in anthologies? We learn that we are not alone, and that letters may leave us both larger and other than we were. These are odd nuggets of unexpected history – history in the present tense, history from its participants. They expose a grand truth, and often the same truth we may feel when we read Shakespeare and Austen: no matter how original we consider ourselves to be, it is evident that our emotions, motives and desires have echoes in the past. We're not so special; someone else has almost certainly been there first.

Let Us Mention Marriage

14232134 SIGMN. BARKER H.C., 30 WING, I COY.,
9 AIR FORMATION SIGNALS, M.E.F.

18th April 1944

Dear Bessie,

I don't know what you will mainly feel at the conclusion of this letter, but I do want to remove the impression I have too pulverisingly included in earlier letters. I cannot withdraw my earlier warnings of instability, and I do not. But I want now to catch you up and carry lovely you to a place where you will forget I was ever so grim, and where you will only think of our possible lives together. Do not worry about 'tomorrow'. You will make your own tomorrow, and I hope it will be with me.

The second thing I want to say is that our association in the future depends on your ability to put up with me and my defects, not my ability to put up with yours. And that if we are spending much of our time regarding the other as a bed mate that is a very natural thing, since we are likely to be in that position before too long; I hope it doesn't mean we are very lustful, but if it does, it doesn't stop me wanting to tell you how I stiffen and ooze as I read your words and imagine you writing them. I shall do all that I can to keep you warm. I hope that we shall always love each other as we do now. Our thoughts are identical. Yes, we are in harmony! I am glad that I am your lover, and you are glad that you are mine.

What a pity we cannot be together, so that I can do what you want me to do; perhaps I should say 'try to do'. I am your servant and your master at once. I will command you and be commanded by you. Your breasts are mine. Whatever I have is yours. I want to have you. I want to awaken you as you have never been awakened. I yearn for your secrets. I want to tell you that you are my dear love, to keep me by you, to see I do not stray. I am not very collected when I think of you, your invitation and your loveliness – I am 'shattered' too, I do assure you.

I WILL ALWAYS LOVE YOU.

I do not feel very happy at the thought of the practical difficulties in the way of setting up house after the war. Every shark in the commercial world will be up and about. Unfortunately I used to donate most of my money to various good causes and I did not start to save until the end of the war in Spain. I think I had about £75 when our own war started; I did not increase this until I joined the Army. At the end of last year I had (my Mother told me) a mere (for my purpose) £227. I think that I am adding to this at about £2.10 a week. I do not know what will be required. Incidentally, I think that engagement rings are jewellers' rackets, and that marriage is more properly transacted at an office than mumbo-jumbo'd at a church. I am sorry you don't already know my views on this. You will have to be told sometime.

Can you see that it is gradually dawning on me that you are too good to be missed? Will you tell me that we may be together really one day, and you will hit me if I start wanting to go? Remember now, that you have a hand in shaping me and making me, and that I want you to speak up where and when you like.

I am strictly limited in the number of things I may send you.

I can only send one Green Envelope weekly, officially, and I shouldn't send any ordinary censored-in-unit mail. I am also rather limited in what I can say because, although it comes under the 'private and family matters' mentioned on the certificate, some of the things I want to say I cannot bring myself to write, as there is another censor outside the unit, liable to breach my envelope.

Now enters logic, sobriety, order, so that I may mention some of the things that have happened lately around here. First, our Sergeant Major has left for England after six years abroad. (We shall be 35 if I wait that long.) There was no chance of making a gift, and we may not give money, so I asked one of the chaps who is good at printing to draw up a testimonial which we could all sign. But this chap alternates between drinking and sleeping, and let me down so that I had to write it out with my own miserable calligraphy. I was sleeping when it was presented to him, but he later came round the tents to say Goodbye. He doesn't drink, but left the price of a bottle of beer for everyone to drink his health in. He is the best boss I have met in the Army. I am very apprehensive about his successor.

When I am writing you I seem to be nearer you. I want to think of you and nothing else. I want to underline a dozen times that I need you and love you. I want you to the exclusion of everything else. I want to surround you and enfold you. My comments may seem hackneyed but you must know that you control me, and that I am filled with thoughts of you, and cry out for you imperatively and urgently. I want to touch your person and possess you. I don't know how long I shall carry on writing things like this, but I shall not stop thinking of you as my partner, as my lover, my wife. The wonderful thing is that neither of us are saying anything that has not occurred to the other. You are necessary to me, whatever I may blithely have thought previously. How I long for YOU! I love you. I love you. I love you. Hurry on the day when I may say these things to you, with all the force I have and be received by your flesh and revived by your loveliness. How near we are despite the distance, how far from contact because of it, Bessie; love, mistress, wife.

No, I am not fooling. I am as serious as yourself. Certainly let us mention marriage. Consider me as the one you will be with always from this day, if you want me and will chance it. I read a life of Donne in a Times Lit. Supp., and gained the impression he was no saint. Gladly and gloriously I would rove, I would grope, I would seek you. My dear and lovely, please believe that we are aroused together, and I am alert to your provocative delight. I know now that in 1946 or 47 we shall still be going strong. I hope, too, that by then we shall have each gazed full upon the other and admitted as we wish, our mutual love, dependence and obligation. By then your banks will have burst and I shall be with you in the flesh. I don't want 'marriage' to 'stagger in and out of these pages'. I want you to regard me as your future husband, to think of me, at least as your companion, at most as your everything. I want you to build on me in the assurance that we are each other's, not that my contribution to our future happiness is less than yours. Try hard to have faith in me, though I be but a man. Tell me you believe in me and our lives together. Tell me that you think of US as a fact and not just a possibility, and that your intelligence guides your thoughts. If you are there, I shall not 'scurry off'. If you are there I shall be with you, to comfort and to soothe, and to be comforted and soothed. Do not hope any longer for a permanent place in my heart; be glad (if you will flatter me) you have it. You are my love.

I shall close this letter at the end of the page, though this time I feel I ought to carry on, telling you that I love you, and that I am discontented and not happy without you. I want to be very very tender and gentle towards you – and, too, very rough. I want to sink into you, to merge with you, to be a part of you. You end one of your L.C.s with a French phrase I interpret (I never had French in my youth) as 'I adore you my good friend'. Thank you. Please hold onto that idea, and for my sake, please hold onto me; let me in, and warm me.

I love you.

Chris

Chapter Nine

Why Jane Austen's Letters Are so Dull (and Other Postal Problems Solved)

It is February 1816, and Jane Austen, aged 40, is beginning to feel unwell. It is seventeen months before her death. One of her lasting and final pleasures, apart from work and the sedentary thrills of spillikins, is her friendship with her niece Fanny Knight, a relationship conducted primarily through letters. 'You are inimitable, irresistible,' Austen writes to her from her home in Chawton, Hampshire. 'You are the delight of my life. Such letters, such entertaining letters, as you have lately sent! such a description of your queer little heart! such a lovely display of what imagination does. You are worth your weight in gold, or even in the new silver coinage.'

Their correspondence continues until the end, and it is the first thing Cassandra Austen, Jane's sister, refers to when she writes to Fanny directly after Jane's death in July 1817.

Winchester, Sunday.

My dearest Fanny,

Doubly dear to me now for her dear sake whom we have lost. She did love you most sincerely, and never shall I forget the proofs of love you gave her during her illness in writing those kind, amusing letters at a time when I know your feelings would have dictated so different a style. Take the only reward I can give you in the assurance that your benevolent purpose was answered; you did contribute to her enjoyment.

Even your last letter afforded pleasure. I merely cut the seal and gave it to her; she opened it and read it herself, afterwards she gave it to me to read, and then talked to me a little and not uncheerfully of its contents, but there was then a languor about her which prevented her taking the same interest in anything she had been used to do.

The letter contains further details of Austen's final day and the plans for 'the last sad ceremony' at Winchester Cathedral. But half a century later, in 1869, Fanny Knight (now Lady Knatchbull) did not have such reverential things to say about either of her aunts, recalling in a letter to her younger sister that Jane 'was not so refined as she ought to have been from her talent' and that

They [the Austen family] were not rich & the people around with whom they chiefly mixed were not all high bred, or in short anything more than mediocre . . . Both the Aunts were brought up in the most complete ignorance of the World & its ways (I mean as to fashion &c) & if it had not been for Papa's marriage which brought them into Kent . . . they would have been, tho' not less clever & agreeable in themselves, very much below par as to good Society & its ways.

Why so ungrateful? Victorian society had sharpened her standards and hardened her expectations, and perhaps dulled her memory and tact. But her condemnation does contain a telling phrase: 'most complete ignorance of the World & its ways'. Sweeping as this assertion was, Fanny was not alone in finding this fault in the Austens, and there is no firmer evidence of it than in Jane Austen's letters.

For a writer whose novels are so steeped in epistolarity as Austen – characters are defined by letters, plots turn on them

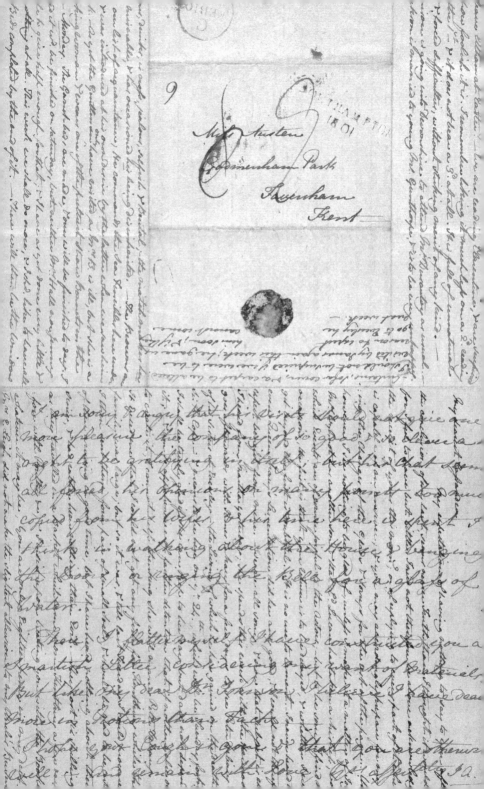

9

SOUTHAMPTON
1801

Miss Austen

Godmersham Park

Faversham

Kent

– it is startling to discover how damn dull so many of Austen's own letters are. Taken in one sitting – some 160 surviving items in all, the majority to Cassandra – you can read a great many pages without finding any insight into their author, or even much to amuse or inform; their domesticity and apparent unworldliness (the thing of which her niece complained: only scant and disparaging mention of the wars raging in Europe, for instance, and no apparent care for industrial revolution at home) are disappointing to her biographers and general fans alike.

In 1801, Jane Austen acknowledged a truth about letters that, if not exactly universal, is at least as true today as it was then, and as much of a cliché too: 'I have now attained the true art of letter-writing,' she wrote to Cassandra, 'which we are always told, is to express on paper exactly what one would say to the same person by word of mouth.' To which one may ungenerously conclude that her conversations must have been more than a trifle on the dry side.

Here's an example from October 1808, written from her home in Southampton when she was 32. She had already composed a draft version of what was to become *Sense and Sensibility* (in letter form), although the final version would not appear for a further three years.

My dear Cassandra,

Edward and George came to us soon after seven on Saturday, very well, but very cold, having by choice travelled on the outside, and with no great coat but what Mr. Wise, the coachman, good-naturedly spared them of his, as they sat by his side. They were so much chilled when they arrived, that I was afraid they must have taken cold; but it does not seem at all the case; I never saw them looking better.

Jane cross-writes to Cassandra in 1807. Good luck with that.

They behave extremely well in every respect, showing quite as much feeling as one wishes to see, and on every occasion speaking of their father with the liveliest affection. His letter was read over by each of them yesterday, and with many tears; George sobbed aloud, Edward's tears do not flow so easily; but as far as I can judge they are both very properly impressed by what has happened. Miss Lloyd, who is a more impartial judge than I can be, is exceedingly pleased with them.

George is almost a new acquaintance to me, and I find him in a different way as engaging as Edward.

We do not want amusement: bilbocatch, at which George is indefatigable; spillikins, paper ships, riddles, conundrums, and cards, with watching the flow and ebb of the river, and now and

'A note for Miss Bennet': an engraving from an 1894 edition of Pride and Prejudice.

then a stroll out, keep us well employed; and we mean to avail ourselves of our kind papa's consideration, by not returning to Winchester till quite the evening of Wednesday.*

Mrs. J. A. had not time to get them more than one suit of clothes; their others are making here, and though I do not believe Southampton is famous for tailoring, I hope it will prove itself better than Basingstoke. Edward has an old black coat, which will save his having a second new one; but I find that black pantaloons are considered by them as necessary, and of course one would not have them made uncomfortable by the want of what is usual on such occasions.

Fanny's letter was received with great pleasure yesterday, and her brother sends his thanks and will answer it soon. We all saw what she wrote, and were very much pleased with it.

The letter continued, anticipating a forthcoming marriage of friends and a possible family move to Kent. And then:

In the evening we had the Psalms and Lessons, and a sermon at home, to which they [her nephews] were very attentive; but you will not expect to hear that they did not return to conundrums the moment it was over. Their aunt has written pleasantly of them, which was more than I hoped.

While I write now, George is most industriously making and naming paper ships, at which he afterwards shoots with horse-chestnuts brought from Steventon on purpose; and Edward equally intent over the 'Lake of Killarney', twisting himself about in one of our great chairs . . . Our evening was equally agreeable in its way: I introduced Speculation, and it was so much approved that we hardly knew how to leave off . . .

---

* George and Edward's mother (Jane Austen's sister-in-law) had just died, and Jane is looking after them. Within this context, her observations on their spirits and games are caring and touching.

We have just had two hampers of apples from Kintbury, and the floor of our little garret is almost covered. Love to all.

Yours very affectionately, J.A.

There is nothing intrinsically wrong with this letter or her others (apart from the examples she 'crossed', writing first down the page in the usual way, before turning the page sideways and writing across it again, a thrifty, eye-straining scheme she refers to in *Emma*). She did write wittily, spitefully and gregariously at times, but these flashes are fleeting. (And these flashes enraged some as being unnecessarily cruel: E.M. Forster, a committed fan of Austen's novels, found her letters loaded with 'triviality, varied by touches of ill-breeding and of sententiousness . . . she has not enough subject-matter on which to exercise her powers', while Austen herself was self-consciously apologetic about her outbursts in another letter to Cassandra: 'I am forced to be abusive for want of a subject, having nothing really to say'.)

It may be unfair to pick another example that shows Austen in a bad light when she writes so much that hardly throws a light on anything, but her comments from her Hampshire fireside on the casualties being reported in the Napoleonic Wars in May 1811 are narrow-minded at best: 'How horrible it is to have so many people killed! And what a blessing that one cares for none of them!' The same letter goes on to describe a visit to a woman 'who is short and not quite straight, and cannot pronounce an R any better than her sisters'.

Cool, dispassionate and occasionally heartless: that's an unexpected combination. Her biographer David Nokes suggests that Austen's letters reveal her to be one thing above others: an instinctive mistress of disguise. Even in her letters to Cassandra, where we would expect her to be most forthcoming, her 'playful pose of sisterly confidence usually falls teasingly short of genuine self-exposure'.

This is the main disappointment in her letters: we occasionally catch her artfulness but rarely her personality; 'the real Jane Austen' remains slippery and elusive, and provides little insight into either her mind or her working practices. Knowing what we do of the intricate sensibilities and rich psychological multi-layering of her novels, surely it isn't unreasonable to hope for more? And how to explain why her fiction should play so irresistibly with letters and her real life should not?

According to the brief author biography in his book *What Matters in Jane Austen?*, Professor John Mullan has taught Austen to university students for more than a quarter of a century. And according to his energetic and surprising book, he is evidently still highly energised by the subject. The book's surprises lie in the originality of the approach that someone so academically steeped in her work can bring to bear on the novels, picking them apart with amusing thematic essays on sex, the weather, sex between sisters, money, and what characters say about the heroine when the heroine's not there. It's the sort of book that will inspire you to read all the novels again in order, to see what you missed.

But the most surprising thing about the book is that there is hardly anything in it about letters. There is a small section on Robert Martin's strategic misjudgement in proposing to Harriet Smith by letter in *Emma*, thus stirring the novel's plot and giving Miss Smith ample time to mull things over and refuse him (had he just come out and asked her directly, she probably would have said yes). But that's pretty much all we get on the subject. To rectify this absence I called on Professor Mullan one morning in his Bloomsbury office at University College London, and he began with a persuasive explanation that we may understand Austen best by first considering her literary forebears and the social context in which she wrote.

Whatever else they were, Mullan observed, her letters were not written with publication in mind; she would have shuddered at the thought. But this was not the general eighteenth-century view of the literary world. Samuel Johnson argued that the likely publication of his letters was one reason why he put so little in them, while the likes of Pope and Swift wrote as if their private letters were destined for the printing press with the ink still wet. Austen wrote for her friends and family; Pope was perennially grandstanding. 'Pope's letters are fantastic,' Mullan says, 'but they are completely contrived. He did things like – he fell out with Joseph Addison. After he died, Pope thought, "God, I haven't got a correspondence with Addison . . ." So he got hold of a load of letters he'd written to other people and rewrote them to Addison, and fabricated this kind of literary correspondence. It was as if Ian McEwan had gone, "Oh God, I hadn't been writing to Hilary Mantel, and now she's gone and died. I'd better produce some Hilary Mantel letters!"'

The key with Austen's letters, then, is to remember that she is not writing as an author. 'I think her letters are a very superior version of what many a person like her would have written about,' Professor Mullan believes, 'interspersed with little glitters of something Austenish. I think Cassandra is slightly resented by a lot of Jane Austen fans . . . because she totally shapes the main effluence of personality that we have. And Jane Austen wrote to Cassandra about what she thought she wanted to know about. "Mrs Blah Blah has done this, and the harvest has been got in and we've all had colds ..."

'The funny thing is, often – even though you can get her letters in a fantastically annotated edition which gives you biographical glosses on everybody – it's amazing, with a typical letter by Austen chosen at random, how much of it we don't understand. You know, "Mrs X has done this again ...", and Cassandra is reading it and going "Oh not again!" and we know nothing.' And Professor Mullan emphasises that while some letters may seen inconsequential on the surface, their context – known to the recipient as well as Jane Austen herself – may reveal hidden values.

We can probably trust what we read in Austen's letters – their lack of theatre suggests an authenticity we have come to expect from daily domestic accounts. But do we dupe ourselves even here? Midway through our meeting, John Mullan scans his wall of shelves for a book about Samuel Richardson with a rewarding quote at the start of it. He reads:

> It has been so long said as to be commonly believed, that the true characters of men may be found in their letters, and that he who writes to his friend lays his heart open before him ... But the truth is, that such were the simple friendships of the 'Golden Age', and are now the friendships only of children. Very few can boast of hearts which they dare lay open to themselves, and of which, by whatever accident exposed, they do not shun a distinct and continued view; and, certainly, what we hide from ourselves we do not show to our friends. There is, indeed, no transaction which offers stronger temptations to fallacy and sophistication than epistolary intercourse.

The quote is from Samuel Johnson's *Life of Pope* from 1781, but is juxtaposed with another that the author sent to his friend Mrs Thrale a few years before: 'In a man's letter you know, Madam, his soul lies naked, his letters are only the mirror of his breast, whatever passes within him is shown undisguised in its natural process. Nothing is inverted, nothing distorted, you see systems in their elements, you discover actions in their motives.'

In Jane Austen's novels we get both conflicting interpretations, often in the same chapter. Indeed, one encounters significant letters in almost every chapter, and so much do they become a part of the furniture that they form a vital character in themselves.

The dutiful-cum-obsessive Austen website pemberley.com has gone so far as to list every significant appearance of a letter in *Pride and Prejudice*, including Caroline Bingley's letter to Jane in Chapter 7, inviting her to come to Netherfield; Darcy's letter to Elizabeth in Chapter 35, explaining his conduct; and Mr Collins to Mr Bennet in Chapter 57, advising against an Elizabeth/Darcy match. There are 18 other game-changers en route, and these are only the letters which are quoted from rather than just mentioned; to include the latter would take up a chapter in itself.

Had she lived and published 20 years earlier, Austen's novels might have consisted of letters and nothing else. Both *Pride and Prejudice* and *Sense and Sensibility* are thought to have begun as purely epistolary novels; her early work *Lady Susan* retained the form to posthumous publication. 'At the end of the eighteenth century writing a novel in letters would have been instinctual,' John Mullan suggests. 'Almost every creative genre appeared in letters in the eighteenth century – travel writing, pornography, political controversy, philosophical writing, even poems take the form of epistles.'

The unchallenged champion of the genre was Samuel Richardson, whose three largely unread great works of mid-eighteenth-century English literature – *Pamela*, *Clarissa* and *The History of Sir Charles Grandison* – were all crowd-pleasing epistolary fictions (to the point where they inspired parodies, most famously Henry Fielding's *Shamela*.*)

The tension in *Clarissa* derives from the unreliability of letters; we're unsure whether to trust the heroine's virtuous version of herself, and we read of letters being forged and going astray. Austen is similarly playful with the form, and uses letters both as an indicator of character and a symbol of intimate engagement. At the beginning of *Emma*, for example, Frank Churchill is judged solely by his writing skills: 'For a few days, every morning visit in Highbury included some mention of the handsome letter Mrs. Weston had received. "I suppose you have heard of the handsome letter Mr. Frank Churchill has written to Mrs. Weston? I understand it was a very handsome letter, indeed. Mr. Woodhouse told me of it. Mr. Woodhouse saw the letter, and he says he never saw such a handsome letter in his life."'

SAMUEL RICHARDSON.

One reason Churchill's writing skills are tapped up early on is because the core of the novel is concerned with his clandestine correspondence from Ireland with Jane Fairfax. And it is this correspondence, later in the book, that entices Jane out to the post office in the rain, and puts her on the defensive with John Knightley, who cares little for Frank Churchill.

---

* Fielding also wrote *The Letter Writers*, a Whitehall-style farce in which two hapless men try to protect their shaky marriages with a plot involving letters, hiding in closets and other buffoonish antics. And alongside his novels, Samuel Richardson also wrote an influential letter-writing manual titled *Familiar Letters*, in which he combined grammatical with moral guidance. Richardson believed strongly that letters were vehicles not just for communication but for education, and most of his template letters had a message, including 'To a Father, against putting a Youth of but moderate Parts to a Profession that requires more extensive Abilities'.

'It is my daily errand. I always fetch the letters when I am here. It saves trouble, and is a something to get me out. A walk before breakfast does me good.'

'Not a walk in the rain, I should imagine.'

'No, but it did not absolutely rain when I set out.'

Mr. John Knightley smiled, and replied,

'That is to say, you chose to have your walk, for you were not six yards from your own door when I had the pleasure of meeting you; and Henry and John had seen more drops than they could count long before. The post-office has a great charm at one period of our lives. When you have lived to my age, you will begin to think letters are never worth going through the rain for.'

There was a little blush, and then this answer,

'I must not hope to be ever situated as you are, in the midst of every dearest connexion, and therefore I cannot expect that simply growing older should make me indifferent about letters.'

'Indifferent! Oh! no – I never conceived you could become indifferent. Letters are no matter of indifference; they are generally a very positive curse.'

'You are speaking of letters of business; mine are letters of friendship.'

'I have often thought them the worst of the two,' replied he coolly. 'Business, you know, may bring money, but friendship hardly ever does.'

A short time later, the subject of letters crops up again, and this time Jane defends the entire institution:

> 'The post-office is a wonderful establishment!' said she. – 'The regularity and despatch of it! If one thinks of all that it has to do, and all that it does so well, it is really astonishing!'
>
> 'It is certainly very well regulated.'
>
> 'So seldom that any negligence or blunder appears! So seldom that a letter, among the thousands that are constantly passing about the kingdom, is even carried wrong – and not one in a million, I suppose, actually lost! And when one considers the variety of hands, and of bad hands too, that are to be deciphered, it increases the wonder.'

Inevitably, it is letters (and the knowledge contained within them) that will expose the relationship between Churchill and Fairfax, and it is a long, self-justifying letter printed in full from Churchill that helps bring the novel to a close. By choosing to have letters do so much work for her throughout her books, but rejecting her initial inclination to use letters and nothing else, Austen goes a long way in bridging the gap between old and new forms of fiction, and between the eighteenth century and the nineteenth.

'It ends really suddenly,' Professor Mullan says of the epistolary novel. 'The high point is the 1780s; 30 years on from Richardson it's still very strong. But in the first decade of the nineteenth century it just goes off a cliff. What are the answers? There's a literary critical answer, which is that writers begin to discover ways of doing interior life – a style that doesn't require this extraordinary artificial form. Austen is a key to that, because she sort of discovers this free-indirect technique which she bequeaths to many of the great nineteenth-century writers, although very few of them acknowledge their debt. And people weren't all going "Jane Austen is a goddess and she's cracked it", so it's hard to make the case for her immediate and dramatic influence.'

So there must have been other reasons, and one of them was simple. At the beginning of the nineteenth century, it became clear to novelists that letters were just too artificial; it came to be seen as an eighteenth-century thing. 'It belonged to a past age,' Mullan says, 'and the whole point of the novel for most writers was that it sell, that it be fashionable, that it be novel. It became clear to everybody that if you wanted to write a novel of today, you couldn't do this letters thing anymore.'*

Leaving Professor Mullan's office as a student enters for a tutorial, I remember one other reason for the dichotomy between the letters in her fiction and in her life: censorship. Some of this she performed herself: as in her novels, Austen knew that letters are often read aloud and passed around, and when Austen learnt that her letters to Cassandra were also being read by her niece Fanny Knight she noted beautifully: 'I am gratified by her having pleasure in what I write – but I wish the knowledge of my being exposed to her discerning Criticism may not hurt my stile, by inducing too great a solicitude. I begin already to weigh my words and sentences more than I did, and am looking about for a sentiment, an illustration, or a metaphor in every corner of the room. Could my Ideas flow as fast as the rain in the store-closet it would be charming.'

But there is a still harsher censorship – the rash and

---

* The form is not quite dead, of course. Although the epistolary novel is still out of favour for its unreliable narrators and limited perspective, the letter and postal service have been star performers in countless contemporary novels – a list that includes Saul Bellow's *Herzog*, L.P. Hartley's *The Go-Between*, Thomas Pynchon's *The Crying of Lot 49*, Alice Walker's *The Color Purple*, A.S. Byatt's *Possession*, Terry Pratchett's *Going Postal* and Mark Haddon's *The Curious Incident of the Dog in the Night-Time*. A letter reliably means 'New information; things are bound to change after this'. As yet, emails don't have quite the same narrative effect, as emails are rarely discovered in lofts or under floorboards, or in boxes when people die. At the moment, emails in fiction often perform the same role as texts, usually alerting the reader to infidelity.

destructive judgements of others that have purposely obscured our view of Austen for all time. Not long after her death, Cassandra burned a large number of her letters and cut others (literally cut: some of her existing correspondence has been scissored and pasted). This was partly to protect her sister's reputation – her vituperative personal outbursts would not have endeared her either to her living acquaintances or future fans; and it was partly to protect herself, as Cassandra had no doubt written about one of the darkest times in her life following the death of her fiancé, and Austen had no doubt replied with heartfelt consolation. We are left with something slightly more than Austen Lite, but we can only guess at how significant this loss has been.

What we do know is that after Cassandra had a good fillet, Jane Austen's more distant relatives also had a go themselves. Her nephew, James Edward Austen-Leigh, amended further letters in his *Memoir* of his aunt in 1869, while her great-nephew Lord Brabourne continued the tradition in the first collection of her letters 15 years later. Brabourne keenly protected her prim and saintly reputation, omitting anything remotely caustic and anything relating to sex or the female body. Austen's observation of 'naked cherubs' on a mantelpiece was deemed unsuitable and disappeared, while a description of a sleepless night caused by having 'too much cloathes over my stomach' was changed to 'over me'. A solid, restored (but still sorely incomplete) edition of her letters only appeared in the 1950s, by which time it was apparent that Austen had written a rather different version of herself than the one we have been allowed to see. 'If I am a wild beast, I cannot help it,' she wrote to Cassandra in 1813, towards the end of her life. 'It is not my fault.'

When Jane Austen died in 1817 it cost 4d to send a light letter from one end of Hampshire to another. The same letter would cost 8d from London to Brighton, 10d to Nottingham and at least 1s to Scotland. The prices had been raised frequently to pay for the Napoleonic wars, and varied according to whether they were carried by mail coach or, for longer and more costly distances, coastal steamer.

Despite the high charges, it wasn't only Jane Fairfax who thought the mail a miraculous thing. Celebrated writers gave a considerable amount of space in their letters on the subject of letters themselves – not least the early nineteenth-century debate over whether it was disrespectful to the Church to write on a Sunday (consensus: personal letters acceptable, business ones less so). And they were particularly interested in the vagaries of the postal service, and what likelihood their letters had of reaching their destination. In 1835, Thomas Carlyle sent a transatlantic letter to Ralph Waldo Emerson in which he marvelled at the divine madness of the system. A letter from Emerson had taken two months to reach him, but still Carlyle felt grateful: 'As the Atlantic is so broad and deep, ought we not rather to esteem it a beneficent miracle that messages can arrive at all; that a little slip of paper will skim over all these weltering floods, and other inextricable confusions; and come at last, in the hand of the Twopenny Postman, safe to your lurking-place, like green leaf in the bill of Noah's Dove?'*

In another letter to Emerson four months later, Carlyle bemoans the state of England; there is poverty everywhere, there is the threat of cholera, and worst of all, it seems, is all this newfangled technological progress, a comment we may hear echoes of today. 'What with railways, steamships, print-ing-presses, it has surely become a most *monstrous* "tissue" this

---

* This was part of a long letter about work, Goethe and health, and at the foot of it Carlyle wondered, 'Have I involved you in double postage by this loquacity?'

life of ours.' Fortunately for him, it was still possible to defeat the technology of the postal service. Writing to his mother in 1836, he is delighted that the parliamentary summer recess is over, because, now that 'certain "honourable members" having got back to town again', he may once more obtain free postage by abusing their free franking privileges (he mentions one particularly obliging member, a man called Mill). And his other cheat, more ingenious, was a personal coding system applied to the mailing of newspapers, which travelled at a much cheaper rate: 'I have sent the *Examiner* forward these two last weeks, to Jenny at Manchester to be sent on to you ... I know not whether either Rob or Jenny care about reading Newspapers; but doubtless they will always like to see the *two strokes* on the back. When I send *them* two strokes, you are to take *their* two strokes for a sign that all is well here too.'

The code of strokes was familiar not only to men and women of letters; in the first part of the nineteenth century the cost of postage ensured that it was a familiar dodge for a great many. As postage was paid by the recipient, the charge could as easily be refused as accepted. But often a letter would be refused and still achieve its sender's aim, for the marks on an envelope – perhaps strokes, symbols or a brief letter code – would indicate everything from a simple yes/no reply to a question or a furtive declaration of love.*

For a century or so before 1840 the Post Office managed all but the very last step of the delivery with moderate efficiency. But the payment by recipient was a slow enough process even if the recipient was available when the postman called; it was like paying a utility bill every day. As disquiet about this inconvenience grew, the outgoing secretary of the Post Office, Sir Francis Freeling, began to feel concerned. He complained

---

* In much the same way as telephone charges would be saved when a caller hung up after a ring or two, the code arranged in advance to indicate that all was well.

that throughout his career he had run the most effective service possible, and carried out his duties to the letter. 'Where else in the world does the merchant or manufacturer have the materials of his trade carried for him gratuitously or at so low a rate as to leave no margin of profit?'*

One of his main parliamentary opponents was Robert Wallace, MP for Greenock, whose admonishing speeches came to the attention of a civil servant named Rowland Hill. Hill conducted his own research into the postal system, and published a pamphlet noting not only the abnormalities and corruptions, but also that revenue from postage had been gradually falling in recent years despite the huge potential profits to be made. His suggested improvements transformed postal networks throughout the world.

Hill proposed a uniform postal charge of one penny per half-ounce for any letter sent within the British Isles, and reasoned that the cost should be paid in advance. To this end he drew on a previous idea of Charles Knight for a prepaid letter envelope, but it was his second idea that guaranteed his place in history: 'A bit of paper just large enough to bear the stamp, and covered at the back with a glutinous wash which the user might, by applying a little moisture, attach to the back of the letter.' How would one prove that postage had been paid? With the application of an adhesive stamp, initially referred to as a 'label'. And Hill envisaged another breakthrough: 'Probably it would soon be unnecessary even to await the opening of the door, as every house might be provided with a letter-box into which the Letter Carrier would drop the letters, and having knocked, he would pass on as fast as he could walk.'

The principal opposition to these novelties came from the postmaster general, Lord Lichfield, who complained that 'of

---

* The birth of universal penny postage is discussed in greater detail in *The Error World* by Simon Garfield (Faber, 2008), from where these quotations are taken.

all the wild and visionary schemes which I have ever heard or read of, it is the most extravagant!' But his was a lonely voice: the House of Commons voted in favour of penny postage in July 1839, and Hill was offered a new job at the Treasury.

But how was the new stamp to look? The basics we now take for granted – the size, the monarch's head, the licking – were all up for discussion. Uniform penny postage was introduced four months before the new adhesive labels were ready, with hand stamps from about three hundred towns being used in their place. There was an immediate increase in the amount of post through the system, despite some bafflement over the need to prepay. But there was an immediate incentive to welcome the new system: prepaid letters would cost one penny, whereas those paid on delivery would cost two.

The Treasury announced a competition to find a design for the new stamp. A notice in *The Times* requested that 'artists, men of science, and the public in general, may have an opportunity of offering any suggestions or proposals as to the manner in which the stamp may best be brought into use'. There were awards of £100 and £200 offered to those who could not only design something attractive, but could also solve the tricky issues of forgery and security. But none of the 2,600 entries satisfied. A Treasury committee praised the public's ingenuity, but finally the stamp, with Queen Victoria's head in profile, was designed and produced by a group of professional men already known to Hill and the inland revenue for their role in the printing of bank notes and other official documents.

Post offices received their first two Penny Blacks at the end of April 1840, with clear instructions on how they should be issued and cancelled (the stamps had to be cut from large sheets – perforations were not introduced until 1854). Postmasters also received an example of prepaid postal stationery, an envelope and letter sheet design by William Mulready containing images of elephants, lions, Britannia and people engrossed in their mail deliveries, an illustration whose parodies by London stationers and satirical magazines hastened its withdrawal.

The stamps – the Penny Black and the Two Pence Blue – went on sale on Friday 1 May 1840, along with the prepaid envelopes, and a revolution got under way. 'Great bustle at the Stamp Office,' Rowland Hill recorded in his diary that evening. On the following day he noted, '£2,500 worth of stamps sold yesterday'. By 6 May, the day the stamps were first intended for use, 22,993 sheets of 240 stamps each had been issued to 253 post offices, and on 22 May, Hill recorded, 'The demand for the labels is enormous, the printers supply more than half a million per day, and even this is not enough.'

The advance was as significant as the birth of inter-city railways a decade before. And like the railways, the postal reforms were a symbol of the popular will. In 1839, one year before reform, the number of letters carried in the UK was 75,907,572. In 1840 the number more than doubled to 168,768,344. Ten years later the number was 347,069,071.

Hill was soon convincing sceptical householders to have rectangular panels cut into their doors, and in London he introduced the concept of postal districts to ease sorting and delivery. By the time of his retirement in 1864, half the world had adopted his reforms; no single person had contributed more to the global communication of ideas.

And beyond this, Hill may be credited with inventing an entirely new hobby, a perfect solitary companion to letter-writing. Men and women began collecting stamps as soon as stamps began, a hobby considered eccentric from the start. Sheets of Penny Blacks and Two Pence Blues contained 240 stamps, and to limit forgeries and enable the tracing of portions of a sheet, each stamp had a letter in the two bottom corners. The rows running down the sheet had the same letter in the left corner, while the right corner progressed alphabetically. The first row went AA, AB, AC and so on, and thirteen rows down it went MA, MB, MC ... There were twenty horizontal rows of twelve, and some people who got a lot of post thought it would be fun to collect the set (while everyone else thought they ought to get out more).

One of the first mentions of the new hobby appeared in a German magazine in 1845, which noted, much in the manner of comedian Bob Newhart describing Raleigh's attempt to promote tobacco, how the English Post Office sold 'small square pieces of paper bearing the head of the Queen, and these are stuck on the letter to be franked'. The writer observed that the queen's head looked very pretty, and that the English

Rowland Hill commemorated – where else? – on stamps
marking universal penny postage.

'reveal their strange character by collecting these stamps'.

The first collector we are aware of was a woman known as 'E.D.', who advertised in *The Times* in 1841: 'A young lady, being desirous of covering her dressing room with cancelled postage stamps, has been so far encouraged in her wish by private friends as to have succeeded in collecting sixteen thousand. These, however, being insufficient, she will be greatly obliged, if any good-natured person who may have these otherwise useless little articles at their disposal, would assist her in her whimsical project.' There were two addresses to which to send the stamps, one in Leadenhall Street in the City, one in Hackney. There are no further records of E.D.'s collection, nor are there pictures of her room, which must have been a shade on the dark side, but these days might have been shortlisted for the Turner Prize. By the following year she had competition. *Punch* noted that 'a new mania has bitten the industriously idle ladies of England . . . They betray more anxiety to treasure up the Queen's heads than Harry the Eighth did to get rid of them.'

There was one more essential accoutrement to postal pleasure in this period – the pillar box. Its stated inventor, a Post Office employee for 33 years, would soon be famous for other things, the overproduction of dull novels. Anthony Trollope, whom Henry James called 'the dullest Briton of them all' (after sharing a transatlantic steamer with him), loved nothing more than the smooth and efficient productivity of modern life, and when he gave up his job at the Post Office in 1867 he continued his fascination with the post in his fiction. His detractors found this entirely apt, seeing him, in the words of historian Kate Thomas, as 'more of a postman than he is a novelist'.

Trollope simply wrote too much. In his autobiography he wrote of how inspiration was for aesthetes and the lazy;

he preferred something he called 'mechanical genius', which meant 18-hour days at a writing desk. To achieve this he had carpenters build special desks in his ship cabins and a special lap apparatus to enable him to write on trains. He was as infatuated as Austen with the fictional potency of the letter,

Trollope: when he wasn't writing, he was putting up pillar boxes.

and not by chance did he consider *Pride and Prejudice* the best novel ever written in English. The fate of the characters in one of his own novels, *John Caldigate* (1879), a tale of bigamy and fraud, turned principally on the forensic detection work conducted on an envelope and stamp. The novel also featured that rarest of things: a postal worker as hero.

Trollope's own postal legacy is still contentious. His biographer Victoria Glendinning states that he was the principal cheerleader for the pillar box rather than its inventor, while Trollope claimed full credit. Trollope began as a postal desk clerk, feeling frustrated in the role. But he flourished in a new role as postal surveyor, taking on responsibility for boosting the rural postal system, connecting a vast administrative system with the most isolated outpost. He was a great supporter of Rowland Hill's reforms, and he perceived his own role as grandly: 'I was,' he boasts in his autobiography, 'a beneficent angel to the public, bringing everywhere with me an earlier, cheaper, and much more regular delivery of letters.'

Before the pillar box was the letterbox, which may have originated in Italy in the sixteenth century. The *tamburi* of Florence were closed wooden boxes in which churchgoers could inform on those they believed had blasphemed or spoken against the state; one dropped a letter with a name through a slit. Postboxes in British post-receiving houses, usually built into walls or windows, existed from the beginning of the nineteenth century.

Anthony Trollope's version of the roadside pillar box, something he called his 'iron stump', also had its roots outside England. In November 1851, Trollope submitted a report after a visit to the Channel Islands: 'There is, at present, no receiving office in St Heliers, and persons living in the distant parts of the town have to send nearly a mile to the principal office. I believe that a plan has obtained in France of fitting up letterboxes in posts fixed at the road side, and it may perhaps be thought advisable to try the operation of this system in St Heliers – postage stamps are sold in every street, and, therefore, all that is wanted is a safe receptacle for them.'

A year later four pillar boxes were in place, including one in New Street 'in front of Mr Fry's, Painter and Glazier'. The first British mainland box appeared in September 1853 in Botchergate, Carlisle, and the first six boxes in central London were installed in April 1855, including one on the north side of Piccadilly, 'Corner of Bolton Street, two yards west of Lamp Post', and one in Fleet Street, 'opposite the centre of the Sunday Times doorway'. The design was by the Post Office consulting engineer E.A. Cowper, who could soon proudly claim 'I am glad to hear that not a single Letter has been stolen out of 212,000 posted'. Two years later the boxes carried iron notice plates on which were painted the times of collection. And thus the postal system came of age, and rapidly became the envy of the world. Its new efficiencies boosted more than letter-writing and the Treasury; it boosted employment too. It was now possible for entire families such as the Barkers to contemplate a lifetime's career dedicated to the post.

More Than Is Good for Me

14232134 SIGMN. BARKER H.C., 30 WING, I COY.,
9 AIR FORMATION SIGNALS, M.E.F.

22nd–30th April 1944

Dear Bessie,

I think that I will now start to tell you something of myself and family from the Year Dot to the present day. I think this is necessary because I want to (it is very difficult to write – all I want to do is tell you I LOVE YOU) marry you very soon after I return to England, and I want us to do most of the 'talking' through the medium of our letters.

I hope that you, too, will give me an abridged 'something', so that when we do, wonderfully, finally meet, we shall know more about each other than could be obtained by a contemporary or current correspondence. My ignorance of you can be judged by the fact that I don't know if the B.I.M. stands for Ivy, Irene or Itma, I don't know your birthday, or your birthplace. I want to know your food dislikes, if any; if and what you drink; whether you still smoke; how you housekeep or if someone else does it somehow. Please, please, please, tell me of and about yourself, so that I may breathe you in, and wallow in news of you. For by now you must have serious doubts of your ability to escape marrying me, and wondering what the Dickens you have done to deserve it.

When I was born, my Father was 34, a postman, and getting about 25/- a week. The family was increased to six (I have two brothers and one sister), and had to move from rooms in one part of Holloway, N.7., to a four roomed house in another part. It came under a Slum Clearance scheme when I was 13, and we were rehoused in a 5 roomed house on the London County Council Estate at Tottenham, until I was 26, when we moved to our present place at Bromley, which my brother owns. I am the baby of the family. My sister is 33, my second brother, Archie is 36, my eldest, Herbert Redvers (after a Boer War General) is 38. Dad is 64, Mum, 62. My early memories are few. I remember digging big holes in our back yard and lining up for the pictures. I don't know how much you recall of the last war? I remember the great fun of making cocoa after we had come back, seeing the R33 [a British patrol airship] which I thought was a Zeppelin; wanting to be a 'Spethial Conthtable' when I grew up; my Dad, a strange, awkward, red faced man, coming home from India.

Things here (I'll leave The Story of My Life II till later) are about the same, except that today we have gone into Khaki Drill which is much nicer than Battle Dress, and can be washed anytime one wants. I am playing chess as usual and bridge at night when possible. I'd like to creep away somewhere and do a bit of hard brooding about you, but I have to go through the motions of behaving normally, like you. Whatever I do I am conscious of the fact that you are in the same world, and it is a pretty great thought to be getting on with, rather overwhelming at times. I hope the time we are away from each other will not seem too painfully long, and that before 1999 we shall be able to TELL each other what now we can only think.

I have enclosed a small photograph which I hope you accept more as a token than a likeness. I have had 'better' ones done since, but only had this one on me. You probably noticed the disappearing hair on the top of my head. Sometimes I think it is falling out quickly, and at others I persuade myself there are positive signs of growth. It is very convenient to have my present amount, but I really do hope I hold on to it.

My autobiographical details seem to have been neglected. I suddenly dropped the idea under pressure of telling you that you are lovely. But I will potter along for a bit now. I was never christened. My mother had a lot to do at the time, it was somehow overlooked! Now she is very keen that I be 'done' but I am quite pleased with my status. I believe that if a child dies without being christened he must be buried in un-hallowed ground. That makes me very keen to rebel against the rubbish of that dictum.

I went to Drayton Park (Highbury) LCC School. I was probably a very ordinary pupil but good at English. I never won a scholarship despite parental ambitions. When I had done very badly at Arithmetic once I had to stand up before a class. The headmaster said that a chap with a noble forehead like mine should have done much better. I was elected editor of a new school magazine, but somehow never got out an issue. I left too soon. I remember, at an Armistice treat when I was very young, putting a banana in my pocket to take it home to Mum. When I got home the banana was just pulp. I had the usual fights during playtime, and before and after school. I supported Cambridge, The Arsenal, and Surrey. (I got these from my eldest brother who has been a big influence on me throughout my life.) I only remember having one good hiding from my Dad, that was when I was about 11, I made a swing, tied one end to the mangle, and smashed it completely when it fell down under my weight.

I started in the Post Office as a Boy Messenger at the M.O.D. on 8th March 1928. I enjoyed the experience. It was good to be earning money, and I spent most of my pocket money on secondhand books. I left in November 1930, when I started at the C.T.O. [Commonwealth Telecommunications Organisation.] The first girl I ever went out with was a Girl Probationer, whom I took to see 'Sunny Side Up', one of the first talkies. I was Secretary of the Cricket Club, but my highest score was 16, and that must have been unusual or I shouldn't remember it. I played little football. I must have been poor. I was 'junior boy' for nine months, and had a terrible time being dragged all over the kitchen by my seniors, ducked in the water, and generally leg-pulled with. One of my jobs then was to clear away the Controller's tea tray. I remember still the pleasure of drinking the creamy milk he used to leave.

I think of your breasts more than is good for me. I am sure you are not entirely disinterested in the fact that I have hairs on my chest. Then we start wondering other things. Where shall we live, do we want children; how about your age. You tell me you have £85.10 in the P.O.S.B. without knowing I am just writing you that I have £227. I think, and you think, of 'Gifts' at the same time because we are falling over ourselves in our desire to pay tribute to the other. Thank goodness you did not send me a cross. Really, I am scornful of such things. I have no patience with its religious intent, and I know very well that the gold-cross-laden women at home wear them as no more than lucky charms. I hope you didn't seriously think of sending me any such thing. I must risk hurting you, my love – I hope you aren't R.C. I'll say no more for the present.

I love you.

Chris

Chapter Ten

A Letter Feels Like Immortality

Let us assume that it is 1794, and you are a farm labourer in New Hampshire named Abner Sanger. What would you hear from others about life beyond the root crops? In early June you learn from someone with your interests at heart that there is a letter from your brother waiting for you in a Boston post office. The letter has been sent from northern Vermont, and may contain important news, because why else would you write in 1794? So you ask a local shopkeeper to pick it up when he next buys supplies in the city. Before this happens, your wife's cousin spots the letter at the post office and thinks she's doing you a good deed by picking it up and bringing it much closer to you; it is now in Keene, a town about 10 miles away. After a few days more farming, you go to Keene to collect it, but despite making enquiries at all the local stores and saloons, the letter is nowhere to be found. About ten days later, some two months after the letter was sent, your own son meets the brother of the shopkeeper you originally trusted with the letter retrieval, and he brings it back for you to read, or for someone to read it to you.*

The story has neither a sad nor happy ending, for we don't know what the letter said. But the postal news was as good as it gets: the letter got through, and two months may not have been considered a bad result. But its journey tells us other things, not least that the United States was not yet geared up

* I am grateful for this letter trail to Richard D. Brown, as related in *Knowledge Is Power: The Diffusion of Information in Early America 1700–1865*, OUP, 1989.

for such specific postal adventures. No one brought the mail unless you organised a search party, and it was unlikely that anyone not involved in pressing matters of the day expected any. In the main, letters were intended for important city people who organised delivery among themselves; everyone else kept on farming.*

The fact that something (or several things) had to change did not go unnoticed. Four years earlier, on 20 January 1790, Samuel Osgood, the postmaster general of the United States, declared the postal service 'very defective' in a variety of ways. The chief defect was that it was losing money; a secondary one was that it was open to abuse, and then there was the point that it wasn't offering much of a service. And so Osgood drew up an official plan for improvement, and at the top of it was a speculative list of why things weren't going so well. In part this read:

1). 'That there may be so few letters written that, under the best regulations, it would not amount to anything considerable.' Remarkably (it may seem to us), Osgood's financial calculations were based on the estimation that only about 100,000 people were sending letters regularly towards the end of the eighteenth century in the US; he surmised that each of these would write, on average, 30 letters a year.

2) 'The franking of letters may have been extended too far.' As in

---

* The bulk of surviving letters from colonial America did, by and large, betray their British roots. Most are respectable, god-fearing and dull, and one is grateful for the occasional flash of desperation and emotion. Newly settled in Massachusetts Bay in 1631, a man called John Pond writes to his father William Pond across the pond. 'I pray, father, send me four or five yards of cloth to make us some apparel, and loving Father, though I be far distant from you, yet I pray you remember me as your child, and we do not know how long we may subsist, for we cannot live here without provisions from ould eingland.' As was to be the case with postal reforms, New England relied on the old. Quoted in *Epistolary Practices: Letter Writing in America Before Telecommunications* by William Merrill Decker, University of Carolina Press, 1998.

Great Britain, free postage was a privilege extended to those in the administration of government, and, as in Great Britain, those in the administration of government frequently extended this privilege to their friends, and attained seats on boards of companies in exchange. One of the most notorious over-frankers was one of Osgood's predecessors as postmaster general in the colonial era, Benjamin Franklin.

3) 'The rate of postage may have been too high in some instances, and too low in others.' It cost 25 cents to send a single sheet the 400-odd miles between Albany and Pittsburgh, as much as a third of a non-farm labourer's daily wage. If you wanted to send a letter between New York City and Alabama, you would pay 50 per cent more than the cost of sending a barrel of flour.*

4) 'Stage drivers and private post riders may have been the carriers of many letters which ought to have gone in the mail.' As in England after the establishment of the Royal Mail, many private services offered unlicensed unofficial alternatives, offering cheaper rates and the promise, often unfulfilled, of a more secure delivery.

5) 'The Postmasters may have consulted their own interest in preference to the post.' This was really a catch-all excuse: because so much of the postal system was inefficiently and randomly organized on a local level, it was ever unreliable and prey to personal whims. Unchecked, it was also open to embezzlement: payment received on the delivery of letters might not make it back to the office; postmasters enjoyed franking privileges too, which would be gifted for other privileges in return.

What did Osgood propose? He suggested a 'more energetic' system based on better maps and surveys of the country, leading to swifter post roads; more accountable postal officers; and

* See *The Postal Age: the Emergence of Modern Communications in Nineteenth-Century America* by David M. Henkin, University of Chicago Press, 2006.

cheaper postage.* But the difference these plans made was modest. Until the mid 1840s, the post in the United States remained in disarray, but the disarray didn't lead to disquiet. Americans seemed to accept the expanding size of their country as just something too vast for a viable post, and even the most literate seemed to reserve long-distance communication for special occasions.

Appended to Osgood's proposals was a detailed chart of the existing chief post offices and their revenues, which in many cases were pitiful. In a three-month period between October 1789 and January 1790, Philadelphia took in $1,530, of which $306 was paid to the postmaster as a salary. In New York the net revenue was $1,067. But in Springfield, Massachusetts the net revenue was $10; in Stamford, Connecticut, it was $3.05; and in Charleston, Maryland, it was $2.19. Samuel Osgood estimated that his country contained 3 million people.

So slow progress ensued; it is possible to construct a new map of the United States by simply tracking the postal statutes. In December 1803, for example, after the Louisiana Purchase from Napoleon had expanded US territory by an area now comprising 15 states, a certain Congressman Thomas attempted to reduce the mail distance between the city of Washington and New Orleans by about 500 miles. As things stood, Thomas noted, mail was transported 'through the wilderness . . . a distance of more than fifteen hundred miles'. But by plotting a direct route, or as direct as the Blue Ridge mountains of Virginia would allow, and by passing through land inhabited by 'friendly Indians', a new post road would not only be more secure, but would also provide regular subsistence for the first time to those charged with delivering the

---

* Osgood was by all accounts a big-brained and generous man, vacating his grand house in Manhattan so that President Washington could live there when the seat of government was still in New York, making this early executive mansion a popular and unexpected stop on the Manhattan city tour.

mail. It was resolved to establish a new route 'through or near' the 'Tuckaubatchee settlement, to the Tombigbee settlement ... and also from the Tombigbee settlement to Natchez'. But that was only one direct route, a journey of about 1,000 miles, and progress across the country was predictably slow.

Those who opposed Osgood's reforms, and the reforms of his successors in the next decades, often did so on the grounds that letter-writing was still a relatively insignificant social act. Government and other official business would find its own private channels if required, and the delivery of news (papers, pamphlets, journals – the prime content of the mail until 1850) would happily continue as before. But the expansion of post roads gradually bore fruit, and suggested that a literate public would respond to a more reliable post. On the Post Office Department's recommendation, new roads were laid between venues not previously on the postal map, and hardly on any map: in 1831 it was proposed to link the then tiny towns of Mobile, Alabama and Pascagoula, Mississippi; in 1833 the Ohio and Mississippi Mail Line was established as an exclusive steamboat postal route; by 1835 there were routes contracted between Jacksonville and Tallahassee, Florida, a distance of 163 miles, to run once a fortnight. And revenue increased. In 1829, net postage revenue for the previous year stood at \$124,530 in New York City, a 30-fold increase from a projected annual income 40 years earlier. The same calculation in Springfield, Mass., was up from \$40 to \$1,407.

But there were still many problems to overcome, not least the accepted social significance of letters within everyday life. Antebellum America was traditionally a place where letters were mainly the domain of business and trade transactions; beyond the leisured class, other more personal communications tended to be brief and important news bulletins. The delivery of private mail was designed to subsidise the delivery of newspapers, which traditionally went at a rate of 1 cent per package. And as in Great Britain before the Penny Black, the cost fell to the recipient. And if you could afford postage for personal letters, there was always the thought that you were spending it in vain. In 1840, when Nathaniel Hawthorne addressed his fiancée Sophia Peabody, he entrusted his message to the fates: 'I know not whereabouts this letter will find thee,' he wrote, 'but I throw it upon the winds'.*

The postal reforms of 1845 and 1851, which included the introduction of the first United States postage stamp in 1847 and the universal rate of 5 cents for a half-ounce letter travelling under 300 miles, did not transform letter-writing on their own, but it was a good start. Combined with the expansion of the railroads, great westward migration and increased literacy, the communication advances of 1850s set in motion the postal notion we entertain still: an organised, trusted, state-run prepaid delivery service that brings letters to our door at great speed and great frequency at minimal cost.** For the majority of people in the United States, the postal service was the first regular contact they had with the administration of government beyond taxation. And it was this new common conversation – whereby ordinary people could maintain reliable contact with people they couldn't see – that made the modern world modern.

* She was almost certainly rather near, probably in Boston. When she replied, Hawthorne went nuts. 'Belovedest . . . I have folded it to my heart, and ever and anon it sends a thrill through me; for thou has steeped it with thy love – it seems as if thy head were leaning against my breast.'
** Steamboats, canals and the introduction of the (relatively costly) telegraph service in 1844 also contributed. The domestic delivery of mail was still some way off; for most of the second half of the century the population collected their letters from the nearest post office.

How did the country celebrate? By writing more letters. In 1851–52, a woman called Mary Wingate wrote regularly from Connecticut to her gold-prospecting husband Benjamin in California, and noted that 'when the new postage law takes effect I shall be selfish enough to want to hear from you by every Steamer.' We don't know how well he heeded this request, but on at least one occasion his wife thought it necessary to pull tighter on his heartstrings by including an emotional appeal from their daughter: 'I want you to come home as soon as you can for we are very lonely without you. I hope I shall learn to write soon so that mother wont have to hold my hand next time I want to write to you. From your own Lucy.'

The great social mobility in the US in the middle third of the nineteenth century benefitted greatly from an efficient and affordable postal service; one could argue that it made great dislocations bearable. But the new postal privileges were not confined to what one may consider the writing classes: there is much evidence of slaves writing to their absent masters, and not always through an amanuensis. 'I hope to write more satisfactory than I have done heretofore,' wrote Lucy Skipworth from Hopewell, Alabama in 1863. '[T]he white people who have stayed on the plantation are always opposed to my writeing to you & always want to see my letters.' Literate or not, slaves swiftly came to appreciate what novelists and playwrights had long known: letters are ripe for subterfuge. Harriet Jacobs, a slave in North Carolina, had escaped from her master, a certain Dr Flint, and was holed up in a nearby house. With the probable help of the homeowner, she managed to send a letter to New York, ensuring it was then mailed back to Flint with a New York postmark to bamboozle his search.

Observing these new freedoms from Edinburgh, *Blackwood's Magazine* expressed a combination of envy, pride and horror at what the postal reforms had unleashed. Young women in America enjoyed concessions not yet seen in Great

Britain, and their parents thought nothing of providing them with 'the privilege of a latch-key if she stays out late at the theatre'. The post provided yet further opportunities for loose living.

> She has the privilege, if she chooses to exercise it, of her own private box or pigeon-hole at the post office of the town where she resides, where she can have her letters addressed, and whither, by a 'Ladies' Entrance' where no profane male can intrude, she can resort when she pleases and unlock her box from the outside, and take away her letters without observation.
>
> To young women at the susceptible age, only half educated, and whose favourite reading is the trashy novels that are reprinted from the English penny papers . . . novels in which there cannot be too much love, or seduction, or bigamy, or murder, for the prevalent taste of a class – the post office system offers a facility for clandestine correspondence which no respectable father or mother on the European side of the Atlantic would think of without a shudder.

So how would a woman conduct herself if she wanted to unlock her box in high-minded Edinburgh? 'They cannot do it easily. They must take the neighbouring pastrycook or stationer into their confidence.'

The number of letters crossing the US annually in the middle third of the century increased from about 27 million in 1840 to about 160 million in 1860. And is it possible, with the flourishing of the mail, to detect also a new blossoming of the spirit of America? In 1855, a Post Office 'special agent' named James Holbrook wrote a book entitled *Ten Years Among the Mail Bags* in which he wrote of how it was now quite impossible to envisage a thriving American life without the post. 'Imagine a town without a post office!, a community without letters!, "friends, Romans, countrymen, and lovers", particularly the lovers, cut off from correspondence, bereft of newspapers, buried alive from the light of intelligence, and the busy stir of the great world! What an appalling picture!'

Certainly we have a large amount of epistolary evidence in this period of widespread optimism and opportunism, and not a little despair. The country was on the move – migration increased dramatically year on year, particularly westward; the gold rush was on, but so was a general boom in trade and geographical expansion exemplified and made possible by the railways. There was inevitably a burgeoning personal development on display in the nation's correspondence: there was a greater need to maintain contact with family members and friends in more far-flung locations, and it was clear that writers increasingly trusted the mail with their confidences. At the end of July 1849, Henry Thoreau wrote from his home in Concord, Massachusetts, to the 10-year-old daughter of his friend Ralph Waldo Emerson; Ellen Emerson was staying with her cousins in Staten Island for the summer, and Thoreau took on a mentoring role just as her father had done with him. The publication of *Walden*, his influential spiritual journey of self-reliance and self-discovery, was still five years away, but there is evidence from the reflective tone of the letter that it was already mostly complete.

Dear Ellen,

I think that we are pretty well acquainted, though we never had any very long talks. We have had a good many short talks, at any rate . . . I suppose you think that persons who are as old as your father and myself are always thinking about very grave things, but I know that we are meditating the same old themes that we did when we were ten years old, only we go more gravely about it. You love to write or to read a fairy story, and that is what you will always like to do, in some form or other. By and by you will discover that you want what are called the necessaries of life only that you may realize some such dream.

... Children may now be seen going a-berrying in all directions. The white-lilies are in blossom, and the john'swort and gold-enrod are beginning to come out. Old people say that we have not had so warm a summer for thirty years. Several persons have died in consequence of the heat, Mr. Kendal, perhaps, for one. The Irishmen on the railroad were obliged to leave off their work for several days, and the farmers left their fields and sought the shade. William Brown of the poor house is dead, the one who used to ask for a cent – 'Give me a cent?' I wonder who will have his cents now!

I found a nice penknife on the bank of the river this afternoon, which was probably lost by some villager who went there to bathe lately. Yesterday I found a nice arrowhead, which was lost some time before by an Indian who was hunting there. The knife was a very little rusted; the arrowhead was not rusted at all.

You must see the sun rise out of the ocean before you come home. I think that Long Island will not be in the way, if you climb to the top of the hill – at least, no more than Bolster Island, and Pillow Hills, and even the Lowlands of Never-get-up are elsewhere.

Do not think that you must write to me because I have written to you. It does not follow at all. You would not naturally make so long a speech to me here in a month as a letter would be. Yet if some time it should be perfectly easy and pleasant to you, I shall be very glad to have a sentence.

Your old acquaintance,

Henry Thoreau

A few days later Thoreau wrote to Harrison Blake, a publisher friend in Worcester, Massachusetts, with whom he corresponded for 12 years. His tone had changed: he was now preachy, transcendental and idealistic, and his admonitions and instructions appeared to reflect the confidence of a new nation. After opening pleasantries, he launched into a woody version of 'Desiderata'.

> Be not anxious to avoid poverty. In this way the wealth of the universe may be securely invested. What a pity if we do not live this short time according to the laws of the long time, the eternal laws! Let us see that we stand erect here, and do not lie along by our whole length in the dirt. Let our meanness be our footstool, not our cushion. In the midst of this labyrinth let us live a thread of life. We must act with so rapid and resistless a purpose in one direction, that our vices will necessarily trail behind. The nucleus of a comet is almost a star. Was there ever a genuine dilemma? The laws of earth are for the feet, or inferior man; the laws of heaven are for the head, or superior man; the latter are the former sublimed and expanded, even as radii from the earth's centre go on diverging into space. Happy the man who observes the heavenly and the terrestrial law in just proportion; whose every faculty, from the soles of his feet to the crown of his head, obeys the law of its level; who neither stoops nor goes on tiptoe, but lives a balanced life, acceptable to nature and to God.

In Blake's later memoir, Thoreau's correspondent said that he never tired of re-reading his letters, and 'I am apt to find new significance in them, am still warned and instructed by them, with more force occasionally than ever before; so that in a sense they are still in the mail, have not altogether reached me yet, and will not probably before I die. They may well be regarded as addressed to those who can read them best.' That's us, in a way. But there is a mild irony that hovers perennially over Thoreau's letters. Famously in *Walden* he wrote of how he had 'received no more than one or two letters in my life that were worth the postage' and that he 'could easily do without the post-office'. He was writing in 1854, at precisely the time when everyone else with even the most basic way with ink and paper was beginning to feel the opposite.

Emily Dickinson began writing letters in 1842, when she was 11, and it took her just three years to find her literate and numinous voice. In 1845 she wrote to a school girlfriend about her absent male crush, imagining him 'changed into a star some night while gazing at them, and placed in the constellation Orion between Bellatrix and Betelgeux'. And she tells her friend she is delighted at the prospect of keeping up a steady stream of correspondence: 'Old Time wags on pretty much as usual at Amherst, and I know of nothing that has occurred to break the silence; however, the reduction in the postage had excited my risibles somewhat. Only think! We can send a letter before long for five little coppers only, filled with the thoughts and advice of dear friends.'

We may hardly find her as happy again: in subsequent years her correspondence resounds with desolation and a strong sense of separation: Dickinson famously became a recluse in later life, and in her letters she revels in the concept of absenteeism and longing. A letter is necessar-

ily a note of absence, but Dickinson took it further, often describing the mail as a sort of heavenly ordained link as it travelled through time and space. Not that she wasn't sometimes up for a bit of divine subversion, as she admitted in a letter in 1852 addressed to her sister-in-law Susan Gil-

Emily Dickinson, founder of the epistolary book group.

bert, a letter which echoed the steamy transactions of Abelard and Heloise in the thirteenth century: 'When [the pastor] said Our Heavenly Father,' I said "Oh Darling Sue"; when he read the 100th Psalm, I kept saying your precious letter all over to myself, and Susie, when they sang . . . I made up words and kept singing how I loved you.'

Eroticism intensified many of her letters, the sort of sentiments one would expect to discover, if at all, in a secret journal; she clearly trusted the postal service with her heart. Other letters to Gilbert express further desires, and strengthen speculation that they were lovers (or put another way, it favours speculation that they were physical lovers; their correspondence leaves no doubt that they were lovers at a distance):

> Susie, forgive me Darling, for every word I say – my heart is full of you . . . yet when I seek to say to you something not for the world, words fail me, If you were here – and Oh that you were, my Susie, we need not talk at all, our eyes would whisper for us, and your hand fast in mine, we would not ask for language.

Dickinson was 31 before she made her blazing talent for poetry semi-public, and the revelation came in the form of a letter to a man called Thomas Wentworth Higginson. Higginson had enjoyed a varied career – abolitionist, civil war soldier, literary critic – and Dickinson soon came to regard him, in his words, as her 'literary counselor and confidant'. But the confidence only lasted so long: in 1891, five years after Dickinson's death and at the height of her fame, he decided 'with much reluctance' to spill the beans. Writing in the *Atlantic*, where he had previously advised hopeful young writers, Higginson explained that his first contact from her came unexpectedly one day in April 1862 when he 'took from the post office in Worcester, Mass' a letter enquiring whether he was 'too deeply occupied to say if my Verse is alive?' He wasn't, and it was. The letter was postmarked Amherst. Higginson found her handwriting 'so peculiar that it seemed as if the writer might have taken her first lessons by studying the famous fossil bird-tracks in the museum of that college town. Yet it was not in the slightest degree illiterate, but cultivated, quaint, and wholly unique. Of punctuation there was little; she used chiefly dashes.'

He regarded the poetry as alluring beyond measure, later claiming that he knew from the first that she was 'a wholly new and original poetic genius'; in one poem of eight lines he found 'a truth so searching that it seems a condensed summary of the whole experience of a long life.' In a letter since lost he sent back a gentle critique, something Dickinson regarded as 'surgery', and asked for more details of the poet. He received a reply that was mystical and coy, and so plainly flirtatious that it was difficult to believe she had been in self-imposed seclusion for the last few years, rather than swishing her skirts in town.

Mr Higginson,

Your kindness claimed earlier gratitude, but I was ill, and write today from my pillow.

Thank you for the surgery; it was not so painful as I supposed. I bring you others, as you ask, though they might not differ. While my thought is undressed, I can make the distinction; but when I put them in the gown, they look alike and numb.

You asked how old I was? I made no verse, but one or two, until this winter, sir.

I had a terror since September, I could tell to none; and so I sing, as the boy does by the burying ground, because I am afraid.

You inquire my books. For poets, I have Keats, and Mr. and Mrs. Browning. For prose, Mr. Ruskin, Sir Thomas Browne, and the Revelations. I went to school, but in your manner of the phrase had no education. When a little girl, I had a friend who taught me Immortality; but venturing too near, himself, he never returned. Soon after my tutor died, and for several years my lexicon was my only companion. Then I found one more, but he was not contented I be his scholar, so he left the land.

You ask of my companions. Hills, sir, and the sundown, and a dog large as myself, that my father bought me. They are better than beings because they know, but do not tell; and the noise in the pool at noon excels my piano.

I have a brother and sister; my mother does not care for thought, and father, too busy with his briefs to notice what we do. He buys me many books, but begs me not to read them, because he fears they joggle the mind. They are religious, except me, and address an eclipse, every morning, whom they call their 'Father.'

But I fear my story fatigues you. I would like to learn. Could you tell me how to grow, or is it unconveyed, like melody or witch-craft?

You speak of Mr. Whitman. I never read his book, but was told that it was disgraceful.

I read Miss Prescott's Circumstance, but it followed me in the dark, so I avoided her.

Two editors of journals came to my father's house this winter, and asked me for my mind, and when I asked them 'why' they said I was penurious, and they would use it for the world.

I could not weigh myself, myself. My size felt small to me. I read your chapters in the Atlantic, and experienced honor for you. I was sure you would not reject a confiding question.

Is this, sir, what you asked me to tell you?

Your friend,

E. Dickinson

The pair maintained their correspondence, initially frequently and then less so when he fought in the civil war and she underwent treatment for her eyes. Dickinson often signed off as 'Scholar', and responded to his request for a photograph with a request of her own: 'Could you believe me without? I had no portrait, now, but am small, like the wren; and my hair is bold, like the chestnut bur; and my eyes like the sherry in the glass that the guest leaves.'

She once wrote revealingly how, to her, 'A letter always feels to me like immortality because it is the mind alone without corporeal friend'. To make matters more material she occasionally invited Higginson to visit, and finally in August 1870, eight years after their correspondence began, he did. He found the event uncomfortable and slightly disappointing, writing later that he found her face 'without a single good feature' and her character diffident and enigmatical.

'When I asked her if she never felt any want of employment, not going off the grounds and rarely seeing a visitor, she answered, "I never thought of conceiving that I could ever have the slightest approach to such a want in all future time" … She told me of her household occupations, that she made all their bread, because her father liked only hers; then saying shyly, "And people must have puddings".'

Higginson found her rather like her poems: elliptical, compressed and inverted. He continued to admire her work, but it appears that he preferred her letters to her reality. But in reality, her true character was hard to define. Biographers have combed her letters for clues (just over 1,000 remain, many more were burned or lost), but it is rarely clear when she was genuinely writing as herself, and when she was writing poetically and for effect. She enclosed many poems in her letters, and scholars have long argued that there wasn't much of a gulf between the themes of her mail and her verse. Certainly her poems addressed the art of letter-writing and letter receiving in a personal way: 'This is my letter to the World,' she wrote ruefully in a poem published in 1890, 'That never wrote to Me'. Lest we take this at face value, she later wrote of how she treasured the many letters she did receive:

The Way I read a Letter's – this –
'Tis first – I lock the Door –
And push it with my fingers – next –
For transport it be sure

And then I go the furthest off
To counteract a knock –
Then draw my little Letter forth
*And slowly pick the lock –**

One cannot underestimate the value of letters to Dickinson and her circle in the nineteenth century, and for us they are valuable for other reasons. They display a relaxed creativity seldom seen before in this American century; again, these are not letters written with posterity in mind (unlike, say, some of Emerson's, who copied letters before he sent them), and they carry a gentle playfulness that explodes all the formulas in the manuals. She wrote her final letter a few days before her death in 1886 at the age of 55, to be opened by her two cousins after she fell into a coma. In its entirety:

Little Cousins,
 Called back.
  Emily

And there is one other epistolary feature that makes Dickinson original: from her teenage years onward she conducted a postal – and virtual – book group. If it wasn't the first it was certainly one of the strongest: a huge amount (perhaps even half) of her letters contained at least some reference to her

---

* She's written better.

current reading material or an oblique literary reference her middle-class friends would be sure to recognise. It is highly likely that she also attended what she may have called a 'corporeal' real-life book club in her early twenties (in one letter she writes to her brother how 'Our Reading Club still is, and becomes now very pleasant'), but when she saw less of the real world she seemed happy to keep in touch with it through books and letters about books. Her first tentative steps towards this occurred in 1848 at the age of 18, writing to a friend 'What are you reading now?' before launching into her own list, and her regular book circle soon expanded to include her brother Austin and his wife Sue, her cousins Louise and Frances Norcross, and at least three friends. The Dickinson scholar Eleanor Heginbotham has observed that her 'book club manners' in her letters are still reflected in book club behaviour today: a sociability, a boastfulness, a competitiveness, a delight. Present-day book club members may well exhibit all of these in discussing the work and life of Emily Dickinson.

She read almost everything. We have seen from her first letter to Thomas Wentworth Higginson that she was reading Keats and the Brownings, but she loved Shakespeare, Milton and Byron too. She read the essays of Hawthorne, Emerson and Ruskin. She devoured *Harper's* and the *Atlantic*. For contemporary novels, much against the wishes of her father she ranged from her fellow popular Americans Helen (Fiske) Hunt Jackson and Harriet Beecher Stowe to contemporary English stars George Eliot, the Brontës and Dickens. Dickens became famous with the publication of *The Pickwick Papers* the year after Dickinson's birth, and his plots and characters became a frequent motif of her letters. 'I will never desert Micawber,' she wrote to her brother in reference to a domestic matter; elsewhere she commented on the manipulative nature of Little Nell, and in a reference to *The Old Curiosity Shop* she once signs herself off as 'The Marchioness'.

The one thing she didn't read was still a relatively experimental genre, at least in the United States: books of collected letters.

💀　　💀　　💀

For all her preoccupation with longing and loss, the loss of Emily Dickinson's own letters didn't concern her unduly; the fact that a small percentage of mail wouldn't make it through was a disagreeable but accepted feature of giving oneself up to the post, an occupational hazard. Where did they go, these lost or abandoned letters? Some may have been stolen, while a few perhaps are still awaiting delivery in a buried sack somewhere in the mud, anticipating their Vindolanda moment.

The postal reforms had improved the cost, efficiency and the geographical reach of deliveries without fuss, but when Dickinson's letters hit upon the winds and didn't find their way home, there was another place they could go, a venue in Washington DC that did a roaring and romantic trade from 1825: the Dead Letter Office. Put simply, this was an office where post went not to die but to be resuscitated. But it was also an office wracked with uncertainty. Was what happened in this place acceptable? Was it right to open other people's mail?

In England, as we've seen, such a state practice was regarded as an obligation, a dark art, particularly for letters that were *not* lost or badly addressed. But in the United States such an action would keep those with a conscience awake at night.

Yet what romance was to be had in an undelivered or undeliverable letter! And what mystery and sadness too. As the *New York Times* reported in Shakespearian tones in September 1852, the most hopeless letters met the most conspicu-

Party in full swing at the DC Dead Letter Office.

ous end, 'transported for the last time to a place without the city, and there solemnly burned, no human being but their writers knowing how much of labor and of pain has been expended upon them, thus to perish by fire and be exhaled in smoke.'

That wasn't the original idea at all. The main purpose of the Dead Letter Office (DLO), which began life in the 1770s, was originally as a repository for unclaimed mail, mail yet to be picked up. In the time before personal delivery, letters could languish at a post office for months awaiting their rightful owner. Our farmer Abner Sanger heard about his letter from his brother in good time at the start of this chapter, but what of other farmers in other fields? They would usually learn they had mail from very long lists pinned up in post offices or community halls – long alphabetical scrolls from a clerk doing his best with tricky handwriting. You usually had three months to make a claim, after which time it was sent to Washington for, in the worst scenario, incineration. In the best scenario your mail would be returned readdressed from Washington to find you through other means, or perhaps poor handwriting would be deciphered and redirected. And in the middling scenario items of value sent in letters and parcels that couldn't be returned would be auctioned, with the proceeds passing to a delighted Treasury. The Dead Letter Office sale catalogue of December 1865 provided a handy snapshot of what some citizens would be getting for Christmas at the unwitting expense of others: alongside many pairs of socks, gaiters and gloves were quackeries named Cheeseman's Pills, Rand's Specific Pills, Dr Clarke's Female Pills, Dr Harvey's Female Pills and Culverwell's Regenerator (not forgetting unguents for the hair and the cure-all Tennessee Swamp Shrub). Other items: 'Syringe, Complete', 'False Bosoms', 'Soldier's Writing Desk', 'President Lincoln's Funeral Car' (engraving of), 'French Preventative', 'Hands for Watches', 'Copying Machine', 'Catechism of Steam Engine', an item merely listed 'Housewife' and an item listed 'Rejected Wife'. The most common items were watches and finger rings. The most intriguing was lot 42: 'Destroyed'.

A portion of literate America received their first impression of the DLO not from the service itself but from a short story by Herman Melville called *Bartleby, The Scrivener*. Published in two monthly instalments in *Putnam's Magazine* in 1853, two years after *Moby-Dick*, the tale is a fable of disillusion, recalcitrance and human empathy, and the moral is a grim one. Bartleby arrives at a law firm one day to smooth out the volatility of the other two staff members – one a drunk, the other afflicted with irritable bowels. Bartleby is employed as the others are, to copy out legal documents, but he soon tires of the work. Very soon he tires of the entire world, and becomes an immovable and ineffective object, his only contribution being his catchphrase 'I would prefer not to.'

The narrator of the story wonders what could have possibly reduced him to his present state, tentatively concluding that it may be an early example of someone 'going postal'.* He had heard a rumour: 'Bartleby had been a subordinate clerk in the Dead Letter Office at Washington, from which he had been suddenly removed by a change in the administration.'

The story ends:

> When I think over this rumor, I cannot adequately express the emotions which seize me. Dead letters! Does it not sound like dead men? Conceive a man by nature and misfortune prone to a pallid hopelessness, can any business seem more fitted to heighten it than that of continually handling these dead letters, and assorting them for the flames? For by the cart-load they are annually burned. Sometimes from out the folded paper the pale clerk takes a ring: the finger it was meant for, perhaps, moulders in the grave; a bank-note sent in swiftest charity – he whom it would relieve, nor eats nor hungers any more; pardon for those who died despairing; hope for those who died unhoping; good tidings for those who died stifled by unrelieved calamities. On errands of life, these letters speed to death. Ah Bartleby! Ah humanity!

In 1899, a woman named Patti Lyle Collins wrote an article in the *Ladies' Home Journal* entitled 'Why Six Million Letters Go Astray Every Year', and she knew of what she wrote: she was head of the 'blind reading' department at the DLO, famed for her ability to detect an envelope's address where others saw only scrawl and foreign phonetics. She was able, for instance, to detect that when someone wrote

---

* The term gained currency when postal workers, driven mad by the monotony and inexorable nature of their task, went on gun rampages in the 1970s. Delivering letters, or in Bartleby's case not delivering them, is seldom a task that rewards efficiency; no matter what you do, the pile never diminishes (an affliction now transferred to the email inbox).

M Napoletano

Stater Naielande,

Nerbraiti Sechem Street

No 41

the correct place to send it would be

Mr Napoletano

41 Second Street

New Brighton

New York

Her world was full of these examples, although none quite as satisfying as the mythic understanding that

Wood,

John,

Mass

should be delivered to

John Underwood,

Andover, Mass.

Patti Lyle Collins estimated that in 1898 about 6,000,000,000 (six billion) pieces of mail were posted in the United States, with about 6,312,731 ending their days at the Dead Letter Office. Of these, 32,000 were posted with no address whatsoever, 85,000 had insufficient postage or none at all, and some 200,000 were unclaimed from hotels; 30,000 contained photographs and 185,000 stamps, while 82,000 contained money or money orders to the value of $990,000.

Her article contained further mystifying addresses, an

endearing combination of the ignorant and the inherently trusting. She recalled one that read 'To my Son he lives out West he drives a red ox the rale rode goes By Thar'. Others had increasingly judgemental challenges: 'Kindly address to largest dealer in old medical books'; 'To the editor of the Best Paper'. The trickier the propositions, the more Patti Lyle Collins loved her job: 'Harold Green and His Mother'; 'on dykton Evnn No 17' (17 Huntington Avenue); and an envelope addressed to a large firm in 'New York, Chicago, Boston, St Louis'. 'Not for one instant would this be regarded as difficult at the Dead Letter Office,' Ms Lyle Collins cheered. 'It is like the alphabet, absolutely simple when the art is once mastered.'

Four years later another insider at the DLO named Marshall Cushing offered a less forgiving analysis. In his book *The Story of Our Post Office* he was keen to berate his customers: 'The total number of errors in the transmission of mail matter in the United States is very small compared with the correct deliveries,' he observed. 'Yet so long as the blundering public make voluntary contributions daily to this office of over 20,000 letters and packages, just so long will it be necessary for the Government to "exercise paternal functions" in the correction of those blunders, nine tenths of which are made by the people themselves. If those who use the mails would only be careful to observe a few simple requirements, trifles in themselves, but in the aggregate of vast importance, the work of the Dead Letter Office would soon be greatly reduced.'

The simple requirements (including putting an address on an envelope) were, however, not simple enough, and we continued to blunder. Cushing explained the intricacies of the daily toil – the Opening Division, the Property Division, the Money Division – and emphasised that the vast majority of dead letters were in fact 'live letters', those that lay unclaimed at local post offices as their recipients moved on. And then there was another category, something he connected with 'green goods', which in itself was connected with the 200,000 letters left unclaimed at hotels. They were green because they were dollars; they were left at hotels because they were part of a nationwide confidence trick.

The green goods postal scam of the late nineteenth century was the first great scandal of the modern mail service, the godfather of pyramid schemes and chain letters, the material precursor to Nigerian email phishing. Its success relied upon human fallibility and greed, but also on a more modern advance: the assured anonymity of the post. The Dead Letter Office made great play of the trustworthiness of its officers, not least those who slit open private correspondence. The men and women selected for this task were deemed above suspicion, and would, according to Marshall Cushing, anyway not have time to read anything beyond a return address.* But when the letter openers began to discover the frequent appearance of a printed circular and a large increase in the transmission of dollar bills, their mission changed: they called in the police.

The circular, printed in 1887, read as follows:

Dear Sir,

Your name was sent to me by a reliable person in your town. He said he knew you to be a man who was not adverse [sic] to making money in any way, manner, or form, and that he knew you were up to snuff. Well, to be plain, I am dealing in counterfeit money of the best material, so fine are these goods, no person dealing with me has ever been in the least trouble, but all have made fortunes fast and safe. I am dealing with prominent men in your county, but of course names cannot be mentioned, some of them holding high positions, but you can bet your last dollar they have made thousands of dollars using these goods,

---

* This was not always the case: in the 1830s the postmaster general banned abolitionist tracts from the mail, and Abraham Lincoln encouraged the opening of mail during the civil war; as in London, the mail became a focus for intelligence.

and no living soul need be the wiser as to how they obtained their money. The plates are very fine, also engraving, signatures, numbers, and coloring, in fact we can say it is the best and safest counterfeit money ever put on the market, and will fool all the detectives in the Government service. But to deal with our gang you must be a man who can keep his mouth shut, and you can bet your life if you ever get in trouble we will get you out all right. My terms are as follows:

Cash $75 for $1,500

$125 for $4,000

$180 for $6,000

$220 for $10,000

$400 for $30,000

If you cannot come here to do biz send me $20 in a common letter and I will send you $1,000. I will trust you for the balance until we meet face to face to show you I have the best of confidence in you, but if you want to come on and see me, stop at the Grand Union Hotel, Forty-second-street and Fourth-avenue, New York City, take a room, and telegraph me and say I am in room, (name the number). I will then call on you and we can do business, and no man on the face of the earth will ever know our business, so if you can't send the money come or send a trusty pard. Direct all letters in square confidence as follows.

A. ANDERSON, care of A. Heltenbecker, 302 East Eleventh-street, New York.

The circular, or something worded very close to it, began to appear throughout the United States in the 1870s with a variety of handwritten addresses attached. Most recipients would not bother to risk corruption at a hotel if they could be corrupt at home, and so they sent money and received nothing

*Anti-counterfeiter
Anthony Comstock.*

in return. There were no stolen Government plates, and there were no counterfeit green goods. There didn't tend to be any public complaints either, for who would want to be seen as corrupt, greedy and stupid?

The operation hit the rocks, at least temporarily, in October 1891, when the cops raided several addresses in New York and seized equipment, postal directories, opium and various individuals with Runyonesque aliases. The main swindlers were named as 'Pretty' Frank Brooks, Terence 'Poodle' Murphy and Sam Little (alias Goldstein), and they were found in possession of the personal details of 60,000 targets, 600,000 circulars, and a great many copies of bogus newspaper reports suggesting that the counterfeit bills were indistinguishable from the real thing. Another New York bust that year yielded the men at the centre of the 'Bechtold-McNally Gang' of Hoboken, New Jersey, who, according to the *Hartford Weekly Times,* had defrauded a great many disappointed 'gullible rustics' of their savings.

The man in charge of the counter-counterfeit operation was a Post Office inspector called Anthony Comstock. Comstock was also secretary for the Society for the Suppression of Vice, a group determined to root out subversive material and stop its transmission through the mail. In the 1870s Comstock had made a name for himself by holding public displays of all the items he had seen travelling through the post that he deemed to be obscene: pornographic photographs and stories, pamphlets, song lyrics. He claimed that he had evidence of 15,000 letters from pupils in American boarding schools ordering such items, and his message was clear: the postal service was an agent of immorality, corruption, and vice. He stopped short of suggesting a complete cessation of the entire system, so he did the next best thing: prosecute and fume. Among the more literary items he campaigned against and seized were works by Zola and Boccaccio, and George Bernard Shaw's *Mrs Warren's Profession*. In September 1915, the *New York Times* reported that Comstock died aged 71 of pneumonia, a ten-day illness 'brought on by over-work and over-excitement'.

Goodness knows what Comstock would have made of the brilliantly seditious work of Willie Reginald Bray. In 1898 Bray, a 19-year-old cycling enthusiast living in south London, obtained a copy of the *Post Office Guide*, a weighty quarterly manual published by the British Post Office to update its clients on its many services. For six old pence one learnt the proper way to address a letter, and that all manner of things could be entrusted to the mail if properly packaged and stamped. You could, for example, send creatures through the post, including a single live bee 'if confined in a suitable receptacle' and 'special arrangements may be made as to dogs'. Liquids could be sent 'provided the bottles are properly closed'. Most enticing was this line, which showed how nicely things had advanced since the Penny Black of 1840: 'Postmasters may arrange for the conduct of a person to an address by an Express Messenger.'

Reginald Bray decided to push these possibilities to the limits. He began modestly by posting a rabbit skull and a turnip, and when they arrived safely back at his house (he

*Reginald Bray (and bicycle)
delivered home.*

addressed the rabbit skull along its nasal bone, and put the stamps on its cranium), he mailed, with no wrapping, a bowler hat, a frying pan, a bicycle pump, dog biscuits, onions, and a handbag (with stamps inside).

Looking back a few years later in the *Royal Magazine*, he explained that 'this course I did not enter upon without much consideration and hesitancy, for it would be most unfair, to say the least of it, to cause a lot of unnecessary trouble, merely for the sake of playing a senseless prank. My object from the beginning was to test the ingenuity of the postal authorities, and, if possible, to vindicate them of the "charges of carelessness and neglect."'*

But of course it was only a matter of time before he grew ambitious. On 10 February 1900 he mailed his Irish terrier Bob; in practice this meant paying the Post Office to get a postman to walk him home at a cost of three pence a mile, but Bray explained it could be doubly useful if you had to get him to a friend or vet. But objects and pets were mainly for show – his main challenge involved letters and postcards. Again he claimed this was to keep the Post Office, and specifically the Dead Letter Office, on its toes: items would be addressed 'To

* See John Tingey, *The Englishman Who Posted Himself and Other Curious Objects*, Princeton Architectural Press, 2010.

the Post Offices around the World' and to 'Any Resident in London'. In 1902 he sent a postcard with a picture of the Old Man of Hoy in the Orkneys and addressed it to 'The Resident nearest this rock'. Another went to 'The Proprietor of the most remarkable hotel in the world on the road between Santa Cruz and San Jose, California'.

It was only a short trip from Santa Cruz to 'Santa Claus, Esq', the destination of a Bray postcard in December 1899 (he may not have been the first to try to reach him, but his

The Suffragettes are mailed to Downing Street.

biographer John Tingey has been unable to find an earlier example). Certainly Bray may claim originality for another stunt: in 1900, he succeeded in mailing himself, paying the Post Office to walk him home. He repeated the exercise in 1903, obtaining a registration form that included, in the line allotted for the word 'letter' or 'parcel', the description 'Person Cyclist'. He did this again in 1932, but by then it was old hat, and the Post Office was getting annoyed. The posting of bees is still acceptable, but the ability to mail a dog or a person has since gone the way of all flesh. Which is a shame, for it was useful, as Bray explained. 'Once on a very foggy night I could not find a friend's house so instead of wandering about for hours I posted myself and was delivered in a few minutes.'

If the Post Office was used for personal stunts, why not also for political stunts? At the end of February 1909, two suffragists, Daisy Solomon and Elspeth McClellan, presented themselves for human postage at the West Strand post office and requested delivery at 10 Downing Street to campaign for votes for women. They were escorted on foot by a telegraph boy and a considerable crowd of well-wishers and journalists, but, refused entry by Prime Minister Asquith, were officially declared 'dead letters' and returned to their headquarters.

All a Housewife Should Be

14232134 SIGMN. BARKER H.C., 30 WING, I COY.,
9 AIR FORMATION SIGNALS, M.E.F.

31st May and 11th June 1944

Dear Bessie,

As I have managed to secure an hour, I hope to be able to convey something of the time I am having in Alexandria, although only three days remain and separate me from the desert.

American-like, I have 'done' the Acropolis, Aquarium, Museum, Gardens, Zoo, Catacombs. I can't get worked up about these B.C. dug-outs, but the gardens are really lovely; I sat in them the other day, reading 'The Good Companions', and around me there were purple flowers, thousands of them; above me, a mass of mauve blossoms. Exotic is the word I suppose, but it sounds pretty hackneyed. I saw dates growing, bananas, cotton. The cactus needs to be seen to be believed. Have seen Waldini and His Gipsy Band, a fair entertainment, not smutty.

The shops were full of 'the wealth of the Indies'. They were chock-full of all kinds of goods, but generally the prices were very high indeed for imported goods, although watches, cameras, refrigerators (things that are difficult to get in U.K.) were in much profusion here. In Alex. you can get what you want if you like to pay for it. Two chaps in our party had nights out which cost them £3 apiece each time. They assured me it was well worth it. Almost anywhere you go, little boys, old men, or the women themselves will say 'Want a woman?' 'Want a –?' 'Hello dearie.' I must say that I shudder somewhat at the thought. A boy about 6 in one street invites you to buy a preventative, with as much loud enthusiasm and as little discretion as the chap who sells newspapers at Oxford Circus. 'Lady Chat's Lover', 'The Well of Loneliness' and other items are on sale everywhere, but although they are advertised as unexpurgated, judging by the disappointment of a chap in the train who had bought one, they are pretty much like tracts.

The Alexandria 'peaches' were mainly Greek or French, and some were really fine-looking. The Egyptian women are horrible after age 30, and many are even horrible at birth. The Greek and French specialise in good figures, no great wonder as they do little work. The South African women – at least the ones I saw – impressed me with the excellence of their figures and looks. Again, they do not lift a finger for themselves, the blacks doing all the work at very little wages. The chaps stationed in the towns have a fine time, though it must be expensive. I do not think the atmosphere is half so good as the desert. I fancy there is quite a 'Bloomsbury' outlook, 'fraightfully intellectual'.

I am sorry, but I don't think I shall be home for Christmas, though with a bit of luck providing 'the divinity' does not pack me off to the Far East, I may manage Christmas 1945. The lap of the Gods is an uneasy resting place.

I am sorry about your gumboils. I should leave your private dentist and pay at least one visit to the Dental Hospital at Leicester Square, which is concerned with saving teeth, not making money through extractions and dentures. Don't have your teeth out before you need to, and without seeing the Dental Hospital. They are good people.

I give you my glad sympathy at your efforts to abate the smoke nuisance. You are a good girl, Bessie. I must again say I don't want you to think of me as a superior. Of course I kid myself I have a sharper perception of some (maybe unimportant) things than most others. But you are better than me at French, Algebra, Arithmetic, and I am confused (and remaining so) about Morse and Electricity and Magnetism. You and I are a couple, a man and a woman. Whatever inequalities of knowledge and ability exist between us they are our responsibility.

You ask me if I want you to be a modern woman par excellence, and you 'rather hope I am the least bit old-fashioned'. Well, I am sufficiently old-fashioned not to want you to work after marriage. I want your main job to be looking after me. But, as I have said earlier, I do not want you to go house-mad. I want you to take an interest in other things, and if necessary, join up with people like yourself who may be similarly interested. I have seen (theoretically!) a woman stop being useful to the world upon marriage. I want you to develop, say, something that the circumstances of your working life have prevented you following. I can therefore be, not the bloke who bangs the Harem gate shut, but the one who gives you the chance to do something; obviously I am marrying you because I am selfish, not because I think a little leisure may make you another Van Gogh.

You amuse me when you say you don't think managing money is my strong point. (I haven't got any strong points except those you make.) I expect you will find me a horrible old skinflint, but I hope you'll agree to have pocket-money, as I shall have it, and that should enable you to be at least independent in little things. In any case, you will be doing the housekeeping, and I shall assist only at your invitation.

I've never really asked you, have I – Will you marry me, Bessie (for better or for worse)? There are no good reasons, but the only excuse I can offer is that I will love you always, my fashion. Reply by ordinary L.C. won't you?

I am sure you will find me easy to cook for; we shall have a fine time making you 'all a housewife should be'. With our understanding of the needs of the other, I haven't any doubt about our happiness. We shall get along well. Yes, we dovetail nicely. It is wonderful how the distance has not prevented our easy flow of meaning. You certainly have made a very large and grand contribution to the union which is 'us'.

Yes, I got those corduroy trousers a few months after the war started, and long before everyone adopted them. When I got them home, my Mother said, 'You silly young ass, only artists wear them!' She was approximately correct. They are grand trousers, though, and wonderful material. I am glad about your non-puritan thoughts based on their contents.

Yes, my Mother will be a bit of a nuisance to her prospective daughter-in-law. Not because she is mine, but because in-laws are nuisances. But I shall be able to help you where necessary and when the time comes. My attitude in similar circs. would be 'Blow the lot of them'. I am not over-fond of relations myself.

I had strawberries today, pal, they were grand. I need hardly say I prefer you to all the strawberries yet or to be.

Thinking of you. Love.

Chris.

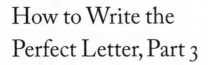

Chapter Eleven

How to Write the Perfect Letter, Part 3

The golden age of letter-writing was not like the golden age of ballooning or the golden age of Leeds United: it is neither easily definable nor much celebrated. But it is a good conversation piece. Madame de Sévigné has already made a case for the seventeenth century, while Lord Chesterfield and the guardians of the epistolary novel have staked out the eighteenth. At the turn of the nineteenth century, John Keats waits coughing in the wings. Amongst the educated public, each decade from 1680 has brought new postal freedoms and delight.

And what of the decline of the English letter? This too has a debatable history. Certainly it began before the fax or email; for many it started in 1840, with the first adhesive stamp. The snobbish and the well-to-do believed cheap postage would lead to the equivalent cheapening of an art form best left to the professionals. When the Victorian writer George Saintsbury considered the history of letter-writing for an anthology, he used a phrase that had already become a cliché: 'the Penny Post killed it'.

And it has apparently been dying ever since. In January 1919, when the *Yale Review* reported that 'the art of writing letters has been lost', it was able to assign other reasons for this sad fact: 'Some lay the blame upon the telephone, the typewriter, the telegraph, upon the railroad that benumbs a letter-writer with the knowledge that his letter, which should ripen in a postboy's bag, will be delivered a thousand miles away at 2.45 tomorrow. Some say the art went out with the goose-quill. But most ascribe the loss to the modern art of leisure.' The theory, sounding somewhat familiar at the beginning of the twenty-first century, ran as follows: we were too busy with work, travel and the pressures and demands of modern life to sit down for a minute, let alone think and write a letter.

Or as Henry Dwight Sedgwick had it at Yale, 'Hurry has been set on a pedestal, and Scurry has been set on a pedestal, and the taste for leisure has been snuffed out.'* There was still some hope: 'There are, and always will be, convalescents, crip-ples, confirmed idlers, guests marooned in country houses on Sunday mornings' – and it was to them that we should entrust the future art of letters. Was there anyone else to blame for this death of letter-writing just after the Great War? Yes: schools. 'Oddly enough, teachers of literature teach almost anything other than the art of letter-writing. Boys and girls from twelve to twenty are set writing essays, theses, compositions, as if Tom, Dick, Molly and Polly were going to write essays throughout their lives to their parents, lovers, husbands, wives, children, and old cronies.' The teaching of English, alas, was 'dominated by the grammarians who desire passionately that every boy and girl shall recognize at sight and call by name a "partitive genitive" or an "adverbial clause", and by educational reformers who regard speaking English and writing English as machinery and not an art. Both sets despise the loafer, and the art of letter-writing.'

In 1927, in the introduction to an anthology of *English Letter Writers*, the compiler R. Brimley Johnson also wondered

---

* In a family association of which one imagines he would have been proud, H.D. Sedgwick was a distant relative of the Warhol protégé Edie Sedgwick, who did write the occasional letter, most famously to Warhol after he was shot: 'I am saying prayers for you . . . don't know how much good they do, but at least you will know I care, and care tremendously.'

whether letter-writing wasn't already a subject for mourning. And what a loss that would be: 'Letters we value reveal the impulse to share beauty and sorrow with another; to give all we have learned and gained from life; to lift a little from the burdens, that, borne alone, would crush and kill; they are of the vision and the understanding which is art.'

In 1929 the *Prairie Schooner* journal in Nebraska was writing a similar obituary. 'It has been said, and with some reason, that the art of letter-writing is to be numbered among the lost accomplishments,' wrote Gilbert H. Doane. 'Certainly there has been a decided decline in the writing of letters. As I go home year after year, and meet old friends and acquaintances, the question is always the same: "Why haven't you written?" And it is always answered: "I'm such a poor correspondent, I'm so busy, and so rarely have the leisure to write a decent letter".'

No one actually used the phrase 'the golden age of letter-writing' in these doomy dispatches, but it was certainly 'golden age' thinking – that bemoaning aura that descends on culture when its once-influential practitioners become aware of their own failing powers. By most sensible standards, or at least quantifiable ones, letter-writing had never been healthier as the nineteenth century drew to a close: more people were writing more regularly over greater distances at lower cost than ever before. Mail volume per head of the population in Great Britain rose steadily throughout the century, from 3.1 items sent in 1839 to 13.2 in 1850, 47.5 in 1880 and 116.7 in 1910.* From 564 million in 1860, the number of letters delivered by the Post Office had roughly doubled every 20 years.

Another indicator of health came from a still booming literary sub-genre: the letter-writing instruction manual. These still consisted of standard lists of correct forms of address and

---

* These were all postal items apart from parcels.

farewells, and their abundance and titles could take up half a market stall: *The Secretary's Assistant: Exhibiting the Varied and Most Correct Modes of Superscription, Commencement and Conclusion of Letters to Persons at Every Degree of Rank* (1842); *The Art of Letter-Writing Simplified; by Precept and Example; Embracing Practical Illustrations of Epistolary Correspondence of Every Age, in Every Station and Degree, and Under Every Circumstance of Life* (1847). It wasn't long, of course, before *Punch* began to rip its way through them with delight. Less parody than reality, the oft-used template of a letter from a regretful son to a father asking for paternal assistance received the reply: 'All your long letter may be boiled down like spinach, into three words: "Pay my debts".'*

Just as they struggled for novelty in their titles, the contents of the Victorian manuals showed about as much originality as their predecessors from earlier centuries. In the 1890s, for example, about two-thirds of the examples in *The Favourite Letter Writer* consisted of letters culled directly from Samuel Richardson's *Familiar Letters for Important Occasions* published 150 years earlier, including such popular examples as 'From an Uncle to a Nephew, on his keeping bad Company, bad Hours &c. in his Apprenticeship'. But the manuals were now appealing to a new class of letter-writer, a cohort made larger by cheaper postage, economic expansion brought on by industrialisation, and greater literacy.

In the United States, there was much strict and practical guidance regarding paper and ink, and a consideration of what may be considered gaudy. 'For all formal notes, of whatever nature,' wrote Richard Alfred Wells in *Manners, Culture, and Dress of the Best American Society* in 1891, 'use heavy, plain, white, unruled paper, folded once, with square envelopes to

---

* As quoted in Laura Rotunno, 'The Long History of "In Short": Mr Micawber, Letter-Writers, and Literary Men' in *Victorian Literature and Culture*, Cambridge University Press, 2005.

match. A neat initial letter at the head of the sheet is allowable, but nothing more than this. Avoid monograms, floral decorations and landscapes. Unless of an elaborate and costly design they have an appearance of cheapness, and are decidedly in bad taste.' Another etiquette guide, *Miss Leslie's Behavior Book* by Eliza Leslie offered further assistance: 'If the tint is bluish, the writing will not be so legible as on pure white. The surface should be smooth and glossy.'

As with Samuel Richardson in the 1740s, the genre was not short of well-known authors willing to join the fray. In 1888, Lewis Carroll produced an item he deemed so indispensible to a fulfilling and creative life that he couldn't understand how anyone could possibly manage without it. 'The Wonderland Case For Postage-Stamps' consisted of a simple folding wallet with 12 pockets marked for various denominations of stamps from half a pence to one shilling. Not a huge revolution in postal technology, but Carroll claimed he invented it after many frustrating encounters with letters to be sent overseas, and other packages requiring irregular postage rates: with a fully stocked 'Wonderland' one would never be short of the correct sums again. It was named, of course, after the Alice books, and it was Alice that would ensure the Wonderland's success. 'Imitations of it will soon appear, no doubt,' he wrote. 'But they cannot include the two Pictorial Surprises, which are copyright.' The surprises were two new illustrations of Alice, one holding a baby, one holding a pig. But there was another reason for buying the case – a booklet entitled *Eight or Nine Wise Words About Letter-Writing*.

This consisted of three parts: 'How to Begin a Letter'; 'How to Go On with a Letter'; 'How to End a Letter'. The instruction was more interesting than the architecture, not least because Carroll assumed that the majority of his readers had barely written a letter before. 'If the Letter is to be in answer to another, begin by getting out that other letter

A stamp for every occasion: Lewis Carroll's Wonderland solution.

and reading it through,' he began, 'in order to refresh your memory, as to what it is you have to answer, and as to your correspondent's *present address* (otherwise you will be sending your letter to his regular address in *London*, though he has been careful in writing to give you his *Torquay* address in full).'

The next instruction seemed a little less obvious: you should address and stamp the envelope before starting the letter. 'And I'll tell you what will happen if you don't,' Carroll predicted.

You will go on writing till the last moment, and, just in the middle of the last sentence, you will become aware that 'time's up!' Then comes the hurried wind-up, the wildly scrawled signature, the hastily fastened envelope which comes open in the post, the address, a mere hieroglyphic, the horrible discovery that you've forgotten to replenish your Stamp-Case, the frantic appeal to every one in the house to lend you a Stamp, the headlong rush to the Post Office, arriving, hot and gasping, just after the box has closed, and finally, a week afterwards, the return of the Letter, from the Dead Letter Office, marked 'address illegible'!

Then there was guidance about where to put your own address, and a command to write this *in full* at the top of the sheet. 'It is an aggravating thing – I speak from bitter experience – when a friend, staying at some new address, heads his letter "Dover", simply, assuming that you can get the rest of the address from his previous letter, which perhaps you have destroyed.' Inevitably Carroll also advised to put the date in full, which will help, years later, in compilation.

How to go on with a letter? '*Write legibly.* The average temper of the human race would be perceptibly sweetened, if everybody obeyed this Rule! A great deal of the bad writing in the world comes simply from writing *too quickly*. Of course you reply, "I do it to save *time*."' Carroll reported that one friend's letters were so badly written that it would take a week to decipher the hieroglyphics. 'If *all* one's friends wrote like that, Life would be entirely spent in reading their letters!'

With regards to content, the best subject at the outset would be your friend's last letter. If one refers to specific points, quote the words exactly to avoid conflict; if there is controversy, take care not to repeat yourself. If you have written anything that may offend, put the letter aside for a day and then read it as if you were the recipient. 'This will often lead to your writing it all over again, taking out a lot of the vinegar and pepper, and putting in honey instead.' Carroll's other rules:

> If your correspondent makes a severe remark, either ignore it or soften your response; if your friend is friendly, make your reply ever friendlier.
>
> Don't try to have the final word: let an issue run its course courteously. 'Remember "speech is silvern, but silence is golden"! (N.B. If you are a gentleman, and your friend is a lady, this Rule is superfluous: *you won't get the last word!*).
>
> If you ever insult your friend in jest, make this very obvious.
>
> If you write that you're enclosing a cheque or someone else's letter, 'leave off writing for a moment – go and get the document referred to – and *put it into the envelope*. Otherwise, you are pretty certain to find it lying about, *after the Post has gone!*'
>
> At the end of a sheet, find another one: 'whatever you do, *don't cross!* Remember the old proverb "*Cross-writing makes cross reading*."' (Carroll admitted to inventing that proverb himself.)

His advice on how to conclude a letter provided a neat update on valedictory habits towards the close of the nineteenth century. He detected 'at least a dozen varieties, before you reach "yours affectionately"', and they are familiar to us still: yours faithfully, yours truly, your most truly. His advice was to refer to your friend's last sign-off and to make yours as or even more friendly. He noted a 'very useful invention' known as the postscript, which had already been shortened to P.S. 'But it is *not* meant (as so many ladies suppose) to contain the real *gist* of the letter: it serves rather to throw into the shade any little matter we do *not* wish to make a fuss about.'

And then there was one final admonition. 'When you take your letters to the Post, *carry them in your hand*. If you put them in your pocket you will take a long country-walk (I speak from experience), passing the Post Office *twice*, going and returning, and, when you get home, will find them *still* in your pocket.'

Two years later, the popular weekly journal *All The Year Round* published its own version of letter-writing instruction, inspired by the new depths to which its anonymous author perceived the art had fallen.* It began with something incontrovertible: 'There are letters, and letters. Though little is needed to write a letter, to write a good letter is another matter.' The highest attainment was to paint in words 'like an artist, and write like an author; but there will be nothing stiff or ungraceful in his pictures, because they keep so close to Nature. No matter how trivial the occurrences related, they are facts in which both writer and reader have a mutual concern and that, together with the easy, chatty style in which they are related, gives them a charm which never fails to make them acceptable.'

---

* *All The Year Round* was established and edited (or 'conducted') by Charles Dickens since its birth in 1859. Following his death in 1870, the task was continued by his son Charles Dickens Jr. There is no doubt that Dickens himself had a keen interest in the development of letter-writing, and it was something he pursued in his novels. The letter-writing styles of Micawber in *David Copperfield* and Alfred Jingle in *The Pickwick Papers* were distinguishing features of their characters, and their author clearly revelled in them. 'I believe he dreams in Letters!' Betsey Trotwood said of Micawber, who considered himself something of an epistolary aficionado and endeared himself to readers with his 'in short' catchphrase, something that invariably heralded the long-winded and exhausting.

Dickens was a great supporter of the new penny post, and a year after it was introduced he wrote to Basil Hall, the naval officer and author, in the style of Alfred Jingle's harried style (signing it with his pen-name):

My Dear Hall.

Post just going – compression of sentiments required – Bust received – likeness amazing – recognizable instantly if encountered on the summit of the great Pyramid – Scotch anecdote most striking and most distressing – dreamed of it – babbies well – wife ditto – yours the same, I hope? – Seaport sketches, one of those ideas that improves in promise as they are pondered on – Good I am certain – Ever faithfully, and at present hastily –

Boz

Charles Dickens in productive pose in 1858.

Not everyone could write like this, of course, and not everyone could be taught to, but *All The Year Round* was keen to provide tips as to how we may at least aspire to greatness. The first referred to the most common bugbear – illegibility. 'If ever there was a time when writing has been made easy it is this present time, when even the poorest are well taught, when schools are plentiful . . . when paper, pens and ink are all good and cheap.' But people just couldn't be bothered to write clearly, the writer complained, or if they couldn't write clearly they just couldn't be bothered to improve their writing, and if they did improve their writing they were often so mean that they would write not on ordinary paper but on scraps or even the margins of torn newspapers. The worst offenders were apparently bishops, the nineteenth-century version of doctors: 'The fact that these right reverend gentlemen are many of them not good, or, rather, are very bad scribes, has grown so notorious, that the saying "he ought to be a Bishop, he writes so badly" is becoming quite a general one.'

But what of those whose writing is fine but just don't write? 'This is more generally the fault of young people, and arises chiefly from thoughtless selfishness. Their thoughts and their time are engrossed with their own pleasures and pursuits. It is more amusing and interesting to write to young people of their own age than to write duty letters to parents and relatives.' Do these terrible people not write at all? 'A shabby, ill-considered, stilted letter is written at wide intervals to those whose whole life has been spent in their service, while folios of trash are lavished on bosom friends to whom they owe no duty whatsoever.'

Could there be worse crimes still? Apparently so. The poet William Cowper was credited with a phrase equally attributed assigned to his contemporary Jane Austen – that letter-writing may be best described as the art of silent speech, the notion that the best letter to a friend was a 'talking letter', something that read as if you were telling it to them over tea. This still makes sense to us today: 'passing from one subject to another, as the thoughts spring up . . . omitting nothing that would be of interest, and telling everything in a simple, natural way.' But very few people actually write in this free-flowing, clear-stream way, and who or what is to blame? It is the letter manuals. Too many people 'assume an unnatural, stilted, verbose style, quite different to their manner in ordinary conversation, using a vocabulary much more polysyllabic

The French explain where to stick it in 1907.

in its nature than is their wont. For "mend" they write "repair",
for "enough" "sufficient" and so on, till their letters are no more
like themselves than if someone else had written them, and
one of the greatest charms of correspondence is entirely lost –
its identification with the writer.'

But there were other, ever more ingenious ways of getting
a message across. Cards have been sent through the post since
the beginnings of the mail (the writing tablets from Vindolanda are arguably the earliest), but their heyday occurred at the
start of the twentieth century, the picture postcard coinciding
with mass coastal holidaying (the British Postal Museum and
Archive estimates that between 1902 and 1914, up to 800 million cards were sent annually). They said what postcards always
did: wish you were here, weather mixed, love to all at home.
But they were an open and unguarded form of writing, open
to prying eyes at every step of their journey, and occasionally a
more intimate message was required. This came in the form of
a code, and was delivered by the tilting of a stamp (in much the
same way as a stroke or symbol on a letter concealed a preor-

dained message prior to 1840). A stamp stuck upside down in the top left hand corner would mean 'I love you'. A stamp on its side in the same position meant 'My heart belongs to someone else'. And so on, through the permutations.*

Further complication arrived by post from Scandinavia. Sweden was particularly enamoured with the possibilities of tilting, as the North Carolina Scandinavian stamp specialist Jay Smith makes clear in his interpretation of a Swedish postcard from 1902. This shows eight stamps at distinct angles and their (translated) meanings: 'Burn my letter'; 'Fidelity is its own reward'; 'I cannot accept your congratulation'; 'You have survived the trial/examination'; and, perhaps reflective of those long dark nights, 'Leave me alone in my grief and pain'.**

In 1938, what may be the most useful manual of all was published in Shanghai. Written by Chen Kwan Yi and Whang Shih, *Key to English Letter Writing* was a guide that served double duty: it taught the Chinese how to compose personal and business letters in slightly creaky English, and it provided its English readers with invaluable insight into personal and corporate Chinese customs we may not have otherwise been aware of. Unlike Anglo-American guides, these letter templates did not usually concern misfiring sons and their long-suffering fathers, or how best to address a duchess. Instead, the examples were both more mundane and, conceptually, more profound.

---

* Upside down, top right corner = Write no more.
Upside down in line with surname = I am engaged.
Centred on right edge = Write immediately!
At right angle, top left corner = I hate you.
** The stamp-tilting tradition is maintained today in situations where mail is subject to external scrutiny and censorship, in particular in prisons and in the military.

They also show extreme generosity, such as this example for the newlywed. 'I have heard from Mr B that you were married to Miss C last Wednesday. I beg your acceptance of the accompanying fish as a trifling token of my affection.' And when that marriage proves fruitful? 'Allow me to congratulate you on the birth of a child in your family. I beg you will accept the accompanying basket of mixed fish which I send you in celebration of the happy event.' Would a promotion, perhaps in the legal profession, also yield a fish gift? Sadly not. 'Sir, I learn with pleasure that you have been admitted to the bar and have established yourself in private chambers . . . Please accept the accompanying bicycle as a slight token of my wishes for your future success.'

The *New Yorker* came across the Chinese manual in New York's Chinatown in the middle of September 1939, two weeks after the outbreak of war in Europe. Everything, even near-calamity, was the excuse for a party: 'The fire which occurred in your neighborhood last night must have caused you considerable alarm,' another letter surmised. 'I was very glad to hear that your house escaped . . . Please accept the accompanying dozen of champagne with best congratulations.'

But one should exercise caution, for the bestowing of presents may be seen as overstepping the mark, particularly when romance has not yet blossomed. 'In the present stage of our relation to each other,' a young woman is encouraged to write to a pushy suitor, 'I do not feel justified in accepting gifts, which in my opinion are only compatible with friendships of close intimacy and long standing.'

Something clearly worked: 75 years on, the average well-educated Chinese person's grasp of English is stronger than the average well-educated English person's grasp of any dialect of Chinese (with letter manuals taking only some of the credit), and congratulatory tokens of fish are no doubt still testing the resolve of Chinese postal workers from Quanzhou to Jinchang. But this is not all. *Key to English Letter Writing* also contains a summary of shortened forms of popular Western Christian names, helping to ensure that letters may be addressed less formally once intimacy is attained. If you have a friend called Charles, you may, after a few letters, address him as 'Chaos'; if he is Thomas, then 'Jommy' will bring him delight; and if he is Stephen, you will have a correspondent for life if you call him 'Steenie'.

Photographs

14232134 SIGMN. BARKER H.C., 30 WING, I COY.,
9 AIR FORMATION SIGNALS, C.M.F.

4th and 12th August 1944

My dear and lovely Bessie,

This will be a short and hurried letter to convey to you the news that I have recently had a short and safe sea journey to the above mentioned Command [in Naples], and am having a most interesting time, as well as looking forward to the times ahead. You can imagine my relief when I discovered I was not bound for India, and my pleasure to be again on the same continent as you. The sand that fell on the stone floor here when I made my bed here last night is the last I may ever sleep on again.

I have no great complaint about Libya, but it is good to get away from the eternal camel, sand, and to see again trees, houses, streets, civilians and other near-England sights. As I have only been here a day, you will not expect much news of the place. Apart from varied uniforms, there is little sign that there is a war on, and no sign of lack of food. Many of the young children present a similar appearance to those in Egypt, but the adults are well dressed and look true to type. The women are attractive, languorous, and their clothes are of many types and materials. (I gave my issue of preventatives to one of our chaps whose appetite is larger than my own.) There is a good NAAFI, and a Y.M.C.A. At the latter I bought 2 cakes (with a penny each) and a cup of tea for – 6d (10 LIRE). There are some fine, but very dear, silks and satins on sale. Strangely, not many ice cream shops, although I had a wonderfully cold Limonata today for 6d. There are plenty of nice tomatoes about, almonds, pears, etc. I was unfortunately unable to travel with my brother, but will shortly be joining up with him again, to recommence our journeyings together and swap recent experiences.

You can imagine how I felt today to get your photographs, on top of these L.C.s I have lately received! How lovely you are! How really nice! How much to be admired! Dear, dear, dearest Elizabeth, what are you doing to me, what are we doing to each other? How did I not see you, why was I blind, what can I do? I do not want to use ordinary words and usual language to tell you how dear you are to me, how I ache and wait for you. You are worthy of so much more than I can ever hope to give, yet your love inspires me, and makes me think I might succeed with you. I shall return later the photographs taken at Great Yarmouth and Rannoch Moor. Both may be a little bit precious to you, and the four (it's grand to have so many) others will be wonderful for me to drink in. Already I have had a dozen quick furtive looks. I am looking forward to the time when I can take my first long look at them, when I am by myself, when I can imagine the better that you are with me. Now, when you look at my photographs, you can wonder if I am looking at yours at the same time. There will be many times when that happens, for I shall look often. Look at you holding your skirt, look at you showing your bare feet, look at you by the boat, and be delighted at the curve of your breasts revealed by the jumper. Look at you with the other girl, at your little velvet trousers, your bare knees. Whew! You have done something now! This is magnificent and marvellous, and you are wonderful and glorious. You are a delight and a delicacy, my wondrous woman! My lovely, lovely wife!

I love you.

Chris

~~~~~~~~~~~~~~~~

28th September 1944

My Dearest,

Your [letter] came today at noon, less than four days from the postmark.

While I applaud any act of decision or resolution on your part, I really do not want you to make yourself unhappy about smoking under the impression that I think it very bad. I hope that you succeed in your cigarette ban. I shall not offer advice, you must have plenty. I know that you are doing it for me, and I can tell you I am proud of you and pleased with you.

You know that, before I left the desert, I had to destroy most of your letters. I kept a very few, I felt that I must because you had said so much to me in them. I had to burn many letters, I have had over twenty since. All of them are precious to me, all of them speak wonderfully to me of your love, of your fragrance. But in the hurry of a move to you know not where, one has to pick out what one can.

We shall not have an easy time immediately I return, because restraint will be necessary. I am hoping you will be able to do something in the way of house-finding before I return, but I know it is difficult. I also hope that when the flying bombs are finally settled you will feel like looking for little things of use in the home. You'll need potato peelers, egg whisks, all sorts of things which if you can get beforehand will save us a lot of trouble and delay.

I have been hearing more of the customs of these folk in this village, and it is probably the same all over this part. There is no courting before marriage. The young man writes his prospective wife's parents. They consent to him coming to tea. They are never left alone, and the first time he holds her hand is when they are man and wife. Some marriages may be arranged in Heaven, but none are around these parts! None of the girls dare be seen talking to men (let alone soldiers), lest they be the subject of gossip. Our chaps are not very happy about feminine availability, although some have had happy moments, though a little expensive.

I met a chap here, eighteen months younger than me, who went to the same school. We had a good talk about teachers and remembered pupils. I have also had a talk with a chap who lives in Leeds. Married a couple of years before the war, one child, been away from England two years. His wife gave birth to a child (by a married man with two children) in June. She asked for his forgiveness, but not unexpectedly, it has not been forthcoming. I have heard many similar cases, or variations on the same theme. They are all very bad, but the separation caused by war is at the bottom of most of them, I think. It is nice to think we live in a world of constancy and adherence to vows, but we certainly don't. Some of our chaps moan about the Yanks at home, but there is plenty of evidence that many Englishmen do not act honourably.

I love you.

Chris

Chapter Twelve

More Letters for Sale

Even Virginia Woolf sometimes went to the beach. She doesn't strike one as a beach kind of girl, not in her writing, and not in her persona. She strikes one (or am I alone in this?) as more of a desk-and-blotter sort, a pallid hair-pinned British Museum Round Reading Room sort, a wet walk through Russell Square type. Passionate about her work and loves, of course, but when she went to the coast she looked out to the lighthouse from gloomy windows. Can you imagine Virginia in a striped swimsuit and headband on the edge of frolicking waves?

No need to imagine – we have a photograph. Taken on the sands at Studland in Dorset, probably in 1908, when Woolf was 26 and still had the surname Stephen, the photo shows her happy, smiling with Clive Bell, who had married her sister Vanessa the year before (the photographer is unknown, but may well be Vanessa herself). The bathing suit was hired, and in her notebooks Virginia described it as 'unisex', and thus a perfect fit. She remembered swimming far out, 'a drifting sea anemone'.

In a letter that accompanied the photograph, written to Clive Bell on 19 February 1909, she described attending a dinner party thrown by her publisher Bruce Richmond at which she 'felt like a cannibal because the dinner was so good, and I knew what went to make it – the blood of respectable young men and women like myself.'

I am afraid that one can't believe nowadays in starving genius, frozen in a garret. We were a dreadful set of harpies; middle aged writers of mild distinction are singularly unpleasant to my taste. They remind me of those bald-necked vultures at the zoo, with their drooping blood-shot eyes, who are always on the look out for a lump of raw meat. You should have heard the chattering and squabbling that went on among them, and the soft complacent coo of those that had been fed. That great goose Lady G[regory?] was the loudest in her squawking; the rest of us sat round and twittered, half in envy and half in derision.*

Woolf was not yet middle-aged, and her claim that she was even of mild distinction may have been wishful thinking. Publication of *The Voyage Out*, her first novel, was still six years away, and her best work up to this point was in literary journals and letters. But her presence within the Bloomsbury group had brought many admirers for non-literary reasons, including advances from Sydney Waterlow, a diplomat in the Foreign Office and an early friend of Clive Bell. In 1911 Waterlow asked Woolf to marry him, an option she declined. But he persisted, and her objections hardened, partly, one imagines, because he was already married, and partly because her feelings for him were indifferent.

'I don't think I shall ever feel for you what I must feel for the man I marry,' she wrote in December 1911. 'I feel you have it in your power to stop thinking of me as the person you want to marry. It would be unpardonable of me if I did not do everything to save you from what must – as far as I can tell – be a great waste.' And then the final dread nail: 'I hope we shall go on being good friends anyhow.'

These letters lie at one end of a career, and at the other lies a remarkable sequence of eight letters written between 28 March and 6 April 1941 by Leonard Woolf, the man she

---

* Vanessa addressed the letter to 'James', and signed off 'Eleanor Hadyng', a childhood game they had.

Not drowning but laughing: Virginia Woolf and Clive Bell in Dorset.

did decide to marry, and her sister Vanessa Bell. They were addressed to Vita Sackville-West, Virginia's fervent friend and likely lover, and documented the immediate period after her suicide.* Woolf had written two suicide notes to Leonard and one to Vanessa, now famous artefacts.** But what happened next is less well known. As of May 2013 the following letter, in green ink, written by her husband on the day of her death on 28 March, remains in private hands.

> I do not want you to see in the paper or hear possibly on the wireless the terrible thing that has happened to Virginia. She has been really very ill these last weeks & was terrified that she was going mad again. It was, I suppose, the strain of the war & finishing her book*** & she could not rest or eat. Today she went for a walk leaving behind a letter saying that she was committing suicide. I think she has drowned herself as I found her stick floating in the river, but we have not found the body. I know what you will feel & what you felt for her. She was very fond of you. She has been through hell these last days.

The following day, Vanessa writes to Vita.

> Leonard says he was writing to you so this is only because I feel I want to be in touch with you somehow – as the person Virginia

---

* Woolf's novel *Orlando* was described by Sackville-West's son Nigel Nicolson, who edited Woolf's letters, as 'the longest and most charming love-letter in literature'.

** I'm not sure why we consistently use 'suicide note' rather than 'suicide letter'; it may have something to do with the anticipated brevity, although this is often far from the case. One of the two letters Virginia left for Leonard read, written perhaps 10 days before she died, in edited form: 'Dearest, I feel certain that I am going mad again: I feel we can't go through another of those terrible times. And I shan't recover this time. I begin to hear voices, and can't concentrate. So I am doing what seems the best thing to do. You have given me the greatest possible happiness. You have been in every way all that anyone could be. I don't think two people could have been happier till this terrible disease came . . . If anybody could have saved me it would have been you . . .'

*** Her last novel *Between the Acts*.

The post office in oils by Vanessa Bell.

loved most I think outside her own family. I was there yesterday by chance & saw him. He was of course amazingly self-con-
trolled & calm & insisted on being left alone. There is nothing
I can do yet. Perhaps some time you & I could meet? It is difficult I know. But we will manage it presently. Now we can only
wait till the first horrors are over which somehow make it almost
impossible to feel much. Forgive the scrawl.

More than a week later, her body has still not been found. On
6 April, Leonard Woolf wrote again to Vita: 'They have been
dragging the river the last week, but are now, I think, abandoning the search.' And then on the same day, Vanessa also
writes to her: 'There is no news of course. It seems to be likely
there never will be which perhaps is best.'

We know what happened, and as we read we know more
than the participants; that this is so often the case with letters – an inherent fallibility – adds to their worth. Letters

with hindsight would be a terrible thing. For here is Woolf just three years before, indelibly delighted with her lot in a letter to her sister about her serene time with Leonard at their house in the small village of Rodmell in Sussex after a visit to what she called the 'scrimmage' of 'appalling' London: 'We get snatches of divine loneliness here, a day or two;' she wrote in October 1938, at the age of 56,

> and sanguine as I am I said to L. as we strolled through the mushroom fields, Thank the Lord, we shall be alone; we'll play bowls; then I shall read Sévigné; then have grilled ham and mushrooms for dinner; then Mozart – and why not stay here for ever and ever, enjoying this immortal rhythm, in which both eye and soul are at rest? . . . We were so sane, so happy.*

Her bliss is spoiled by the intrusion of visitors who wouldn't leave ('An interval of sheer horror; of unmitigated despair') but in the end it was her sanity that failed her. Two weeks after Vanessa wrote to Vita about the non-appearance of her sister's body, she wrote again, by which time the body had been found by children on a far bank.

> It was another shock of course & one had so hoped it wouldn't happen. But I think Leonard meant it when he said, as he did to me, that it was no more horrible than all the rest. . . . He arranged for cremation at Brighton yesterday & didn't want me to go so I didn't. There was no ceremony. Nothing. Poor old Ethel,** who had written to me, apparently wanting a country church yard,

---

* Madame de Sévigné was Woolf's epistolary heroine, if not her inspiration. In *The Death of the Moth and Other Essays*, published posthumously in 1942, she wrote: 'This great lady, this robust and fertile letter writer, who in our age would probably have been one of the great novelists, takes up presumably as much space in the consciousness of living readers as any figure of her vanished age.'

** In later life, Woolf wrote frequently to Ethel Smyth, a composer and prominent member of the suffrage movement who became infatuated with her, although it is clear that Woolf found her partly insufferable, in one letter calling her 'a catastrophe'.

will be disappointed, but after all anything else would have been too uncharacteristic.

The image of Virginia Woolf walking to the edge of the nearby River Ouse and filling her pockets with stones is another indelible one, more so perhaps with the contrasting image we have of her smiling on the beach in her twenties in that photograph. But the epistolary story doesn't end there. Woolf once defined letter-writing as 'the humane art, which owes its origins to the love of friends'*. So it is fitting that her story continues among her friends after her death; there is another sequence of five letters between Leonard Woolf and Vita Sackville-West that occurred between May and June 1941 to settle Virginia's will.

These are typed (in contrast to the autograph death letters), and unravel a friendly dispute. 'Virginia has left you one of her MS with instructions to me to choose it,' Woolf wrote on 24 May, 'and now the probate people have asked me to inform them which it is to be.' Woolf suggests giving her *The Years* or *Flush*, her highly successful biography of Elizabeth Barrett Browning's cocker spaniel (inspired by her reading the Brownings' letters), but Vita evidently wanted something else, perhaps *The Waves* or *To the Lighthouse*. Five days later, Woolf writes: 'I am glad you are outspoken, as always, and I will be.' The manuscripts became the subject of fierce bargaining: he wishes to retain *The Waves*, but offers her *Mrs Dalloway*. He also requests that Vita sends him the unpublished pages of *Orlando* in her possession, and in a subsequent letter he returns them with the belief they are 'incohate [sic]'. Sackville-West then apparently suggests that she should inherit the manuscript of *To the Lighthouse*, which Woolf declines.

---

* Quoted in the introduction to *Leave The Letters Till We're Dead: The Letters of Virginia Woolf, Vol VI*, edited by Nigel Nicolson. Nicolson, the son of Harold Nicolson and Vita Sackville-West, said of Woolf, 'A letter was a wine glass to hold her delights, or a sump for her despair.'

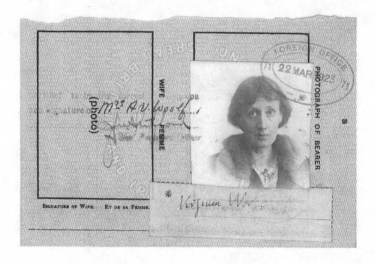

His final, unpublished, letter to her on this matter reads:

Dear Vita,

Here is the book. I am also sending the MS of *Mrs Dalloway*. I presume that it is legal for me to do so before the estate is settled. The first vol. is called *The Hours* which is what V. intended the title to be originally.

The garden here had been rather knocked about by the weather. I think we have less fruit than any year since we came here.

Yours,

Leonard Woolf

The letters, all but one confined to a single leaf, are written on light blue or beige-coloured paper and composed with an eager but legible hand in green or black ink. They are a thrill to hold. I held them in an unlikely location: a sixth-floor office on West 18th Street in downtown Manhattan, the New York premises of Glenn Horowitz Bookseller Inc. I took the Woolf letters in and out of plastic slipcases on a large table in the middle of what, as with letters, I took to be a fading and fusty concern: a rare book dealership where one may buy inscribed first editions and browse obscure and tantalising items one would never discover online.

But the office of GHB is neither fading nor fusty, because it is something else as well: a trader in literary souls. Horowitz, late fifties, curly grey hair, something of a steely Marx Brother about him, runs a literary brokerage firm that deals in the archives (essentially manuscripts, notebooks and letters) of

'They have been dragging the river . . .' Letters to Vita Sackville West in 1941.

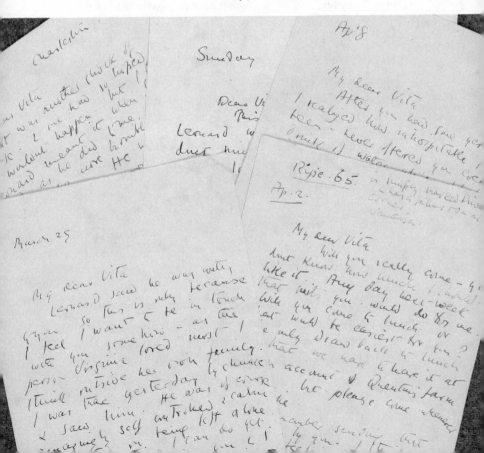

great and famous writers. Horowitz has handled the archive sales of Vladimir Nabokov, Norman Mailer, Bernard Malamud, Joseph Heller, Kurt Vonnegut, Nadine Gordimer, J.M. Coetzee and David Foster Wallace (among others). He has also bought letters from presidents, and sold the Watergate notebooks of Woodward and Bernstein for a reported $5m. The smaller archives may be bought by private clients, but most of the big ones will end up at institutions: Emory University in Atlanta, perhaps, or Harvard, or the Berg Collection at the New York Public Library, or the British Library, or the splashiest and seemingly most insatiable of all, the Harry Ransom Center at the University of Texas in Austin.

Horowitz is not one to sit back and wait for something to enter the open market; he will actively seek out the writers he believes will have something valuable to sell. He has, for instance, recently been having discussions with Tom Wolfe; he is trying to persuade him that buying his archive is not a sign that he is creatively dead, nor even no longer a Master of the Universe, but rather that his manuscript of *The Kandy-Kolored Tangerine-Flake Streamline Baby* and *The Bonfire of the Vanities*, with editor's emendations and the attendant letters from nutzoid fans, may be worth more while he is still alive, when he can join in the purchase celebrations and benefit from the not inconsiderable mountain of loot.

Glenn Horowitz is, as one might hope for, something of a showman. He speaks a showman's language, a strange combination of hyperbole and litotes, his wrangled vocabulary finding drama in the everyday. Take his account of how he added the archive-selling business to his rare book business in his mid-twenties. 'I didn't know shit from Shinola,' he told me. 'But I obviously had instincts. I come from a background of Jewish peddlers, people who had come over as immigrants and literally pushed and pulled carts through the streets.' His first archive negotiation, in 1981, was between the Pulitzer Prize-winning poet W.S. Merwin and the University of Illinois. 'I put together a deal that began with the institution offering me $25,000 for his papers, and ended up with us settling at $185,000. I was entitled to 15 per cent of the transaction, and when the cheque for $28,000 arrived on my desk, it was not only the largest cheque I'd ever seen with my name on it, but it didn't take me very long to realize that it would take me a long time to earn that sort of profit selling books. So I looked at it and saw that this was fundamentally a very interesting spin on the traditional buy-sell dynamic within the world of books.'

He handled several other collections in the next decade, but nothing spectacular. Then in 1991 he was 'summoned' to Switzerland by Vera and Dmitri Nabokov to 'help them unwind the seemingly unsolvable problem of what to do with Vladimir's archive. I shuttled between Montreux and New York, and after six to nine months of intense negotiating, prevailed upon the New York Public Library to buy these papers for a million and a half dollars.' This, he observes, was 'the transformational transaction, the one that suggested not only to me, but to those watching me, that not only did I have a negotiator's skill to bring various parties with disparate interests together, but I was also able to find what was then an historic amount of dollars to attach to an archive.'

And from there, it was seemingly inevitable that he would go on to handle the Woodward and Bernstein Watergate papers, John Updike, Mailer ('which took up a small tractor trailer'), Cormac McCarthy, the photographs of Elliott Erwitt, the Magnum photographic archive, 'on and on and on'. He calculates that about 85 per cent of his market consists of not-for-profit research institutions 'extending their brand of scholarship'.

But these institutions had clearly obtained many fine collections before Horowitz and others like him arrived on the scene, and in a far cheaper way – through donation. Writers considered it an honour to have their paper life stored by Harvard, and there was an issue about whether their estates would have to contribute to their upkeep. Things changed gradually after the war. Libraries and universities enjoyed increased capital and patronage; places like Texas University saw the accumulation of unique literary material as a way of establishing themselves as a world-class research institution. Horowitz established what he calls 'a competitive environment' for these papers, but maintains that he will only be paid his fee if he represents the interests of both seller and buyer. In this mission his spirits have not dulled. The excitement, he says, 'is to identify bodies of work that heretofore people had not thought about having significant research value, and to prevail upon an institution to share that vision.' It is a vision that, prior to his involvement, 'was only shadows and fog'.

I was guided through the Woolf letters by Sarah Funke Butler, the firm's senior literary archivist. Funke Butler is in her late thirties, and has been with the company for 15 years, joining shortly after completing her Nabokov thesis at Harvard. She calls herself 'a self-confessed letter fetishist', a passion that began with a pen-pal assignment with a French grammar school in the 6th grade. 'Their handwriting was uniform, legible, full of curlicues, and they all wrote on graph paper,' she says. 'I didn't find that better or worse than our American scrawl on a range of unlined notepaper, just different, but distinct. At the age of 10 I wasn't thinking in terms of "cultural consistency" though – mostly I was just embarrassed that my new friend Joel had signed off, "Lots of love".'

In recent years she has handled the archives of Don DeLillo, Tim O'Brien, Cormac McCarthy, Erica Jong (with fan letters from Sean O'Connery and others expressing admiration for *Fear of Flying*), John Updike (with dozens of form letters rejecting his work), Norman Mailer (who preserved carbon copies of his outgoing letters for decades), Hunter S. Thompson (who taught her how to shoot), James Salter, David Mamet, Alice Walker, Timothy Leary, 'and so many more'. In this time she has naturally generated many letter-related archives of her own, most memorably a multi-page fax from a nonplussed Dmitri Nabokov complaining about the use of certain phrases in a book she was compiling about his father. He wrote 'that the standards for English instructions at Harvard had clearly changed since his time there'.

Before I examine the Woolf letters, Funke Butler gives me the lavish Woolf catalogue. This includes not only the correspondence mentioned above, but also many other documents and rare items surrounding her work and personal life. There are proofs and inscribed first editions of all the major works of fiction and non-fiction. There is the photograph page from her 1923 passport, attributed to A.V. Woolf (her seldom employed Christian name Adeline). And there are also other great letters, including one from Virginia to Vanessa written on the eve of her sister's wedding, signed with the affectionate pet names Billy, Bartholomew, Mungo and Wombat, commending Clive Bell as 'clean, merry and sagacious, a wasteful eater and fond of fossils'. And then there is another one from Leonard Woolf to Vita Sackville-West, circa 1927, with instructions for his wife's care. 'I am entrusting a valuable animal out of my menagerie to you for the night. It is not quite sound in the head piece. It should be well fed & put to bed punctually at 11. It will be v. good of you if you will see to this & pay not attention to anything wh. it may try to say for itself.'

There are 77 lots in the catalogue, many containing multiple items. The collection had been put together over four decades by Bill Beekman, now a senior finance partner at the New York City law firm Debevoise & Plimpton. What had ignited his V.W. bug? In the late 60s he was majoring in the history and literature of modern England and France at Harvard, and although Woolf wasn't part of the main curriculum, a self-directed tutorial led him to read *To the Lighthouse*. 'It moved me very much (as it does so many people)' he told me via email. 'I had grown up with bound volumes of the old *Vanity Fair* and was familiar with her image and mystique as a highbrow modernist, and was really moved to read her by reading Albee's play [*Who's Afraid of . . .*] in another class.' He ended up writing his undergraduate thesis on 'Character and Characterization in *Madame Bovary* and *Mrs Dalloway*'.

The first letter he bought was fairly insubstantial, from Leonard to someone who inquired about buying a book at the very beginning of the Hogarth Press. Beekman acquired the suicide sequence directly from Vita's descendants, via a dealer, and remembers being 'very moved by Leonard's terse thoughtfulness'. His favourite is the one Virginia wrote to Vanessa on the eve of Vanessa's marriage, 'complete with little doodles of animal paw prints and bound with a red ribbon – very childish.'

I wondered what had persuaded Beekman to part with them. He was retiring in a few years, he said, and he felt he could no longer really afford to buy the stuff that would enhance the collection. 'When a collection becomes static, it becomes much less interesting.'

The Woolf items are only for sale *en bloc*. Glenn Horowitz Bookseller is asking $4.5m for the collection although Funke Butler tells me this is a 'soft' $4.5m, perhaps because it has been on sale for more than a year and has yet to be purchased. But soft may also refer to what one would have to be in the head to spend such money on the (albeit fascinating) cast-offs and daily amassments of a writer who's not exactly flavour of the month. For a soft $4.5m one could buy half a million new paperbacks of *Mrs Dalloway* and give them out to first-year literature undergraduates – would one not be spreading the word about Woolf better that way?

'The collection is an exquisite example of what a dedicated private collector can do,' Glenn Horowitz says. 'I'm very proud in the hand I had in helping Mr Beekman build it. Those very poignant letters between Leonard and Vanessa to Vita are sensational.' But the price? 'In this particular case I probably permitted some element of the sentimental to overwhelm my fine-honed critical acumen, and conceded to the aspirational wishes of my friends the Beekman family, who had worked themselves into a heightened state of consciousness over what they had accomplished.' Rather than sell it as a collection, he now believes 'it should be put back on the market object by object over a number of years'.

And what would Virginia Woolf have made of the price? Perhaps, in a post-post-structuralist world, she would have come round to the idea. But she certainly wasn't thrilled with the prospect of a literary afterlife in a dealer's New York office when she died. The very last words she wrote, in the margin of the second suicide note she left for her husband, read, without a question mark, 'Will you destroy all my papers.'

'It's a very good time for letters at Glenn Horowitz Book-store,' Sarah Funke Butler says. This is particularly true, it seems, if you are a fan of women's writing. They have not only Woolf in their files, but also many fine things from Louisa May Alcott, Margaret Atwood and Susan B. Anthony, Pearl Buck, Jane Bowles and Fanny Burney (to take just the As and Bs) as the company strengthens its archive of feminism and Judaica; the firm's catalogues are purchased by libraries as valuable artefacts in their own right. 'We quote so heavily from letters that you almost don't need to get a copy of it,' Funke Butler says. 'But of course you don't want to trust some book dealer, you want to see the primary source, you want to hold it and sniff it.'

We talk about copyright issues in her catalogues, and how much they can get away with without spoiling the value of exclusivity to a prospective collector. Most copyright holders and purchasers are generous with their permissions, she says (the copyright of a letter traditionally rests with the original writer or their estate, rather than the recipient or present owner). But some estates and owners are more restrictive than others. Funke Butler studied James Joyce at Harvard, and is now thrilled to be handling many of his letters. But when she recently wanted to blog about a Joyce letter (she contributes news of interesting letters to the *Paris Review* online), she found the Joyce estate less than keen. And when she contacted the owner of a Joyce letter she had recently sold to ask permission to post a scan, this was also declined. 'She said, "I want my Joyce letters to be *my* Joyce letters,"' Funke Butler remembers. 'There's something about the temperament of the Joyce collector that breeds this. Joyce definitely draws a different temperament.' She says the estate is 'famously bad' by which she means famously protective, which may be famously unfortunate for letters dealers. 'I don't know why that [attitude from the estate] would impact the actual collectors except that it might breed a sense that this sort of behaviour did give you some kind of power.'

She has noticed a greater interest in literary letters in recent years, and an attendant price rise. 'I'd like to romanticize it and say, "it's because people feel there aren't going to be any more letters," but I'm not sure that's it.' Who's buying? Manuscript material almost always goes to institutions; inscribed books almost always go to private collectors; but correspondence can be the one middle ground. 'If an institution has a big Don DeLillo archive they're not going to pay a premium for six more letters. Whereas a collector of the twentieth century will pay a premium for a few Philip Roth and a few Don DeLillo.'

Is there a difference between selling a letter that has never been seen and one that has already been quoted by a biographer? 'You get more of a bang promotionally with the unpublished one. It's more of a brass section than a violin section.'

The purchase of archives has been buoyant since the birth of institutions built to house them, which is to say the universities in the thirteenth century. But the refined and proactive brokerage of such things is a more recent art, not least when it comes to actively ferreting out letters for sale and resale. But firms like Glenn Horowitz Bookseller are now an integral part of the chain. 'If Texas want to get a tax benefit from the material, they need to get an appraisal done first,' Funke Butler says. 'And they don't want you showing up with a suitcase full of stuff and having to deal with you. You're probably crazy, you're probably going to be calling them and annoying them a lot afterwards. So we provide a layer of interference for which we get a commission. A university does not want to be a retail operation. If you turn up with a suitcase here and say, "this was in my aunt's attic" we'll write you a cheque and you'll walk off happy and we'll be thrilled.' Or, if the firm suspects you have an attic as yet uncharted, they'll come to you. 'With David Foster Wallace we know who his friends and associates and colleagues were, so we can reach out to them individually and ask, "Don't you have a few letters?" And perhaps we can then sell them to Texas to add to their archive, or we can feed off the power of the archive and sell them for more money to a private collector.'

A recent intervention pulled in quite a haul. For more than 25 years Horowitz had been in patient contact with a man in Denver, Colorado called Ed White. From 1947 to 1969, White had been in close contact with Jack Kerouac, and their correspondence spans the writer's rambling rise and fall, with the madness that attended the publication of *On the Road* in 1957 pitched firmly in the middle. One letter from Kerouac, written in pencil at the beginning of September 1951, informs White

Jack Kerouac (below) addresses his friend Ed White.

that he is 'completely rewriting the Neal-epic', referring to Neal Cassady, the model for Dean Moriarty in *On the Road*. Kerouac was in hospital in Virginia recovering from phlebitis, and the back of the letter contained fragments with a heading, torn at the corner, that reads 'On the Ro-'. These wouldn't make it into the published work, the 'rewriting' instead appearing in his subsequent novel *Visions of Coady*.

White had met Kerouac at Columbia University, and became a travelling companion before settling down to his career as an architect. He appears in *On the Road* as the character Tim Gray, and in *Visions of Coady* as Ed Gray, but it is a feature of the early letters in particular that White is the one encouraging Kerouac to adventure out and travel more. Kerouac also acknowledges White for encouraging him to try 'sketching' in his notebook as he walks the streets, which Kerouac, in a letter to Ed White in March 1965, credits with having 'led to discovery of modern

Sept. 1

Dear Ed— (ps. Am completely rewriting Neal-epic)

Believe it or not, this is all the paper I have. I'm in the Kingsbridge VA Hospital recuperating from my fifth attack of thrombophlebitis since 1945 — the worst; so I have to stop smoking altogether, take blood-thinning pills & penicillin & take care of myself the rest of my life, or, if the condition spreads from legs upwards I get brain, heart or lung thromboses that prove fatal anytime. I just received yr. marvelous letters yesterday via John Holmes, who visited me here last week (been here 3 weeks, previous to that laid up a month in No. Carolina.) Yes, my (present) work has flown, and good riddance, I've work to do and fun to concentrate on. Your coming to New York is going to enrich my life. Bravo for fate in this case! — she finally got us in the same town, I'll be devouring at my mother's house at 94-21 134th St. Richmond Hill as soon as I get out of the hospital next Friday. Of course, a born celebration is in order for us battered Knights of the cross. Really, Ed, I'm exhilarated you're coming; think of the fun; I have mad new places to go to (tell you later); and women galore all over. Yes, I think you made the right choice in architecture — architecture is better than teaching and all that sissy shit — architecture is a noble thing — it was Faust's last dream — and you are a born architect, sir! Think of the honor, sir, in this age, of being the exact opposite of a psychoanalyst! I look forward to meeting you at the train — shoot me the coming-time. All's well. Sir, to be your admirer is not to be meek. Jean

'I've work to do…' Kerouac writes to Ed White with a plan for
On the Road.

spontaneous prose', the literary pulse of the Beats, and, in this instance at least, a modern American urban counterpart to Virginia Woolf. The whole collection, comprising 63 letters and postcards from Kerouac and some replies from White, was, on the day I visited, for sale for $1.25m.

It is not the first time that Glenn Horowitz Bookseller has offered Kerouac letters for sale. A few years before it offered an individually priced list of 76 items, the majority unpub-

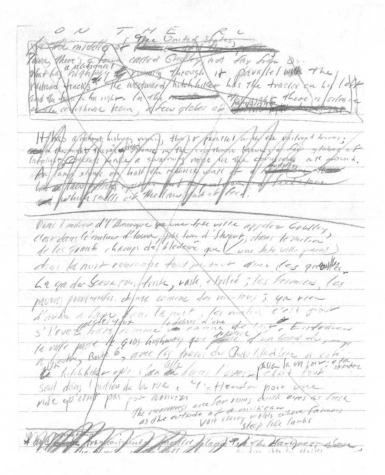

lished, including a poem dedicated to Allen Ginsberg, a rant after the assassination of JFK, a cheque made out to Nonzie's Wines + Liquors for $10.50 from 1961 (that was now valued at $3,500), and a set of notes written in a New York bar at the age of 22 in which he waits for a companion called Celene and sets out an early tale of woe. 'If she does not come I shall go to a movie to postpone the anguish,' he writes on paper headed 'Ballantine Ale and Beer', going on to invent a maudlin third-person narrative in which he ponders Thoreau's dilemma, 'how to make the getting of one's living poetic'.

But it is the letters, to Neal Cassady and to Kerouac's family and other friends, that flesh out a picture of the writer through key stages of his life, codifying his distorted thoughts as he bebops from disillusion to acclaim to despondency. One doesn't have to be Beat to marvel at his bug-eyed idealism as he makes heady plans for California with Cassady and their wives in January 1951 ('I bring mambo drums and you bring flute and we play on side of road while Joan [Haverty, Kerouac's second wife] spreads peanut butter on bread and whatall.') Cassady alerted him to the pitfalls of such a move from one coast to another, but Kerouac seemed possessed by the pioneering spirits of Lewis and Clark: 'I see everything working out fine; a thousand hassles that will only be wonderful because we are taking that big trip to the coast. I feel wonderful about it . . . great, wonderful, grand, fine magnificent.'

More than any other mid-century writer, Kerouac's letters open up to readers a sense of the vast size and opportunities of the United States; his bid to become great was linked in his mind with this spatial adventurousness. In the autumn of 1947 he wrote to his sister Caroline (whom he called Nin) of his ambitious travelling schedule, surmising 'I'll certainly do 90 per cent of it, I'll have seen 41 states in all. Is that enough for an American novelist?'

But it wasn't. Kerouac floundered, discovered that his demons travelled with him, ventured back and forth from San Francisco several times, lodged again with his mother, found Buddhism, and in 1954 wrote to Allen Ginsberg that 'Unless I suddenly sell *Beat Generation* [*On the Road*] . . .' the fates would forever turn against him. His new-found religion would offer some solace, but his writing ambitions had hit the rocks. 'I am finished, I know the dream is already ended and all I see is the blur of it like in or through water and I wonder why men rush so straightforward and interested thru the fantasy.'

And then, three years later, after six years of rejection and revision, *On the Road* made him, overnight, the voice of a generation. In 1968 he told the *Paris Review* that he 'got the idea for the spontaneous style for *On the Road* from seeing how good old Neal Cassady wrote his letters to me – all first person, fast, mad, confessional, completely serious, all detailed . . . The letter he sent me is erroneously reported to be a 13,000-word letter . . . no, the 13,000-word piece was his novel *The First Third*, which he kept in his possession. The letter, the main letter I mean, was 40,000 words long, mind you, a whole short novel. It was the greatest piece of writing I ever saw, better'n anybody in America, or at least enough to make Melville, Twain, Dreiser, Wolfe, I dunno who, spin in their graves. Allen Ginsberg asked me to send him this vast letter so he could read it. He read it, then loaned it to a guy called Gerd Stern who lived on a houseboat in Sausalito, California, in 1955, and this fellow lost the letter: overboard I presume.'*

Initially, Kerouac was euphoric with the success of *On the Road*. 'Frisco is jumping', he wrote to his latest big crush, the writer Joyce Glassman (later Joyce Johnson), on a postcard from Berkeley, California in May 1957, 'millions of poets & jazz clubs & novelists 19 years old . . . waiting for my type-writer to write you regular letters.' Five months later he reported to Glassman from Orlando that he had used all his penny postcards to reply to 'ALL my fan letters', and three months after that, 'Have 3 new offers to make album readings, bigtime companies too'.

But the sheen faded. *On the Road* drew as many detrac-tors as admirers, and Kerouac soon came to loathe the idea of heading a movement that would inevitably suffer media burn-out. His literary heroes were more permanent and more poetic: Thomas Wolfe and Rimbaud. After a six-day alcohol

* When we spoke, Glenn Horowitz was negotiating with Gerd Stern to sell his archive; the letter is still believed to be overboard, alas, and is not part of it.

binge in May 1959, and the onset of severe stress and paranoia, Kerouac berates the forces that secured his reputation.*
'It was better for our writing souls and abilities when we were
obscure,' he wrote to Allen Ginsberg. 'I am being destroyed
by wellmeaning admirers ... they have no conception of how
much they outnumber me and all their enthusiasm and mail
piles up meanwhile with further demands from everywhere
including insane 10,000 word letters from girls who try to
write in subterranean style etc.'

But even worse, it's the wrong sort of attention: he claims
he seldom gets the credit for starting a new literary movement:
'and Hollywood doesn't even know I originated beat generation or that it all comes out of on the road, which they didn't
buy and won't buy because everyone is hysterically crooked.'

Ginsberg escaped to India, and on his return secured a firm
grip on the politics of the 60s. Kerouac, embittered and overwhelmed by his own creation and date-stamped talents, failed
to do so. He died from complications from internal bleeding
due to alcohol poisoning in 1969 at the age of 47. One may
play the same poignant trick with his letters that one played
with those of Virginia Woolf before her self-destruction, an
exercise in glimpsed epistolary autobiography from a happier and earlier time.** For Kerouac this too takes place by the
water's edge, in one of the earliest Kerouac letters to survive,
written to his sister in late summer 1941 at the age of 19. Nin
was four years older than Jack, and had not joined the family
when they moved briefly to New Haven, Connecticut from
Lowell, Massachusetts. But Jack wanted her to reconsider:

> Oh, I tell you, it's beautiful. Every time you look out the parlor
> window you can see the ocean, and sometimes the high tide

* The letter is also dated May 1960.
** Although one could also argue that a more representative picture of the way
things would turn out could be gleaned from the 'Celene' bar letter three years
later.

splashes sprays over the sea wall across the street from our little cottage . . . I tell you Nin, this place is a resort. We look like millionaires, and what fun . . . The day we moved, I went in for a quick swim in the cove and there was a high wind. The waves were rolling in on me in great grey mountains and I was being billowed high and then low.

An important letter, punctuation perfect, some sticky imagery, typed on three leaves of paper with handwritten corrections. Yours for $17,500.

⊥　　　⊥　　　⊥

A few weeks earlier, on 8 May 1941, not quite six weeks after Virginia Woolf drowned herself, Leonard Woolf wrote again to Vita Sackville-West in reply to a request to visit her. 'Later on I might feel I want a day or two away & then I should like to see you at Sissinghurst. At present I feel I'm better here . . . I keep on thinking how amused Virginia would have been by the extraordinary things people write to me about her.'

Many of these extraordinary things have been gathered at the Leonard Woolf archive in the Special Collections department of the University of Sussex, not far from where they lived. Reading through these condolence letters, 208 in all, one is struck not only by their starry variety (T.S. Eliot wrote, as did E.M. Forster, H.G. Wells, Elizabeth Bowen, Edith and Osbert Sitwell and Radclyffe Hall) but by the absolute sincerity of what they say and the kindness and elegance with which they say it. There is no hint of obligation in these letters; the common themes are shock and love.

Woolf died at what may be regarded as the very lowest point of the war for Britain, and many of the condolences are tinged with a general mood of despair. They vary a great deal in length and the large variety of stationery, some of it distinctly

From THE HEADMASTER, CHARTERHOUSE, GODALMING.

4. 5. 41.

Dear Mr Woolf,

I feel tonight to begin this letter by saying that I have never written one like it before. When a great author dies it is not the business of her admirers to thrust themselves at her relations. But for some reason, (which I suppose is really understandable, though not very pleasant to contemplate,) people seem to have taken the occasion of Mrs Woolf's death to write and print things which are intolerable. I can only write to you as representing a "class", those who were the undergraduates of the early 'twenties. But because people have written these things I feel I should like to let you know something of whether books meant to me and I hope you will forgive my intrusion.

I shall never forget reading "Jacob's Room" for the first time, because it was a real moment in my life. I shall not try to express what I felt because that would be attempting a criticism which I am not competent to make. I can only say that since then I have waited for each one of her new books, so firm and sympathetic, like strong, delicate fingers unravelling the hardest knots, as I have waited for those of no other living English writer. For twenty

'I have never written one like it before...' The Headmaster of Charterhouse addresses Leonard Woolf.

ragged (particularly that from the general public), again shows the effects of the war. The letters from fans are perhaps the most moving, coloured with trepidation for intruding upon private grief but overwhelmed by gratitude towards Woolf and her work. One of these, from Isabel Prentice, was written from Montreal on Easter Sunday:

Dear Mr Woolf,

From all over the world where English is read, you will be receiving letters such as this. So many will come, that they will probably be a trial to you. And yet, people like myself must be allowed to send you some small comfort for your great personal loss.

We have all lost so much in the disappearance of a lovely person like Virginia Woolf. There must be many like myself who have read her books since schoolgirl days and who regarded them as personal treasures. We still have the beauty and the sensitive personality expressed in her writing, to turn to again and again, but how sad to know that there will be no more.

A letter like this, from a complete stranger intruding on your grief should be apologetic; and I have hesitated long before writing. If I didn't feel so torn with anxiety about England, and so constantly wishing to help all English people who are suffering so today, I should not be writing. It has seemed to me that a brief message to say that others are sad and share in your grief might be welcome now.

Please do not answer this, but accept for what small comfort it may bring.

I was in England last Spring at this time and regret very much that I am not there now to share the trials you are all so bravely enduring. Many of us have no wish to survive in a world where there is no free England and would be only too glad to be there to help.

Very sincerely yours

Isabel Prentice (Mrs Norman A Prentice)

Some of the letters were angry, not least at the negative connotations attached to Woolf's suicide following a misquote in the *Sunday Times* of one of her suicide notes, which suggested

'A weak and inadequate thing': The Woolf condolence letters become an archive at the University of Sussex.

that Woolf killed herself on account of her inability to cope with pressures of the war rather than her own depression, that she was a defeatist rather than a depressive.*

Other letters, including one from P.H. Wallis of Hampstead, London, said that they would not have dared to have written were it not for the fact that Woolf had once composed such a generous letter to them, 'that I treasure to this day'. On 5 April, John Farrelly Jr. wrote from Allerton, Missouri.

My dear Mr Woolf

I was shocked and saddened by the news of your wife's death. For two days I have been stunned and sick at the thought. You may question this from a person who knew absolutely [nothing] of Mrs Woolf's private life, who had never even met her. But

---

* The misquote may not have been entirely accidental. A few days before her death, *The Times* had run a hostile editorial entitled 'The Eclipse of The Highbrow' condemning the 'esoteric parlour games' and inefficiency of high intellectualism during the war, aiming its arrows specifically at the Bloomsbury group; subsequent replies to the editorial, by Kenneth Clark and others, likened this criticism to the book burning of the Nazis in 1933. This dispute is tracked well in *Afterwords: Letters on the Death of Virginia Woolf*, edited by Sybil Oldfield.

I think that anyone who has known her books feels the same. Through all her writing runs the thread of a lovely and lovable person, so that one naturally felt a personal affection for Mrs Woolf herself. And we knew her at her very best.

I know that so many felt this from the way many of my friends speak. Hers is not just the death of a public figure for them. [St Louis] Post Dispatch (our main newspaper – and a hard-boiled political sheet, at that) ran a sympathetic and admiring editorial about her last night. And my English professor (I am a freshman at college) devoted yesterday's class to an enthusiastic lecture on her. They all felt a deep personal loss.

So if it is any consolation to you to know that so many everywhere share your sorrow, draw upon that consolation.

I wrote a letter to Mrs Woolf last fall which she answered. I mailed another one from St Louis about January 15. I wonder if she ever received it. Sympathy is a weak and inadequate thing – particularly from a stranger, but one needs to do or say something – yet is left gaping. I know that I feel much that words would only falsify and make clumsy and ridiculous. In a sense, I write this for myself. Not only for you am I grieved, but with you.

Sincerely yours,

John Farrelly Jr.*

And how did those closest to her respond? On 31 March, Vita Sackville-West wrote to Leonard three days after his letter to her reporting her disappearance.

* John Farrelly Jr.'s son George kindly passed on to me the following story: 'My father wrote a letter to Virginia Woolf a few years before the one to Leonard. He was perhaps 18 or so. I was told by one of his brothers that he was uncertain whether or not to send it. In the end he decided not to send it, and threw it out the window of the family car as they were driving into St Louis from their home in the country. Someone must have found it and posted it, because it did in fact reach Virginia Woolf (who I think replied to him).'

My dear Leonard

I have no words of grief. Your letter stunned me, and at present I can only think of you, with feelings I will not attempt to express. The loveliest mind and spirit I ever knew, immortal both to the world and us who loved her. It was so utterly unexpected as I did not know she had been ill lately and had had a letter from her only about a fortnight ago.

I do not like to send you a telegram as you may be trying to keep it private for the moment, but you will know that that was my only reason.

This is not really a hard letter to write as you will know something of what I feel and words are unnecessary. For you I feel a really overwhelming sorrow, and for myself a loss which can never diminish.

Vita

I am more touched than I can say by your having written to me.

And on 7 April 1941, with Woolf's body still undiscovered, Sackville-West also wrote to Woolf's friend Ethel Smyth. 'Darling Ethel I wish I could say something comforting. All I can feel is that it is better for her to be dead than mad, and I do thank God that she has not been found. The river is tidal so she has probably been carried out to sea. She loved the sea.'

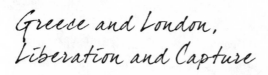

Greece and London,
Liberation and Capture

The following letter was written two weeks after the Germans withdrew from their occupation of Greece. Chris and Bert Barker had sailed towards Athens in the same homecoming fleet as the Allied Forces leader General Scobie and Greek prime minister George Papandreou.

27th October 1944

My Dear Bessie,

Athens is a city on holiday, a people celebrating after years of suffering, a great communal smile; laughter, happiness, joy, jubilation everywhere. It would do jaded Londoners good to see what I, treading on the heels of the Germans, have seen. It would do them good to have the Athenian welcome as I have had it.

Imagine travelling with half a dozen other chaps in a truck, running through banner-bedecked festooned streets hung with bright coloured declarations of welcome and praise for England, being cheered and applauded, loud and long, by single individuals or groups of people, as we rushed along. Imagine everyone sitting outside a cafe getting to their feet and clapping. Imagine that happening at a hundred cafes. Turn a city into a stage, make the British Army the players and hear us warm to the genuine joyous proud applause of the appreciative audience. Imagine every house flying flags, some-times only the Greek, but generally our own, the U.S., and the Red Flag. Imagine every wall painted with well-meant slogans and salutations, many in English (some pidgin English!) and many in Greek: 'Welcome Our Liberators' – 'Greetings Allies' – 'Good Luck to our Greit Allies' – 'Hip [Hooray] for the British Army' – 'Welcome Heroic English' – 'EAM-ELAS Welcomes You'. Great signs, little signs, printed posters, chalked or painted walls. Bright posters, streamers, banners carried by processions, signs flung across streets (dangerously low in some cases, one chap in my truck was hit on the head, and had three stitches in it). Imagine having flowers thrown into the truck. That is our luck as we make our way through the beautiful avenues and squares, the first non-goosesteppers since 1941.

Don't get thinking that these announcements about home leave are of any earthly use to you and I, by the way. The state-ment about 6,000 men a month is just useless to all but a very few of the men. It is window-dressing. I am afraid that we must reconcile ourselves to at least another year apart, and probably two. It is pretty bad, but thank the Lord there are letters to give visible evidence of belief and interest in one another. You must always remember that I am interested in you, vitally interested, wholly, completely conscious of you, and how you and I are one, no matter where we are.

How can I tell you I want to implant myself; how my lips need to meet your flesh everywhere, to kiss your hair, your ears, your lips, to kiss your breasts; to kiss you, to put my face between your legs, in homage, in love, in obedience – and because I must. You are my aim in life, you are my goodness, and I must and will claim you, claim you for ever. I want to run my hands on, over, around the vital, vibrant spot. I want to warm my hands by being there. I want to warm you, inflame you, too. It is a wonderful thought to think that one day I may really touch wondrous, lovely you.

I love you.

Chris

The socialist-led anti-Nazi resistance movement EAM, and its military wing ELAS, had won control of most of Greece, apart from the large cities. This led to civil war between EAM and the right-wing, royalist EDES party. Churchill was alarmed at the prospect of communist rule, and with the return of George Papandreou and the British forces, confrontation with EAM seemed inevitable. After 15 communist protesters were shot dead, fighting broke out between ELAS and the British on 3rd December. Chris Barker would soon be involved.

5th December 1944

Dearest,

I expect the news of Greece has by now nicely alarmed you, and that you are not without concern for me. I hope you will take this as a token of my continued safety and welfare. I am enduring no hardship or privation, and am subject to very little inconvenience. Later on I shall doubtless be able to tell you something about the present happenings, but for the present you must put 2 and 2 together and – if you are wise – not be too sure that the answer is 4. I listen to the wireless news from London with great interest, and find much food for thought in this whole proceeding. A flickering oil lamp illuminates this page as I write now, for it is night, but when I wrote before, there was a smoke pall over the city and I could hear the 'PUFF-BOOM, BOOM-PUFF' of the guns. I should very much like to tell you what I think and know, but this is not possible with me a soldier. Perhaps you will feel aggrieved and misled that I did not tell you this was liable to take place. I could not have done so without breaking the regulations, and in any case, I did not think it would be so soon.

It is true that some of our rations are going to the Greeks. I hope it is going to the many poor and not the few rich. I went round the market in town the other day, saw some lovely fish on sale – octopus! I didn't like the look of them at all but they are said to be very nice to taste. There is no coal here for domestic consumption. Wood is the only agent, and the use of charcoal is usual.

I saw 'Citizen Kane' and thought it remarkable, extraordinary, puzzling, different. A far better film than 90 out of a hundred others, and one certainly possessing qualities that none of the others I have seen had got. Welles may be mad. But he is not Hollywood mad.

Regarding your cookery programme. I have no doubt you'll be alright. I reckon I'd be alright myself after the slight Army training in independence that I have had. It could be a fair idea to buy a cookery book if you feel you need one, and I should get a secondhand one for preference. But you should certainly be doing some cooking now. I know that if I was back home I should want to 'have a go' at things, although probably only while the novelty lasted.

I love you.

Chris

27 WOOLACOMBE RD, LONDON SE3

6th December 1944

Dearest,

So very worried about what is happening in Greece. On the news tonight it spoke of it spreading and seems to have become a battle, my worst suspicions of what the British Army went to Greece for are fulfilled. I don't know how this is affecting you and whether the ordinary people are involved. Of course you won't be able to tell me much, I can only just hope for your safety. Your safety – oh! Darling! The trouble seems to be centred in Athens, and you spoke of visiting it, so I presume you aren't billeted there. We should have them to settle their own troubles, we will regain the name of perfidious Albion again before this war is through.

All but 16 of Bessie's letters to Chris Barker have perished. Many were burnt by Chris as he moved billets to save them from prying eyes. Others were burnt after the war at Bessie's request. This is the first letter to have survived.

Darling, I have no complaints about your letters, I am too happy that it is my body that you want, that occupies your thoughts. If you didn't write and tell me these things, I should suspect you of being interested in somebody else's body; you keep concentrating on mine, my breasts, my vital vibrant spot, my hands and my desires.

Well, I am glad you have 4 blankets to keep you warm – if I was there you wouldn't want any, you'd be hot enough. Here am I, a blooming iceberg of a maiden waiting to be roused into a fire, not just melted but changed into a fire, and there are you, miles and miles away, needing an extra blanket.

During this last month I have reached rock bottom, I now feel something like a convalescent – no longer need a nurse, Christopher, I need the whole vital man in you, your strength, your energy, when, when, when will you make me a whole woman, when will I be one with this frustration, when? Stunted growth, that's what I am suffering from! My body is stunted, my affections are stunted, even my blooming mind suffers from this incompleteness. I want to be your mistress, to be used to the uttermost, I want to fuss you, look after you, I want to be your companion in arms – away with depressions, fed upness, waiting. Angel, I want to feel human, I am so sick of being a cold, haughty virgin. Crikey, talk about untapped resources. Did I have to find the man of my life in the middle of a blooming desert, who then goes on a Cook's tour and then gets himself into a hot spot of trouble – oh! Christopher, I do hope you'll be alright.

'My apprenticeship' – books, books, books, I am sick of those too; I want to live, live with you, oh! Why couldn't you have come home instead of going to Greece, why can't I come out to Greece, so that I could stand in the way of any stray bullets.

Write poetry to me Chris? You have already written poetry to me, music as well, I doubt whether you could surpass it, it isn't easy to express these things in words, but you have done it, you have moved me, right down, down to the foundations, you have accomplished what I shouldn't have thought was possible, you have opened a vision of a new world, a new experience for me, I cannot help but be so very very grateful to you. With that in front of me, I can overcome my black moods and rise up again and know that this life is worth the living.

Pancakes, yes we had your lemons with them, that was why I made them. I rather think your lemons helped to get rid of my cold, maybe your letters as well. All those things help, you know, the lemons on the practical side, and the letters on the mental side.

Thank you for the sultanas which are on the way, I do feel considered, my thoughtful lover, such a nice sensation. You don't know what a relief it is to have a pair of slippers, I have been wearing my shoes in the house, it was wretched not having anything to slip my feet in, you know, for when you get out of bed, after a bath, for evenings.

I had to giggle about my 'bravery' in bombed London. I live here, work here, and there isn't anything else to do but live here and work here, and like most things up to a point, you get used to it. It's one's low resources that one has to be brave about, all one's usual aches and pains get you down easily, any extra effort tires you out, but as we are all in the same boat, that isn't so bad as it sounds, it's communal you know, makes a difference, besides the battle fronts sound so much worse, I concentrate on that when I feel pathetic. I shall be concentrating on Greece, can't help it, the situation sounds so much worse, the news tonight says civil war. Darling I love you, love you, so very much.

Bessie

27 WOOLACOMBE RD, LONDON SE3

8th December 1944

My Darling,

The stop press of tonight's evening paper says it is quieter in Athens today. It is horribly difficult for us to get at the truth.

The weather sounds lovely there, whereas here, well –! It tried to snow today, horribly cold. I don't know whether I told you that I bought a pair of lined boots (getting all prepared for the worst), I wore them yesterday and it wasn't necessary, and didn't today when it was. What is a girl to do in this climate, had cold feet all day, very breezy these luxury flats – we have such a palatial entrance hall and carpeted stairs, but inside the flat, it's bare boards, the lavatory is always going wrong, and the water in the bowl won't run away – luxury? Our trouble now is that we have heard that our British Restaurant is being taken over by the War office, so that will mean 2/6 lunches, without any improvement on the B.R. I brightly asked one of the WVS women if it was true, and if so were they opening anywhere else – yes it was true, and there were plenty of places for us to go to, and anyway the B.R. wasn't meant for us in the first place, it was for bombed-outs.

Xmas is a family time, children's time, I expect you will enjoy yourself in Greece with your friends' families, anyway I hope you will be able to. Am just listening to the 9 o'clock news and it's most disheartening, it says it's spreading not slackening. Oh! Dear! Christopher! I really can't think of anything else, Darling, I do really want to be cheerful, but it's so blooming difficult, Xmas! And you out there. I love you, I love you, I love you, and my heart is aching, it is so lonely and desolate without you. My mind keeps going into such flights of fancy on how to get to you, from stowing away on a ship, to applying to the war office, so blooming silly, but it does get so bad sometimes.

I went to see 'The Circle', John Gielgud's production, a play by Somerset Maugham, didn't think much of it, so was glad you couldn't come. Lil Hale wasn't very impressed either and she is rather keen on Gielgud's acting, to me he seemed such a milk and water specimen, no fire, no life in him, just a beautiful voice, too too cultured. I think I have got a bit choosy over the theatre, have seen some really fine plays during the war, my standard has got a bit high.

I have been horribly chatty in this L.C., that's the result of worrying, I have kinda got you on my mind in a different way, the situation in Greece is getting in my hair, despite all efforts to remain calm. Keep calm is my motto. But I do wish I knew how things were with you. Keep well, keep safe.

I Love You.

Bessie.

27 WOOLACOMBE RD, LONDON SE3

18 December 1944

Dearest,

I shouldn't really feel anxious about your possible conduct while you are away, because we love so much, we do really care. I know it's just as unthinkable for you as it is for me, my heart is in Greece and nothing else can touch it. But I know of so many people whose lives have gone awry it's a bit horrifying, and I think you might feel tempted in a lonely moment, I don't mean cheap temptations. No, as I write that, I don't believe it, because like me you don't allow the situation to arise, there can't be temptation when all your heart and mind and body is straining to somebody so far away, no I won't worry further, we are one, we really do care, in each other we can rise above the second rate, you make me feel that. You do brighten the scene, indeed you do, we will, will it so, in those future days, grand days – we trust, oh! We do trust, Chris.

To go out together – knowing that we shall go home together, knowing that we shall pass the night together – to go out together knowing that – I think of that so often, really just belonging – that makes my inside sing, to be together so that I can answer your demands, make my own, just put my arm around you at any time, sometimes in public, would that embarrass you? I know it's rather a possessive thought, but I do feel rather proud that you are mine, I could be rather blatant over that in front of your friends, am I being too awful, but I can't help that proud elated feeling, to put it baldly, you are a wonderful catch, I want everybody to know you are mine.

Have given up present-giving with my pals by mutual consent, thank goodness, in the end it becomes a racket, much too wearing to keep up, most of 'em can't afford it, so found it kinder to cut it out. It's most awkward this business of being unable to give people anything without they must return it, most natural I suppose, but difficult with present financial straits. Funny how people get the urge at Xmas time for a holocaust of present giving, you should see the crowds in town, all trying to buy what isn't there. Dear oh dear what a game.

I wonder how you will spend Xmas.

Oh Darling, I Love You.

Bessie

On the day this letter was written, Chris Barker was stationed in Athens' Hotel Cecil. He awoke to shouts from ELAS (the Greek People's Liberation Army), of 'Surrender comrades, we are your friends'. He wrote in his notebook: 'At 11.30, ELAS started serious attack: shells, Bren, rifle, mortar. The last was quite frightening . . . Mortars started firing and got very close . . . Panic in the passage. 'Close the door!' The Bren gunner still outside . . . got more ammo, then with Bert and Jack sat on the first floor landing. Ordered downstairs, then upstairs again. Bofors or dynamite through end passage. Much glass falling under shelling . . . Then, suddenly, 'Cease Fire!' Joyously, all over the building the cry was taken up . . .

Came downstairs, laid down our warm weapons and was greeted by long-haired partisans, with 'Hail, Comrades!' during the dark hour, before dawn.

Led away in small parties while above us the Spits (Spitfires) looked wonderingly on ... Walk about 4 miles to a mansion. Lady partisans. Lovely, interested and approving. Water and 2 ozs of bread. Then about 15 mile march through the woods and forest glades. Led away to a mountain fastness blindfolded.'

Chapter Thirteen

Love in Its Later Forms

Each day Charlie Brown would look, and each day he would be disappointed. It was like the Carpenters' hit *Please Mr Postman*: he'd be waiting so patiently, and all he wanted was a card or a letter, and could the postman check one more time and see – but nothing. What Charlie Brown wanted specifically was a Valentine's card, from anyone in particular one imagines, although something from the Little Red-Haired Girl would be particularly fine. But every time he folds down that metal hatch on his mailbox and stretches his stubby arms to the very back . . . he gets only air and fluff. Ah well, maybe next year. Some hope.

When Charlie Brown failed to get even one card in his comic strip, and when the humiliation was compounded by the TV broadcast of the animated *Be My Valentine, Charlie Brown*, sympathetic observers sent him hundreds of cards, such is the power of the media, such is the poignancy of the post. Charlie Brown later sought to capitalise on the response: 'There must be millions of people all over the world who never get any love letters,' he surmised. 'I could be their leader.'

Early on in the TV animation, Lucy is leaning against Schroeder's piano as he plays his usual Beethoven sonata, and she begins to read cheerily from a book: 'It says here that it is probable that the Valentine was the first of all greetings cards. The paper Valentine dates from the sixteenth century.' Lucy smiles at Schroeder, who carries on playing obliviously. 'By 1800 hand-painted copper plates were produced to meet the

large demand. Get it, Schroeder? To meet the large demand
for *Valentines*?' He plays on, deaf to her suggestions, but she
perseveres. She plays with her hair and smiles at him, but
Schroeder doesn't look up, so she throws the book away and
asks whether he is sure he really wants to suffer the tortures of
a memory of a lost love. Schroeder finally looks up in aston-
ishment, and Lucy starts destroying his piano. 'You'll wake
up at night SCREAMING!' she wails. 'You'll wanna smash
things!'

In the United States Valentine's cards were certainly not
unknown before 1840 – in that year some 1,100 were sent in
New York – but their popularity blossomed with the introduction of stamps and cheaper postage, and in 1847 some 30,000
Valentines were mailed. February 14th became a unique thing
– a *postal* holiday, and the Post Office was aided in its windfall

by advertisers seizing on the possibility of attaching gifts to this transaction. Mothers' and Fathers' Day would follow suit, but they would be modest in comparison with the 'heaving postbags' and 'thronging crowds' that dominated cartoons and comment pieces in the newspapers at the time. In mid-Victorian Britain and antebellum America it emphasised powerful things about the post that had not been evident before: that the mail could be used for leisure and provocation, and that these things could be conducted more or less anonymously. When the San Francisco *Daily Evening News* reported in 1855 that 'The rap of the postman, on the morning of 14th February, causes many a maiden's bosom to throb with love and curiosity,' it was clear that the mail had found a new purpose: a service of pure, inessential pleasure.

But the popularity of Valentine's Day has ebbed and flowed. In 1958 *Harper's Weekly* wrote that 30 million cards were sold in the United States, while three years later in the UK the *Daily Mirror* reported a figure of 27 million. This was quite a recovery from an inter-war slump that had seen the same newspaper ask 'Is St. Valentine Dead? . . . The young . . . are no longer sentimental. The cinema has formed a generation with unabashed methods of courtship – if indeed it can be called by any such old fashioned name.' But by 1962, sentimentality was back: 'This year, Valentine's Day will be spelt with a capital R for Romance.'

The appeal of a Valentine's card is that it says nothing and everything all at once. One doesn't have to be very skilled at expressing love or longing to send one, for someone has done that for you with a poem or illustration of a rose, and the real work is done by the recipient. And the recipient is never obliged to reply to one, merely to cherish it and wonder. They are not real love letters, and these days they are unlikely even to be a prelude to them; they are date-appropriate arousals, really not much more than the Facebook poke, and they may ever teeter on the brink of timidity and alarm. Real love letters are something else, and soon we will all be like Charlie Brown, reaching for what isn't there.

No art flourishes in a vacuum. In November 2012, Sotheby's New York was delighted to unveil the line-up of its pre-Christmas Books and Manuscripts sale, a predictably eclectic array of Isaac Newton, F. Scott Fitzgerald and George Gershwin, and a fragment of the first bible to land on the moon. But the noise around the auction was generated by another lot, described in the catalogue as 'the largest and most significant group of correspondence and drawings by Charles Schulz ever offered at public sale', documenting 'the romantic pursuit of Tracey Claudius by the celebrated creator, author, and artist of *Peanuts*'.

Schulz and Tracey Claudius sent each other Valentines all year round. Tracey Claudius (whose name would not have been out of place alongside Peppermint Patty and Linus van Pelt in the comic strip) was 25 when she first met Schulz in March 1970, when the cartoonist was 48. A friend of hers was interviewing Schulz for a magazine, and Claudius tagged along to take photographs. She was a huge fan, and explained that she really just wanted to meet her hero. She admitted as much in a letter she sent him after returning home the same day: she adored Charlie Brown and 'that stupid beagle', she wrote, and meeting their creator 'was like being Charlie Brown and getting to meet Willie Mays . . . Happiness is discovering your idol's feet are not clay, but pure and durable gold.'

According to his biographer David Michaelis, Schulz fell under her spell from the off. His marriage was apparently in disarray, and he was in need of another woman to anchor him. 'From the start,' Michaelis writes, 'the unspoken assumption between them was that Tracey was going to make him happy.' In the following week the couple met often – ice-skating, an outing to a bookstore in San Francisco, a hotel dinner. And then Schulz recreated their meetings by sending Claudius a series of letters and cartoons, casting himself as Charlie Brown and his new squeeze as Lucy. In the first, Charlie Brown asks 'Remember?' and in the second his speech bubble says 'March 16th was the day we met.' Subsequent drawings depict other early meetings, and in the sixth, Charlie Brown asks, 'On April 22nd you squeezed my hand in the Dark! Remember?' Another drawing, in which Schulz apparently recalls their first night together (and what may have been his first infidelity) in a Monterey hotel, says, 'May 1st and 2nd were so neat I can hardly stand to think about it.'

In July 1970, four months after their meeting, Schulz sent Claudius a postcard from Honolulu, where he was vacationing with his wife and another couple. 'Aloha – Like Gatsby, I'm pursuing the "green light" . . . Hope to see you soon – I miss you very much.' The green light, Schulz reminds Claudius in another letter, is Gatsby's interpretation of 'the orgiastic future that year by year recedes before us.'

The Sotheby's catalogue claims that many other letters

> rehearse all of the features that Schulz finds most attractive about Claudius. More often than not, her name is written in longing triplicate: Tracey Tracey Tracey. Schulz variously comments on her sweet voice, her nose and beautiful profile, her prettiness, her beautiful eyes, her fascinating weirdness, her deeply musical laughter, her golden eyes, her soft hands, and her marvelous face. One letter is actually a compilation of Tracey's 'Good Points', which includes charming, cute, beepable, huggable, buggable, sensitive, athletic, and bookable.'

Frequently he tells her how much he loves her; occasionally there are red hearts.

Charles Schulz didn't always keep his love private; he also wrote syndicated letters to the world. David Michaelis has detected the parallel appearance of certain words and themes in his correspondence with Claudius and his speech bubbles in *Peanuts*. Snoopy had previously referred to himself as 'buggable and huggable'; in two letters to Claudius, Schulz writes that his wife had found out about his many long-distance phone calls to her, and in a *Peanuts* strip at about the same time Charlie Brown berates Snoopy for his obnoxious behaviour when he is denied a visit to 'that girl beagle' he met. In the fourth panel, showing Snoopy picking up the telephone, Charlie Brown yells at him, 'And stop making those long-distance phone calls!' In another strip, Charlie Brown calls at Lucy's psychiatric help stand ('The Doctor Is In') and asks, 'Do you think monogamy is possible for humans, given how we're wired?' And then there's the one where Peppermint Patty dozes in class and says 'Tracey! Tracey, I love you! Tracey, do you hear me, I love you?'

According to his biographer, Schulz twice proposed to Claudius. She declined, she later said, because she doubted whether she could make Schulz happy, and because she despaired of wrecking the public image of the creator of a comic strip she considered 'holy'. The couple remained in contact until 1973, when Schulz, a year after his divorce, married someone else.

The emergence of the letters did not delight members of Schulz's family, who declared their sale tasteless and heartless; the image of Schulz that Claudius was keen to protect while Schulz was alive clearly no longer applied (he died in 2000 at 77). The media reported that the family of Tracey Claudius was selling the archive (44 letters in all) to finance her deteriorating health, at which point close readers were able to deduce that the collective childhood memory of one of the most popular cartoons in America was being sacrificed on the altar of a health system that was failing to adequately care for its seniors.

The letters didn't sell.

What makes a great love letter? Truth, vulnerability, passion, secrecy, vulgarity, fervour, delusion, exquisitely painful ecstasy? Something so intense you want to shout it or burn it? Something that speaks to us all through the ages? Something Goethe called 'the most immediate breath of life, irrecoverable for ourselves and for others'?

Love letters catch us at a time in our lives where our marrow is jelly; but we toughen up, our souls harden, and we reread them years later with a mixture of disbelief and cringing horror, and – worst of all – level judgement. The American journalist Mignon McLaughlin had it right in 1966: 'If you must re-read old love letters,' she wrote in *The Second Neurotic's Notebook*, 'better pick a room without mirrors.'

But of course there are exceptions, those letters whose shelf life is everlasting and whose lessons are immutable. We may look at Petrarch's and Shakespeare's sonnets this way, and there are correspondences with equal weight. We would expect the Romantic poets to come up trumps, and so too the buttoned-up Victorians: the courtship between Robert Browning and Elizabeth Barrett is one of the great mythical romances, created entirely through letters. But the catalogue extends deep into the last century too, with Henry Miller/Anaïs Nin and Robert Lowell/Elizabeth Bishop leading the glittering literary way through a million less celebrated heartbreaks in wartime. And they all have a patron saint, wittingly or not.

On 1 November 1820, John Keats wrote to another Charles Brown, his great friend back in London. Keats was in Naples, on his way to his final lodgings in Rome, an increasingly futile attempt to find warmer air and recovery from tuberculosis. A tortuous month-long crossing had been followed by a 10-day ship-bound quarantine, Italian officials worried that its passengers would export London's latest cholera outbreak. To add to his woes (the whole blood-coughing consumptive ordeal), Keats was also lovesick, and his longing took up the greater part of his letter to Brown. The object of his affection, of course, was his fiancée Fanny Brawne, the woman he would never marry. They had known each other for two years; he had

'I cannot bear to leave her': John Keats ponders his fate in this engraving by Joseph Severn.

left for the continent certain that he would never see her again. His regret worsened with his illness.

> The persuasion that I shall see her no more will kill me . . . My dear Brown, I should have had her when I was in health, and I should have remained well. I can bear to die – I cannot bear to leave her. Oh, God! God! God! Every thing I have in my trunks that reminds me of her goes through me like a spear. The silk lining she put in my travelling cap scalds my head. My imagination is horribly vivid about her – I see her – I hear her.

Keats, ever financially embarrassed, had begun to share Charles Brown's house in Hampstead named Wentworth Place in December 1818; Fanny Brawne and her mother lived next door. Brown subsequently observed him writing some of his greatest poems in the house and garden, most famously 'Ode to a Nightingale' (although Brown's account of this is disputed). The two went walking in Scotland together and discussed literary matters, and when doctors advised Keats to move to Italy he tried to persuade Brown to accompany him. But Brown stayed behind, and resolved to write often. In one letter to Italy he told Keats: 'If I have a right to guess, a certain person next door is a little disappointed at not receiving a letter from you, but not a word has dropped. She wrote to you lately.'

Brown was unaware that Keats had determined never to write to Fanny Brawne again, or read anything she sent to him. He hoped this might ease their separation; he found it did not.

> There is nothing in the world of sufficient interest to divert me from her a moment. This was the case when I was in England; I cannot recollect, without shuddering, the time that I was prisoner at Hunt's,* and used to keep my eyes fixed on Hampstead all day. Then there was a good hope of seeing her again – Now! – O

* Leigh Hunt, the English writer and poet, a close friend of Keats.

that I could be buried near where she lives! I am afraid to write to her – to receive a letter from her – to see her hand writing would break my heart – even to hear of her any how, to see her name written would be more than I can bear. My dear Brown, what am I to do? Where can I look for consolation or ease? If I had any chance of recovery, this passion would kill me ...

My dear Brown, for my sake, be her advocate for ever. I cannot say a word about Naples; I do not feel at all concerned in the thousand novelties around me. I am afraid to write to her. I should like her to know that I do not forget her. Oh, Brown, I have coals of fire in my breast. It surprised me that the human heart is capable of containing and bearing so much misery. Was I born for this end? God bless her, and her mother, and my sister, and George, and his wife, and you, and all!

Your ever affectionate friend,

John Keats.

One can view Fanny Brawne's gold and garnet engagement ring every afternoon from 1–5 p.m. at Keats House, as Wentworth Place is now known. There's also Brawne's bodice and bracelet on display, and two mementoes containing Keats's hair. There is also a letter on show to Fanny Brawne's mother, which Keats composed at the start of his quarantine in Naples in October 1820. 'I dare not fix my mind upon Fanny. I have not dared to think of her. The only comfort I have had that way has been in thinking for hours together of having the knife she gave me put in a silver-case, the hair in a Locket and the Pocket Book in a gold net. Show her this.'

Keats writes further of his illness and his dimming wits, before adding 'My Love again to Fanny.' And once again, after the valediction to her mother, he adds a line beneath: 'Good bye Fanny! god bless you.' He died four months later, his epistolary legacy as great as his poetic one.

In fine health, Keats was among the finest letter-writers in the English language. His letters are all that Jane Austen's are not: a creative torrent, a cascade of insight and illumination, a daily record of a young mind working out a philosophy for life. For a poet whose poems are possessed with a sheen of language that appears, as a recent editor of his work has it, 'too much like bright monuments in winter sun', his letters by contrast are spontaneous, sometimes genial, sometimes fiery, consistently chatty.* They are, dare one say it, fun. His letters have their 'greatest hits' – their talk of 'Negative Capability' (the happy allowance of scholarly doubt and mystery 'without any irritable reaching after fact and reason'), and his comparison of life to a large 'Mansion of Many Apartments' (only two of which he had encountered by the time of his formulation: the 'infant or thoughtless Chamber' and the 'Chamber of Maiden-Thought', where 'we become intoxicated with the light and the atmosphere'). But these are not conscious showstoppers; they are thinking aloud, and Keats is as ready to make a fool of himself as he is to appear brilliant. His letters show a mind exploding with activity, the big thoughts colliding with the mundane.

His letters were not always so well regarded, but the most famous positive approval (and a resurrection) came from T.S. Eliot, who reviewed a published collection as 'the most notable and most important ever written by any English poet', seeing in them 'what letters ought to be; the fine things come in unexpectedly, neither introduced nor shown out, but between trifle and trifle.'

Keats's letters to Brawne are something else. They are not all possessed of the same exploratory flights of intellect, and they have led some of Keats's greatest admirers, W.H. Auden among them, to believe his mind tainted after 1820 with the

---

* The most accessible collection is *Selected Letters of John Keats* edited by Grant F. Scott, Harvard, 2002.

twin diseases of lovesickness and consumption, and to wish that his love letters had not been published alongside his more literary output. Certainly they can be imperious, histrionic, chastising, contradictory and self-pitying (and Brawne was rightly reticent, and suspicious of his caprices). But they are daring nonetheless, and – in speaking of the universal lightness and illusions of an emotion that has infected men in their twenties since the concept of love began – they achieve their stated aim of immortality. They reveal a true self. Those from 1819, before his sickness took fatal hold, can be beautiful. Keats is unduly fond of himself in his love letters, but it is his muddled soul on show, not his art.

'My dearest Lady,' he wrote from Shanklin on the Isle of Wight on 1 July 1819. The couple had been secretly engaged for several months.

> I am glad I had not an opportunity of sending off a Letter which I wrote for you on Tuesday night. 'Twas too much like one out of Rousseau's Heloise.* I am more reasonable this morning. The morning is the only proper time to write to a beautiful Girl whom I love so much, for at night, when the lonely day has closed, and the lonely, silent, unmusical Chamber is waiting to receive me as into a Sepulchre, then believe me my passion gets entirely the sway, then I would not have you see those Rhapsodies which I once thought it impossible I should ever give way to, and which I have often laughed at in another, for fear you should think me either too unhappy or perhaps a little mad.
>
> I am now at a very pleasant Cottage window, looking onto a beautiful hilly country with a glimpse of the sea; the morning is very fine. I do not know how elastic my spirit might be, what pleasure I might have in living here and breathing and

---

* A highly popular epistolary novel by Jean-Jacques Rousseau from 1761, *Julie or the New Heloise* documented the correspondence between two lovers and referred directly to the letters of Abelard and Heloise.

wandering free as a stag about this beautiful Coast if the remembrance of you did not weigh so upon me. I have never known any unalloy'd Happiness for many days together. The death or sickness of someone has always spoilt my hours, and now when none such troubles oppress me, it is you must confess very hard that another sort of pain should haunt me. Ask yourself, my love, whether you are not very cruel to have so entrammelled me, so destroyed my freedom. Will you confess this in the Letter you must write immediately and do all you can to console me in it? Make it rich as a draught of poppies to intoxicate me. Write the softest words and kiss them that I may at least touch my lips where yours have been.

For myself I know not how to express my devotions to so fair a form: I want a brighter word than bright, a fairer word than fair. I almost wish we were butterflies and liv'd but three summer days.

Three such days with you I could fill with more delight than fifty common years could ever contain . . .

Though I could centre my Happiness in you, I cannot expect to engross your heart so entirely; indeed if I thought you felt as much for me as I do for you at this moment I do not think I could restrain myself from seeing you again tomorrow for the delight of one embrace. But no, I must live upon hope and Chance. In case of the worst that can happen, I shall still love you, but what hatred shall I have for another! . . .

Do write immediately. There is no Post from this Place, so you must address Post Office, Newport, Isle of Wight. I know before night I shall curse myself for having sent you so cold a Letter; yet it is better to do it as much as in my senses as possible. Be as kind as the distance will permit to your

J. Keats

'My dearest Girl,' Keats began in August 1820, in what is believed to be his last letter to Fanny.

I wish you could invent some means to make me at all happy without you. Every hour I am more and more concentrated in you; everything else tastes like chaff in my mouth. I feel it almost impossible to go to Italy. The fact is, I cannot leave you, and shall never taste one minute's content until it pleases chance to let me live with you for good. But I will not go on at this rate. A person in health, as you are, can have no conception of the horrors that nerves and a temper like mine go through . . .

I do not think my health will improve much while I am separated from you. For all this, I am averse to seeing you: I cannot bear flashes of light, and return into my glooms again. I am not so unhappy now as I should be if I had seen you yesterday. To be happy with you seems such an impossibility: it requires a luckier star than mine! It will never be.

I enclose a passage from one of your letters which I want you to alter a little: I want (if you will have it so) the matter expressed less coldly to me.

If my health would bear it, I could write a poem which I have in my head, which would be a consolation for people in such a situation as mine. I would show some one in love, as I am, with a person living in such liberty as you do. Shakespeare always sums up matters in the most sovereign manner. Hamlet's heart was full of such misery as mine is, when he said to Ophelia, 'Go to a nunnery, go, go!' Indeed, I should like to give up the matter at once. I should like to die. I am sickened at the brute world you are smiling with. I hate men, and women more. I see nothing but thorns for the future ...

I wish I was either in your arms full of faith, or that a thunderbolt would strike me.

God bless you. J. K.

It is through Keats's letters that we have one of the great histrionic romances in a romantic century. The poet must have hoped we might remember him this way, despite his requested tombstone inscription that his 'name was writ in water'.

'The fire is at its last click,' he wrote to his brother,

I am sitting with my back to it with one foot rather askew upon the rug and the other with the heel a little elevated from the carpet ... Could I see the same thing done of any great man long since dead it would be a great delight: as to know in what position Shakespeare sat when he wrote 'To be or not to be' – such things become interesting from distance.

The devotions of Robert Browning and Elizabeth Barrett spawned a courtship correspondence no less fiery and rather happier in its ending: as one review of their collected letters concluded, 'Reader, I married you'. It commenced in 1845, and concluded with another fleeing to Italy when her father's disapproval demanded elopement.* One of its joys is its swift 20-month crescendo from endearing fandom to all-consuming craving, from the airiest lines about poetry to the logistics of meeting in secret and the luggage-smuggling that will facilitate their joint escape. Modern readers are within their grip in just three letters:

Robert Browning to Elizabeth Barrett, 10 January 1845: 'I love your verses with all my heart, dear Miss Barrett, – and this is no off-hand complimentary letter that I shall write.'

The following day she replies, 'I thank you, dear Mr Browning, from the bottom of my heart. You meant to give me pleasure by your letter – and even if the object had not been answered, I ought still to thank you. But it is thoroughly answered. Such a letter from such a hand!'

Two days later: 'Dear Miss Barrett, I just shall say, in as few words as I can, that you make me very happy.' His valedictions progress from 'Yours ever faithfully' and 'Ever your most faithfully' (January) to 'Ever yours, dear Miss Barrett' (April) to 'Yours' (May) to 'My love, I am your R.B.' (November).**

When he first wrote, she was the more famous. She had attracted other male admirers with whom she had previously corresponded on literary matters, and she assumed that Browning's correspondence would pan out in the same way. Besides, she liked it like that: a correspondence was the most

---

* The couple chose Italy for the same reason Keats did: she had a lung condition, probably tuberculosis, and sought the warmth of the air in Florence and Rome.
** On Valentine's Day 2012, in a joint venture between Wellesley College and Baylor University, a facsimile of all the Browning/Barrett love letters were made available online for the first time.

- Casa Guidi - June 3 -

My dear Mr. Ruskin   we send to you every
now & then somebody hungry for a touch
from your hand... we also are famished for
it ourselves - But this time, we send
you a man whom you will value per-
-fectly for himself & ~~maybe~~ be kind to
from yourself, quite spontaneously. He
is the American artist, Page, an earnest
simple, noble artist & man, - who carries
his christianity down from his deep
heart to the point of his brush - Draw
him out to talk to you, & you will find
it worth while - He has learnt much
from Swedenborg, & used it in his
ideas upon art - much of it (if new)
may sound to you wild & dreamy.

346

tightly controlled of relationships, the pace and tone malleable, the scholarly flirtation calibrated line by line. Her poor health and overbearing father ensured that letter-writing was the risk-free option; both elements undoubtedly contributed to the grand, Brontë-like gestures of her romance with Browning – the man who swept her away and liberated her passion.

It took more than 20 letters and five months before they met; there would be 574 letters in all before they fled for Europe. Barrett's biographer Alethea Hayter has compared their correspondence to a tennis match, 'the long breathless rally back and forth from every corner of the court ... Excitement and enjoyment shine through their "heart-playing", their absorbed search for the exact word, phrase, image, to express every shade of feeling.' The key line in their correspondence may be the very last that Barrett wrote to Browning as a single woman: 'I begin to think that none are so bold as the timid, when they are fairly roused.' She was referring to the actions of her maid in Wimpole Street, but of course also to herself. We may detect echoes of this in much wartime correspondence: it is not just distance that binds two lovers' letters, but the security of that distance – the fact that the real world does not intrude on an ideal, the possibility of writing perfectly and without looking your target in the eye.

The Barrett-Browning letters facilitate their marriage – which was, by most accounts, a happy one through its 15-year life (Barrett died in 1861) – and they ensure the longevity of their reputations. Even those who cannot quote a line of their poetry beyond 'O, to be in England/ Now that April's there' may know of how their initial intellectual revelations in their letters give way to more instinctual ones, and then to practical considerations of escape, including their rendezvous in a

'An earnest, simple noble artist': The Brownings write to John Ruskin in 1859 about their artist friend William Page.

bookshop and consultations of train timetables. The fact that the letters are often self-conscious and rhetorical (they are both poets after all) does not detract from one's enjoyment any more than a great Rembrandt is dismissed for being too painterly.

And a week after they are married – no more letters.* It is the agonising nature of love that it flourishes best with doubt and poetic imagining, and there is but one hope for the epistolary historian after love-locked correspondents meet: a separation. With Barrett and Browning it never came; but with a few others we have been more fortunate (it's yet another delight of letters – their agony is our pleasure).

Of course, to hope for both an early passion and a prolonged continuation of letters once it subsides is just being greedy; and so it is with fervour that one falls upon the prolonged postal relationship of Henry Miller and Anaïs Nin. They too could be said to have written their most valuable work away from their fictions – Nin in her scandalous diaries, Miller in his copious correspondences with Nin, Lawrence Durrell and many others.

Miller certainly knew the value of communication. Long before he achieved condemnation and literary acclaim with his sexually explicit autobiographical novels, Miller worked for the Western Union Telegraph Company in New York City. In 1920, at the age of 28, he began working as a personnel manager in charge of more than 2,000 uniformed telegraph messengers in the city, a role he held for almost five years. In heightened form the job became the subject of Kafkaesque descriptions in *Tropic of Capricorn*, with Miller depicting

---

* Not that they didn't carry on writing to everyone else (about literary matters, the Crimean War, the Great Exhibition at Crystal Palace).

long days of menacing and senseless monotony as he tried to replace all the people who had quit the day before; like delivering the post, the job was never done. Miller spoke of some telegraph boys who lasted only hours on the job before abandoning their messages in waste bins or the sewers, and he found that colleagues who lasted any length of time had often developed their own swindles, such as shortening a long telegram and pocketing the difference in cost. Miller attempted to reform the system with limited success, and when he quit to become a full-time writer in 1924 with the encouragement of his new (second) wife June he was convinced of two things: the business world, with its insistence on rules and service, wasn't for him; and a 20-cent telegram allowed you just

NIGHT LETTER
THE WESTERN UNION TELEGRAPH COMPANY
INCORPORATED
25,000 OFFICES IN AMERICA   CABLE SERVICE TO ALL THE WORLD
ROBERT C. CLOWRY, PRESIDENT   BELVIDERE BROOKS, GENERAL MANAGER

| RECEIVER'S No. | TIME FILED | | CHECK |

SEND the following NIGHT LETTER subject to the terms on back hereof which are hereby agreed to

"NIGHT LETTERS" EASILY SENT

There are three ways of sending a "Night Letter"—you can hand it in at one of the 25,000 Western Union Offices—you can telephone, or ring a call box, and have a messenger come for it—you can dictate it over the telephone and have it charged in a monthly account.

"Night Letters" are telegraphed at night and delivered the next morning, but they may be sent in at any time during the day or evening, up to midnight.

A fifty word "Night Letter" may be sent at the day rate for ten words, with one-fifth of this rate for each additional ten words.

10 words. For a man who would write long letters every day to a great many people – and could, at the end of his long life, claim to have put more words in the post than any other writer in history – it was no great surprise that he opted for a cheaper and longer-lasting form of getting a message through.

'All I can say is that I am mad about you,' he begins a letter to Anaïs Nin in March 1932, three months after their first meeting. He had already apologised to Nin in a previous letter for sending her an 'avalanche' of mail (the word is apt: she was in Switzerland on a rest cure from her demonic and adulterous crushes, not just on Miller but his wife June too).

The Miller-Nin correspondence initially follows a course we are familiar with: thunderstruck, diehard, sleepless infatuation, combined with the conviction that they are the first true lovers on the planet. There is this from Miller in Paris, also from March 1932:

> Three minutes after you have gone. No I can't restrain it. I tell you what you already know – I love you. It is this I destroyed over and over again. At Dijon I wrote you long passionate letters – if you had remained in Switzerland I would have sent them – but how could I have sent them to Louveciennes? [Where she lived with her husband.]

> Anais I can't say much now – I am in fever. I could scarcely talk to you because I was continually on the point of getting up and throwing my arms around you. I was in hopes you wouldn't have to go home for dinner – that we might go somewhere to dine and dance. You dance – I have dreamed of that over and over again – I dancing with you, or you alone dancing with head thrown back and eyes half shut. You must dance for me that way. That is your Spanish self – your Andalusian blood.

> I am sitting in your place right now and I have raised your glass to my lips. But I am tongue-tied. What you have read to me

'I wrote you long passionate letters': Anaïs Nin and Henry Miller.

is swimming over me. Your language is still more overwhelming than mine. I am a child compared to you, because when the womb in you speaks, it enfolds everything – it is the darkness I adore. You were wrong to think I appreciate the literary value alone. That was my hypocrisy talking. I have not dared until now to say what I think. But I am plunging – you have opened the void for me – there is no holding back.

And this was true: they went at it like an American/French rewrite of Abelard and Heloise, enough heat in their letters to burn down the Louvre, let alone destroy two marriages. They met when they could, and their early literary passions (they were both critically supportive of each other's work) soon engulfed itself in a physical one. Miller was a literary satyr, Nin a sensualist on any sheet that came to hand, and both flew flags for their own particular war of the sexes.

Nin's early letters speak of a similar excitement to Miller's – a *universal* excitement even. There is a well of pleasure to be gained – even 80 years on – from reading her falling in love. It is still March 1932, and she has just been to the *Beggar's Opera* in German with her husband, a banker whom she finds honourable but charmless; she is not much interested in property prices and a predictable future. She thinks of Miller during the opera, of how he has turned her life 'symphonic':

> god, Henry, in you alone I have found the same swelling of enthusiasm, the same quick rising of the blood, the fullness, the fullness . . .

> Before, I almost used to think there was something wrong. Everybody else seemed to have the *brakes on.* A scene in a movie, a voice, a phrase was not for them volcanic. I never feel the brakes. I overflow. And when I feel your excitement about life flaring, next to mine, then it makes me dizzy.

> . . . Do you think we are happy together because we feel we are 'getting somewhere', whereas you had the feeling that with June you were being led into more and more obscurity, mystery, entanglements? And suppose the 'getting somewhere feeling' meant simply reaching a clarity, a knowledge, the very opposite of Dostoevsky – and that the clarity I have I may throw away, discard, repudiate entirely . . . You see, I often return to this conflict – the passion for truth, and also the passion for darkness.

But the desperate needs (and the sexual intimacy that followed) inevitably cooled. Five years after their *coup de foudre* Nin was able to write to Miller of his 'twisted, ingrown, negative love', of a pain no longer exquisite. 'I want to try and explain to you, Henry, how it is you make things so inhuman and unreal that after a while I feel myself drifting away from you, seeking reality and warmth somewhere,' she wrote from Paris in March 1937.

> You repeat over and over again that you need nobody, that you feel fine alone, that you enjoy yourself better without me, that

you are independent and self-sufficient. You not only keep saying it regardless of the effect on me, but you never once make a gesture or a sign like a human being ... Everything in you pushed me away, your collective life, your constant life with others, your incapacity to create nearness or relationship with a person, always with a crowd. I seek, on the contrary, to keep you at the centre of my life ...

The need of expression ... one can put a finger on and say: there it is, it's a heart beating; if I move, this person feels it; if I leave, this person knows it; if I drop away [this person] feels fear. I exist in him, there is something happening there. But when I walk into your place I see the most expressionless face ...

I glanced over what you were writing in *Capricorn*, and there it was, the great anonymous, depersonalized fucking world. Instead of investing each woman with a different face, you take pleasure in reducing all woman to an aperture, to a biological sameness ...

With you and me, I don't understand, because there was no reason for our relationship to be tragic. None, as far as I am concerned. But it has become so for me because you do nothing to make it real. All you do evaporates, dissolves, decomposes it. You volatilize.

Remarkably, perhaps, after these two extremes, what remained between Miller and Nin was something lasting. It was a deep literary groove. He commented on the naivety of her early writing but was a great supporter of what she had shown him of her explicit diaries; her criticisms of his most famous novels were commonly shared by other readers, particularly women. What makes their correspondence compelling is not just their passion, but the fact that there is nothing else. For more than 40 years, and for hundreds of thousands of words, there is no talk of the mundane. There aren't really any pleasantries either, and politeness is supplanted by directness. It is as if we are

always arriving at an action film 30 minutes in, with everything hot and explosive from the start.

Their public notoriety increased with each publication
and each ban or each court case, and they struggled creatively
until the end of their lives (they each remarried, Miller several
times). They saw each other occasionally over their 45-year
friendship, and yet they were bound throughout by their
struggle in writing and by their letters. And it is their letters –
showing their writing and personal lives intermingled – that
stand as their truest and strongest legacy. In the early 1950s,
Anaïs Nin writes with tenderness again, and tries to sum up
their friendship: 'probably if I had the sense of humour I have
today and if you had then the qualities you have today, nothing would have broken.' And in another letter from the same
period: 'I have a feeling we are all going back to Paris ultimately, where we were happiest.'

As is the pattern, most of the Miller-Nin letters were published only after their deaths (Nin's in 1977, Miller's in 1980).*
Nin and Miller both lived long and full lives: their reputations
were secure, as was their notoriety. When the letters emerged,
the philandering, self-delusion and destructiveness of their
earliest correspondence couldn't cause any more damage than
their published writing had already done. Indeed, the reverse
turned out to be true: their letters revealed fuller and richer
selves, and a half-chance at least of understanding wholly
complicated lives.

---

* Miller's letters to Lawrence Durrell, the poet James Laughlin and the painter
Emil Schnellock also make worthwhile reading, tracing (as with the Nin letters)
a proper arc from searing young iconoclasm in Europe to an eventual acceptance
of the world (he writes less, paints more, and, only in late-middle age, finds the
pleasures of solidity and domestication: 'When you surrender, the problem ceases
to exist.').

Days Become Weeks

27 WOOLACOMBE RD, LONDON SE3

21st January 1945

Dearest,

I am hanging on to the old old theory that no news is good news. The papers and wireless say that the exchange of prisoners of war has commenced, am hoping that this affects you, gosh I hope so badly. Churchill said in his speech that prisoners would be coming home and that the truth would come out, just supposing this also affects you. Oh Dear! Is that too much to hope to come home, to see you after all this worry, if it only could be true? I hope you aren't hurt or ill, that you have been warm and at least [had] enough to eat, feel sure you haven't been overfed, for they haven't enough for themselves.

Oh Darling, perhaps it won't be too long before I hear, I wonder how long the exchange will take, they do fiddle so, over these sort of things. What thoughts have you been having during all this long time? About Greece, I mean, I would so like to know, for it is such a muddle, politicians lie so glibly about such important things; doesn't make post war years look very hopeful.

Just another missive, Christopher Darling – Keep Safe. I Love You.

Bessie.

27 WOOLACOMBE RD, LONDON SE3

26 January 1945

Dearest,

I have studied all the newspapers, but there isn't any reference to prisoners in Greece. Surely there will be something in the press when prisoners are exchanged, a few small exchanges have been made, but nothing about the 600 prisoners that the RAF have been dropping supplies to. Unless I have missed something in a corner – don't think so.

Where oh where are you Christopher my Darling, days have become weeks and still no news. I can't settle down to read, not even in the train, so I am knitting up into vests the spurned coupon-free cotton-cum-wool instead of writing loving letters to you, am I bottled up –

I Love You.

Bessie.

~~~~~~~~~~~~~~~~

14232134 SIGMN. BARKER H.C., 30 WING
SIGNAL SECTION, G COY., AIR FORMATION
SIGNALS, CMF.

24 January 1945

[Following a telegram informing Bessie he was safe.]

My dear Bessie,

Technically this is my second day of Freedom though I have only just got off the truck which has carried Bert and myself through the cold Greek mountains over tracks that once were roads, and now, with the thaw, are becoming quagmires. The most satisfactory journey of my life. Now, the warm hands of the British Army are about us and we are as comfortable as possible.

The great worry of my non-arriving letters probably cannot be effaced from your 'system'. I must have added many grey hairs to those you have already. But now you can stop worrying, and get drunk tonight with easy conscience. (I have happily gulped two rum issues since I was released.)

Will write you very fully later. Use the usual address, and be sure I shall write as often as I am able.

Our future moves are a matter of conjecture. Most of the optimists think we will be coming home. If you think we should there is nothing to stop you writing to the Prime Minister, suggesting our return to allay relatives' anxiety. Verb sap.*

Forgive this note. I hope you are well and undisturbed by aerial terrors.

I love you.

Chris

27 WOOLACOMBE RD, LONDON SE3

1st February 1945

My Darling,

This is so wonderful. Oh Gosh! Christopher, I have just received your telegram – how can I tell you how beautiful

* *Verbum sapienti sat est*, meaning 'a word is enough to the wise' or 'enough said'.

the world is, contact again with you, contact with life – Oh Darling of my heart. I did not realise what a benumbed state I had been reduced to, it took about a quarter of an hour to sink in, I did not whoop or prance but my knees went weak, my tummy turned over, since when I have been grinning happily to myself with a beautiful inward pleasure. FREE, FIT and WELL, such wonderful words, the relief from these last weeks of possible sickness, you Blessed Darling, I just haven't any words, no words Christopher, just all bubbles and tremblings. I had been cheering up because as there was no news, felt you just must be a prisoner, but you know how your mind keeps worrying away in circles at all sorts of awful possibilities, well that's what mine had been doing, and now Golly – how I love you!

Ouch. I want to hug you to bits, eat you, come to my arms you bundle of charms. Hurry up mail, I want to hear your voice again, hear you, loving me, wanting me as always. I have not been able to look at your photos or read your letters, much too painful, but I have now, I have now – you know you have been with me in all these bad days, I used to talk to you, inside myself, and I always made you answer that you were alright, and I used to hope that it was the right answer. Am I a silly dope? But I have a few more white hairs. You are there, you are alive. You are in this world with me, we are together, we, we, we, US. Deep breath here!

Dearie me, things are looking up, though this business of Germany fighting to the last ditch sounds rather appalling. Some silly blighter, an MP too, was asking for indiscriminate bombing of Germany, I should have thought what was happening now was grim enough to satisfy even the most bloodthirsty. I really can't understand how Russia has managed to do this, what about supplies etc, surely she can't go on much farther, good luck to her if she can, but what a performance?

I feel in that excited state that anything can happen any moment, something is in the air, with all this news from everywhere. I really should say that it's me that is in the air, bounce, bounce, bounce. I am going to the pictures with Iris tomorrow, golly, I shall have to treat her. It's so wonderful, you are wonderful, the world is wonderful, everything is wonderful. Please come home, home, home. Please do, Darling. Such dreams of our being – Oh My Love.

I Love You.

Bessie.

Chapter Fourteen

The Modern Master

Is it possible to write the perfect letter? Is it possible to even consider writing such a thing?

In the 1970s at Bedales, a vaguely alternative public school in Hampshire where a lot of famous parents sent their children, the school secretary would gather the morning post, walk past the classrooms, cross the orchard and enter the quad of the main building, and at the far side by the kitchens there would be a wooden tray with sorting slots arranged alphabetically. At 10.55 – mid-morning break – pupils would get drinks and a snack and look for mail, which, if they were lucky that day, they would take to their dorm room or the library to read.

Towards the end of the summer term in 1975, Frieda Hughes, 15, went to the far end of the quad to pick up a letter from Devon.

Dear Frieda,

How did the exams go? Did you manage to get into a nice fluent gallop with your answers?

The rain came just as we were finishing loading the bales – we had a wild rush to get them in, bales into the landrover, bales into Jean and Ian's van, bales into the horsebox, bales into our ears, bales into the backs of our necks, bales in our boots, bales down our shirts. So we tottered home towering & trembling & tilting & toppling & teetering. And there in front of us was some other tractor creeping along with a trailer loaded twice as high as ours, like a skyscraper. All over the countryside there were desperate tractors crawling home under impossible last loads in the very green rain.

The rain is making everything grow again. Including your alpine strawberries, which are luscious – the ones the birds don't get. Since we mowed that jungle of weed over the tennis court and the upper part of the orchard, there seem to be whole flocks of blackbirds and thrushes hunting there. And the doves. And Ginger-dandelion. He's discovered a great metropolis of mice up there, that were beyond him before. He's a fine mobile ginger flower.

It's still raining, Thursday evening.

. . . Well, here we are, all aches and stretched joints, like broken down five bar gates, after our baling.

And here are all the holidaymakers, sitting in their sauna-bath cars under the downpour, staring at the sea, with their transistors turned up, & their ice-cream running down to their elbows, like cars stuck in a car washer. See you very soon.

love, Daddy

Ted Hughes wrote about the baling again in his poem 'Last Load' in *Moortown*, but the verse may seem less necessary to us now, now that we have the letter. It is not *the* perfect letter, and it probably wouldn't rank in the top 100 letters that Ted Hughes wrote in his lifetime, but it is still a very fine one. It is lovely to read now, almost 40 years on, the sender dead, the cat no longer finding mice, and the recipient a middle-aged painter, because it is funny, observant, personal, vivid and warm. It is also, of course, high-school poetic: his letters were making hay.

There is alliteration and exaggeration and people doing animal-like things while animals go hunting, and the whole letter has the rhythm of a pecking bird, coming back to a point for effect. Sometimes the words are perfect and clear (the luscious strawberries), and sometimes they are perfect and arresting (the very green rain).

But the letter works so well because it conjures up so many images on a single sheet. The hay baling is hot, rushed, scratchy and slightly obsessional all over Devon; the land is lushly and soakily productive; those who work it are honestly

'Very literary swaggering': Ted Hughes in 1960.

worn; that five-bar gate is still creaky and stiff; the poor tourists are trapped in steamed-up cars – the whole day summed up swiftly in a dutiful hand and then shared as a gift, and in so doing capturing both a personal picture and a documentary record. (No one listens to 'transistors' any more.) How attractive did Hughes find this life? He claimed elsewhere that Devon was a respite from the real world in London, but also, when he escaped to Yorkshire, that it was too deadening for good work. It probably didn't seem too appealing to a teenager at the dawn of punk.

The letter forms part of an invaluable literary archive at Emory University in Atlanta, Georgia. But the main question is: could this letter have been written as an email? I don't think so. It's too thoughtfully composed, too layered and laden. It's not self-conscious; it's just a proper piece of work, homey and chatty and naturally lyrical, and I think as an email it would have appeared too writerly, too out of step with the technology that created it. If it *had* been an email, would Frieda have cherished and kept it? If it had been an email, would we have ever found out about it? And should we have done?

Ted Hughes never sent email. He never used a computer either. He distrusted these things, even though, by the time he died in 1998, the potential for sending one-click messages from a screen had existed for almost a decade. He was one of the last great writers to reject the new medium as something superfluous to his needs. We know this because Christopher Reid, Hughes's editor at Faber and Faber for the last eight years of his life, says he received from Hughes only letters at a time when there were already easier options; most writers who still shun the word processor in favour of a legal pad or an Underwood 5 for their proper work have long succumbed to email as a form of easy communication. ('He was rather averse to any kind of mechanical means of writing,' Reid told me when we spoke on the phone, which serves well enough as a summation of everything he produced.)

In 1995, Hughes was asked by the *Paris Review* what tools he needed to complete his work, and he replied, 'Just a pen.' He says he made an interesting discovery about himself when he worked as a script reader for a film company in his mid-twenties. He was writing directly into a typewriter for the first time, and he noticed that his sentences had become three times as long: 'My subordinate clauses flowered and multiplied and ramified away down the length of the page.'

Then he made another discovery. For several years he was a judge on the W.H. Smith children's writing prize. In the early days of the competition most of the entries were just a few pages long, but in the 1980s they suddenly started stretching to 70 or 80 pages. They were usually fluent and commanding, but they were 'without exception strangely boring'. Not long afterwards he found that these stories were all composed on word processors, and reasoned that as the tools for putting words on a page 'become more flexible and externalized, the writer can get down almost every thought or every extension of thought.' Rather than being an advantage, Hughes found 'it just extends everything slightly too much. Every sentence is too long. Everything is taken a bit too far, too attenuated.' But the old-fashioned alternative continued to exert the same 'terrible resistance': when writing by pen, 'every year of your life is right there, wired into the communication between your brain and your writing hand . . . As you force your expression against that built-in resistance, things become automatically more compressed, more summary and, perhaps, psycho-logically denser.' He wondered whether this was perhaps an age thing: whether, if your first experience of writing is on a computer screen, your wiring is necessarily different, dictated by a different syntactic experience in the brain. The brain-to-hand synapses aren't absent from computer work, when one is merely tapping a keyboard. 'Maybe the crucial element in handwriting is that the hand is simultaneously drawing.'

Letters of Ted Hughes was published in 2007 and is one of the great modern collections. (It's not *The Letters of Ted Hughes*, because that might denote some sort of completion or finality. This collection runs to 700 pages; its editor says the complete letters may fill four volumes.) The author didn't write his memoirs (or at least not in prose), and no full biography yet exists (his wife Carol Hughes announced in 2013 that she planned to write her memoirs before she forgot what they were). But the letters may be all you really need. The collection functions as a narrative of a life (it pulls you through all the career shunts and geographical turns, all the emotional hotspots), but it also lays a clear path for the reader to follow his progression as a writer. There is so much passionate thinking about the creative process, so much hard-won wisdom about the core of living and the behaviour of others, that when one learns about this particular life it is hard not to reflect upon one's own. Hughes described letter-writing as 'excellent training for conversation with the world', but it is easy to believe that his letters were not training at all; they were the entire polished dialogue.

He had an apprenticeship of sorts. 'Those early letters, when he's writing to Edna Wholey, the slightly older woman with whom he's kind of infatuated, they're very literary swaggering aren't they?' Reid suggests. 'They're him swanking and saying, "Here I am – I can be clever, I can be clever and wise".' Here, still a teenager in 1947, proudly, comically and incomprehensibly pretentious, he is indeed writing just for effect.

Cherie Edna,

I have seen many strange things in my 17 years . . .

I have seen things, which, when placed before a camera that memories for posterity may wonder at their form, invariably shattered the lens, burnt the film and slew the photographer. I have seen things which, when taken within the city limits (To the extreme personal peril of the man responsible) stopped all traffic in the streets, paralysed the policeman and covered with green mould the money in the tills inside the shops.

His point, and it's some time coming, after many other things he's seen, is that all these things can't stack up against the 'terror that is Edna,' not exactly something which might endear her to him. If the approach is a little reminiscent of Dylan's biblical-nuclear 'A Hard Rain's A-Gonna Fall', the rain does indeed arrive some two years later, when Hughes is in RAF uniform in barracks on Merseyside. And it's a fairly lyrical rendition: 'Edna, I've seen rain and I tell you this isn't rain, – a steady river, well laced with ice, tempest and thunder, covers all this land, and what isn't concrete has reverted to original chaos of mud water fire and air. Morning and evening its one soak and the sun's more and less a sponge.'

'Once he learnt "how to do" a letter,' his editor says, 'the sense of how you make a letter interesting, whatever the topic, whether it's writing to his son Nicholas to sort out a problem, or whether it's just reporting a bit of literary gossip, he knows how to do it, he's learned the technique.'

The first proper example of this comes in letters to his brother and sister-in-law Gerald and Joan Hughes, and to his sister Olwyn. There is no side to them, and they carry no attempt to impress. Instead they are straightforward, practical and gently scheming. In October 1955 Hughes is considering a property scheme that will earn him enough to write without diversion.

My life lately has been such a turmoil I haven't felt like writing to anyone, though I'm sure I don't have to wait til I have special news . . .

At present I work as a security guard – sitting in a little office at a girder factory all night – I spend the whole time writing and I draw £8 a week, so it's OK till I get something better. I feel very angry at the bottom though . . .

My idea is to save everything for about five years, then buy a house in Oxford or Cambridge & farm it out to students & nurses at £3 a room – offer a landlady free living in the basement. One of my acquaintances does this, and spends his time pottering about the world on the income. Then two and three houses. What different lives we would lead if we had a bit of money.

Early the next year, at the age of 25, we glimpse both ambition and a hint of the extraordinary. 'I have discovered my secret,' he wrote to Olwyn,

I only write poems when I am busy writing prose at the same time, and also when I am taking regular exercise. I published one or two poems in a magazine which were not very satisfactory, but they drew some very gratifying criticisms from the right kind of people. If I could write whole poems as good as odd little bits I'm sure I really would have something, and something quite different from the meanness and deadness of almost all modern verse – with which I feel not the slightest affinity.

Within a few weeks his life had changed forever. At the end of February 1956 he met an American woman at a raucous party to launch a Cambridge magazine he contributed to with his friend Lucas Myers, and three weeks later he is asking for news.

Dear Luke,

I shall expect you any day.

If you have time, drop me a note and tell me when you are coming. If you see Sylvia Plath, ask her if she's coming up to London, give her my address. Get her somehow, free lodgings for her as for you.

(He described his plans to go to Australia on a free passage as soon as possible, but that was before his meeting with Plath junked his schedule.)

See you this week sometime.

Don't forget Sylvia, and discretion.

Ted

It took another 42 years for Hughes to express publicly all his joys and frustrations with Sylvia, and when he did so he elevated the form of the letter to the level of poetry. *Birthday Letters*, his celebration/explanation/evisceration of his life with Sylvia Plath, became an instant bestseller on publication in 1998, and is regarded by some as his greatest work. Written over about 25 years, the 88 poems – the same number as there are constellations, the number also representing a multiplication of Kabalistic ritual, none of this lost on the poet – have neither greetings nor sign-offs, but they are written with enough spontaneous eloquence for the reader to believe that Hughes was not using the word 'letter' in his title in a purely figurative way: they are indeed personal and directed addresses, albeit of the rhetorical, expository and open sort, and of a sort that have the tang of legal 'he-said, she-said' correspondence about them (the title 'Birthday Letters' on the other hand makes a wider point, given that so much about Plath stacks up against her death rather than her birth). Of the form, Hughes wrote to Seamus Heaney shortly before publication that 'I hit on the direct letter as an illegal private transaction between her & me – then simply followed the clues, and they piled up'. Heaney reckoned that 'to read [*Birthday Letters*] is to experience the psychic experience of "the bends". It takes you down to levels of pressure where the undertruths of sadness and endurance leave you gasping.' The red inferno of the book jacket was painted by Frieda Hughes.

Birthday Letters covers not only Hughes and Plath during their courtship and marriage, but Plath's many torments and their aftershocks. In many of his verses he analyses *her* verses, like letters bouncing back and forth. Writing in the *New Yorker*, Al Alvarez, once a close friend of both poets when he was the influential poetry editor of the *Observer* in the 1960s, clocks the unique biographical picture of Plath that Hughes has unleashed, just as he once unleashed her malign genius. 'He takes the bare bones on which the biographies have been hung – Cambridge, Spain, America, Devon – and does what no biographer, however diligent and impartial, could ever do: he describes what it felt like to be there with her.'

Birthday Letters suggests it felt fairly terrifying, and no less so with the passage of time. As readers we feel privileged for the insight, and – more than with his actual letters to the living – we feel as if we're intruding on private matters. It was this, perhaps more than anything, that helped Christopher Reid press on with his own collection. 'To my mind the publication of *Birthday Letters* gave me licence to enter the same territory, and to try to do everything as tactfully and as kindly as Ted would have wished.'

He began compiling the letters in 2003, four years before publication. 'What happened was that Carol, his widow, wrote to a number of people who had had associations with Ted, and asked, "What do I do next, how do I handle future publications?" I wrote back, and I imagine other people did too, saying, "actually a volume of letters would be amazing, and change the public notion of Ted completely, and give people a truer picture". About nine months later she came to me and asked whether I would think of doing a volume, and how could I say no?'

Reid had never edited a collection of letters before, but he did play a significant role in the publication of the Philip Larkin letters following his death in 1985, one of his first jobs as poetry editor. 'Anthony Thwaite [the man commissioned to edit Larkin's correspondence] came in with a great bag of letters that would have made a volume of some 2,000 pages. He said, "I'm up against a brick wall – I don't know how to make this any smaller." And obviously it had to be smaller. As I came to it fresh it was much easier for me. I just slashed out letters which would have been perfectly printable but there were just too many. So a cruel culling had to be done.

'When I came to do Ted I had a similar problem. I had about 2,000 pages of brilliant stuff, and I just thought, "Well how do I make something that's publishable out of this?" What I learned was that when you're making such a drastic selection, it helps to keep in mind that there's a story being implied by the letters if they're in chronological order, implied if not actually stated, and that actually keeps your mind on the straight and narrow. You're just thinking, "Story, narrative." That's the most sensible guiding principle – you don't make a leap from one thing to another thing entirely different – you try to smooth things out, paint the fullest picture. But I thought, "This is a literary story, rather than a story about tragedies and love affairs. Although very obviously they come into the picture."'

The vast majority of the letters were handwritten, and there were no carbon copies. So how does one gather such a collection?

Mostly by post. Reid visited Carol Hughes at Court Green, her home with Ted where she still lives, and she gave him Ted's address book. 'I copied out as many addresses as I thought might be useful, which was pretty well nearly all of them. And then I just wrote to everybody. I got a fairly good response. A lot of people wrote back saying, "We were friends but we didn't correspond", and one or two people said, "I regard this as an intrusion on Ted's privacy and I'm not going to help you". I thought that was fair enough. I think they were being protective of Ted. I can think of one or two cases where I doubted the motive, but in most cases, and there were half a dozen at the very most, they'd seen what a rough time he'd had when his privacy had been breached in his own lifetime, and they thought, "May he rest in peace and we can keep on protecting him." I didn't do much arguing with people. In most cases I don't imagine that I missed a great deal. I may have done.'

That first trawl landed him with at least half of what he wanted. He also visited the collections at university archives and posted a request for letters in the *Times Literary Supplement*. 'I did tell people not to send originals but to send photocopies, although one or two disobeyed me. I did worry about my custodianship of them – some of them were very frail and vulnerable. But it was thrilling enough to see Ted's hand in photocopy. It varied a great deal, and the hand of a person tells you a lot about their emotional state and circumstances – you get plenty of information about that that you don't get from a typewriter or email.'

The collection of letters was published to widespread acclaim, but the early focus – the glare, really – was on one thing: on what Hughes, in a letter to the *Guardian* and elsewhere, had called the public's 'fantasia' with Sylvia Plath, by which he meant the volatility of her torment, the occasion of her death, her mythically heroic life beyond it, and the demonisation of her supposed tormentor (Hughes). And there was much to get excited about. Hughes had maintained an exasperated public silence about Plath, for he soon became aware that almost everyone regarded anything he said as self-serving. Apart from the poetry he was writing in secret, Hughes made it clear that he had officially withdrawn from the Plath industry.

But now the letters to Plath enriched the picture beyond measure. His first letters to her were full-blooded, hurtling and vulnerable. We read them now with too much baggage, but they still disarm with their freshness and momentum. And so much happens so fast. In the first, from March 1956, he writes:

> Sylvia,
>
> That night was nothing but getting to know how smooth your body is. The memory of it goes through me like brandy.

About a fortnight later:

> Sylvia,
>
> On Friday I shall be home about 8 – expect you then.
>
> On the principle that to every sentence of prose there should be six of verse –
>
> *Ridiculous to call it love.*
> *Even so, fearfully I did sound*
> *Your absence, as one shot down feels to the wound,*
> *Knowing himself alive . . .*

A month on, on 22 May 1956, he writes to his sister Olwyn:

> I have met a first-rate American poetess. She really is good. Certainly one of the best female poets I ever read, and a damned sight better than the run of good male. Her main enthusiasm at present is me, and she thinks my verses are as good as I think they are and has accordingly and efficiently dispatched about twenty five to various immensely paying American Mags.

The pair married secretly three weeks later. Her mailings paid off, with Hughes winning a prize not long afterwards that kick-started his career. In the same letter, his work perhaps set free by love, he concludes that he is 'miserable and fit for nothing if I don't write continuously. I shall from now on shape my life round writing instead of squeezing writing into my life whenever I can.'

The couple were separated after their marriage – Hughes living with his parents in Yorkshire, Plath living as a student in Cambridge. It is now – in the autumn of 1956, when all the brief extracts below were written – that their correspondence flourished, as both energised careers begin to take off. She has poems published in influential magazines, he is writing poetry, fables and a play, and there's a sense of 'us against the world'. His greetings are still crush-like: 'Darling Sylvia Push-Kishy'; 'Dearest Sylvia kish and puss and ponk'. His tone is all thrill, the God-like Hughes (as Plath described him to her mother) brought down to the level of mortal teenage lovesickness. He writes of the rabbits he saw on his walks, the Yeats he is reading for an hour a day, and what the horoscope has in store for them – this latter news brought forth like an act from the grand stage at Maskelyne's Theatre of Mystery: 'Sums of money, heavy expenditure, outbursts of passion all likely it says as always. I shall buy no more but go now on my own predictions where I can. One excellent thing I predict about you is that you will be famous and another is that you come into vast fortunes and happiness by marriage to an amazing strange provider of these.'

But there is unease too, a vague admonition. 'I must go to Spain,' he writes at the beginning of October. 'Then we shall have all our lives. You keep watch on our marriage Sylvia as well as I shall and there is no reason we shouldn't be as happy as we have said we shall be. Don't let any stupid thing interfere. Goodnight darling darling darling darling'

Frequently he records the joy in receiving her letters.

Sometimes a new letter arrives while he is in the middle of a reply to an earlier one. In this alone their letters are typical; a passion in ink, both showy and tender, that marks out exploratory passions. The value that the letters hold to Hughes are immediate – their current news, their current crush – but Hughes sees that they may also be valuable in the future; not for the biographer or a collector at auction, but for their children. On 3 October 1956 he writes to Sylvia of wasting a day doing nothing, roused only 'by the nearest thing to your own ponky warmth, which was the wonderful letter. A relic for our fifteenth child's fifteenth child.' If we read these letters unencumbered, we could well ask: why shouldn't their love endure?

Hughes's letters immediately following Plath's death are amongst the plainest and shortest he composed. They are not literary affairs, and, as far as one can read, they were not written with posterity or reputation in mind. But they have, instantly upon publication, taken on the mantle of historical documents. 'Dear Olwyn,' he wrote a day or two after Plath's death on 11 February 1963,

> On Monday morning, at about 6 a.m. Sylvia gassed herself. The funeral's in Heptonstall next Monday.
>
> She asked me for help, as she so often has. I was the only person who could have helped her, and the only person so jaded by her states & demands that I could not recognise when she really needed it.
>
> I'll write more later,
>
> Love
>
> Ted

And then to their friends Daniel and Helga Huws shortly afterwards:

Dear Dan & Helga,

Sylvia killed herself on Monday morning.

She seemed to be getting in good shape, she was writing again, she was making enough money, getting all sorts of commissions, good reviews for her novel – then a series of things, solicitors letters etc, piled up, she flared up, the doctor put her on very heavy sedatives – and in the gap between one pill and the next she turned on the oven, and gassed herself. A nurse was to arrive at 9 a.m. – couldn't get in, & it was 11 a.m. before they finally got to Sylvia. She was still warm.

The Funeral's in Yorkshire on Monday.

I was the one who could have helped her, and the only one that couldn't see that she really needed it this time. No doubt where the blame lies.

I shall look after Frieda & Nick here, & get a Nurse of some sort.

Ted

These letters might have served his reputation well had they been made public at the time of writing, but that would have given them precisely the sort of self-justifying air his detractors accused him of. More than a month after her death he wrote to Plath's mother Aurelia, and there is a timid, regretful and still grief-stricken tone. But he was already writing against a reputation created by letters from Plath, a pre-emptive reconciliation:

Dear Aurelia,

It has not been possible for me to write this letter before now.

... I shall never get over the shock and I don't particularly want to. I've seen the letters Sylvia wrote to my parents, and I imagine she wrote similar ones to you, or worse.

... We were utterly blind, we were both desperate, stupid and proud – and the pride made us oblique, she especially so. I know Sylvia was so made that she had to mete out terrible punishment to the people she most loved, but everybody is a little bit like that, and it needed only intelligence on my part to deal with it. But the difficulties caused by that, the fact that on the surface the situation was no more difficult than the normal one for separated couples – it was better than most in that she had money, fame, prospering plans and many friends – all these things delayed the workings of our conciliation.

I don't want ever to be forgiven. I don't mean that I shall become a public shrine of mourning and remorse, I would sooner become the opposite. But if there is an eternity, I am damned in it.

To us now, weighing the value of letters through years, this is another revelation: letters change their power (to shock, to explain, to placate) over time; the expectation that they become less powerful is – only too clearly here – plainly reversed. At the time he wrote of his wife's death, letters were not history-in-the-making for Hughes; they were private matters, the full fantasia not yet begun. Things changed after it did: letters became tipped arrows.

When Hughes wrote to Frieda about hay-baling in 1975, he was shielding her from other things on his mind. Only a few weeks before, he had written to Aurelia Plath in an attempt to contain the publication of Plath's own letters. After ten months of apparently amicable negotiations by letter and phone with Aurelia and Frances McCullough (the editor of the letters at publishers Harper & Row), solicitors have become involved. Hughes feels his attempt at control slipping from his grasp, and at the end of April 1975 he repeats what he had requested when he first saw a rough assemblage of Plath's letters in the summer of the previous year. It's an attempt to protect his own privacy and that of his children and their friends, but in so doing he is curtailing, and perhaps corrupting the true record.*

> I'd be very grateful Aurelia if you could ask your lawyers to make the necessary moves on the two points I've mentioned. First of all, the agreement about not publishing in England except in a form I've approved (that would be called an abbreviated version of your book for English readers and the friends of Sylvia's children). Second, that you allow me to settle with Frances exactly which and which parts of the letters describing Sylvia's first meeting with me we cut out. I'm sure you like those letters, but you will see they are for me somewhat sacred documents which I would prefer not to have every kid and viperous reviewer and thesis writer pawing over.

Plath's *Letters Home* was published by Harper & Row in 1975 and by Faber in the UK the following spring. We do not know – because we don't have the first draft of the collection – how many letters Hughes succeeded in withdrawing from the British edition, nor the extent of his edits in both editions. But it is not a short book, running to 500 pages. Plath is not as good a letter-writer as Hughes – that is to say, she is neither as studied at it nor, paradoxically, as relaxed. Her imagery is not as intense, and there is a great neediness too. But if it often seems as if she is straining for effect, either to impress her reader or prove something to herself, there is also more raw emotion – more unfettered gusto, more exclamation marks – on display when she writes to others (her mother, her brother Warren) than Hughes manages when he writes to anyone but Plath.

* This letter, and others to Aurelia Plath, reside in the Lilly Library at Indiana University in Bloomington.

Her first account of him to her mother may be one of the most frequently quoted passages of modern breathlessness: 'I met the strongest man in the world, ex-Cambridge, brilliant poet whose work I loved before I met him, a large, hulking, healthy Adam, half-French, half Irish (and a good deal of Yorkshire farming stock, too), with a voice like the thunder of God – a singer, story-teller, lion and world-wanderer, a vagabond who will never stop.'

But this idolatry passage has a preceding line that is less familiar: 'The most shattering thing is that in the last two months I have fallen terribly in love, which can only lead to great hurt.'

Her letters in *Letters Home* are more domesticated than Hughes's, and more descriptive of the daily round. The account of a gentle outing on 31 March 1960 tells of a

Daffodils and smiles: Sylvia Plath with Frieda and Nick in the early 1960s.

natural and treasured freedom she may have detected was drifting away: 'Ted and I took a lovely, quiet walk this evening under the thin new moon, over the magic landscape of Primrose Hill and Regent's Park; all blue and misty, the buds a kind of nimbus of green on the thorn trees, daffodils and blue squills out on the lawns and the silhouettes of wood pigeons roosting in the trees.'

Perhaps it was a bliss she would never quite know again. The following day, at 1.15 p.m., she wrote to her mother again, filling in the detail of news she had just communicated by telephone.

> Ted brought me breakfast – I'd vomited up all that meat loaf at the start of labor – and a tuna salad, cheese and V-8 lunch, which I have just finished with gusto. I feel light and thin as a feather. The baby is, as I told you, 7 pounds, 4 ounces, 21 inches long and, alas, she has my nose! On her, though, it seems quite beautiful. [Her birth was a fairly straightforward affair, with Hughes in attendance throughout.] Well, I have never been so happy in my life. The whole American rigmarole of hospitals, doctors' bills, cuts and stitches, anesthesia etc., seems a nightmare well left behind. The midwife came a second time at 11 a.m. and will come again at tea time to wash me and care for the baby.

She signed off with love from Sivvy (her childhood nickname), from Ted, and, newly blinking in the light, from Frieda Hughes.

Hughes does not write often about letters as a form or a tool, for the same reason that a squirrel rarely contemplates trees; they are so much a natural part of his world. But there is one notable exception, an observation that underlines the power of the letter to come back at you, to harm the future.

On 9 February 1964, one year after Plath's suicide, the emotional exhumation in full dig, he wrote to the woman who catalysed their break-up. Assia Wevill was described by Hughes as dark and dangerous, and he detected that their letters held similarly combustible properties. 'Sweetmouth,' he began, 'all our difficulties blow up out of these long absences.' She was in London expecting her only child, Shura, while he was in Devon, and things were clearly tempestuous when they spoke on the phone.

'Do you know what oppresses me?' Hughes asked.

the thought that you save my letters. You said recently – I forget what, but enough to make me think some day somebody might get hold of those letters & make hay. Assia, I'm foolishly oppressed enough as it is with bloody eavesdroppers & filchers & greedy curiosity, & if you're going to be sitting on all that for some Suzette suddenly to lay her hands on, then I can't write freely.

This is the first and only indication we have of Hughes holding back his pen, but he claims he's been doing it for a while.

As it is I'm always expecting my notes to get intercepted so I don't write a fraction of what I would.

Past experience is bad enough to cope with, but it clears itself – it doesn't really oppose our present lives, whereas those letters & that diary of yours do. They're in our way. They've already caused enough trouble. So please burn all my letters.

If it ever strikes you that my letters are cool or cramped, now you know why. In fact, in my letters I sometimes get perverse about that reader over your shoulder.

He may be talking about you and me here. Of course, she didn't burn his letters. The week before, he wrote about getting the flu, with an interesting side-effect. 'The train back was tropical forest inside. Arctic outside – so yesterday dragged by half-conscious, – today's a sore throat, & Monday will be a cough with pains, & Tuesday tuberculosis – Anyway, it's good for letters. My life has gone over completely to the production of letters.'

So what makes Ted Hughes's letters so compelling, the ones that got through? And what makes them, like the letter to Frieda, still so alive decades after he dropped them in the post? One answer is that they were essential in the development of character and ideas, a working out. There was news too, but seldom mundanity. As his fame and public stature grew, the letters became more self-aware, more conscious of the future biographer's drumming fingers; the belief that an honest letter may not also be a self-serving one is illusory, and no letter-writer, famous or not, could claim otherwise.

But imagine trying to describe a whole life without them. Despite their limitations, letters are still, in the parlance of the rapper, dropped bombs – explosions of life and criticism, urgent observations, repeated evidence of a questing, clarifying mind – and, in Hughes's case, certainly highly pleasurable. The poet Simon Armitage, to whom Hughes wrote towards the end of his life, has written of the thrill of finding a hand-written envelope on the doormat with a Devon postmark: there was always going to be something vital in there. In the introduction to his collection, Christopher Reid writes of receiving his own letters from Hughes with no less delight: 'They were like none I had ever received before. Dealing with publishing affairs, they were invariably direct and business-like, with an extra ingredient of confidentiality and candour that at first surprised me. In addition, though – the extra extra

*'Luxury is stuffed down your throat': Ted and Sylvia write
to Olwyn Hughes.*

– they were written with so much more concentration, force, choiceness of expression, vocal immediacy, grace and wit than the occasion usually, if ever, demanded.' Above all, Reid found them 'generous'.

In the archives at Faber there is a perfect example of just such a letter. *A Choice of Shakespeare's Verse*, chosen by Hughes, was originally published in 1970 but had now been republished, and he was not impressed with the results.

'Between you and me Christopher,' he writes, (a phrase always guaranteed to engender a large readership)

> handling the 1970 Shakespeare paperback Choice and the 1991, leafing through them as a reader might, aren't you startled at the change – typeface half the size, book twice the thickness and weight. Instead of a subtle, elegant bold typeface that enfolds the whole nervous system like a bedful of Geisha girls – a hard spattering of gravel from under the back wheels of an articulated truck on a dark night.

Had his letter been a poem, the image of the truck may have been reworked before we knew about it. But because it is a letter, we know about it. 'Back wheels of an articulated truck wouldn't spatter, would they. Back wheels of an Autobahn bus maybe, the reader a sort of racing cyclist tucked in behind, gulping the carbon monoxide, and all these gravelly letters coming up between his teeth and under his eyelids.'

'What Ted Hughes is doing with his letters is keeping trim,' Reid says, 'and the same with Henry James and Virginia Woolf. They're writing for the sake of writing, by and large at the best of their ability. And then there's the intimacies you wouldn't get in a work of literary fiction. But that's less important to me than just hearing the sound of the voice.'

Reid also noticed something else: Hughes's letters almost always ended, perfectly formed, at the foot of the page. As with a good verse, nothing is wasted; this is not a consideration we require with email. 'I think in a case like his,' Reid says, 'when you're half way down the last page you're thinking, "the coda has got to happen now". So you get into the right gear for that. Something like a musician – a sense of shape comes into play.'

The letters in Reid's 2007 collection are not the final word – far from it. In 2010, the British Library purchased (for £29,500) a great box of tricks from Olwyn Hughes, including an unpublished play, early drafts of poems that later appeared in *Lupercal* and *The Colossus*, and 41 letters written between 1954 and 1964, a few written by Hughes and Plath jointly. Writing from Massachusetts in 1957, he observed how 'luxury is stuffed down your throat – a mass-produced luxury – till you feel you'd rather be rolling in the mud and eating that'.

Perhaps one day, with all letters gathered and sold, there

will be the definitive collection.* Not that Christopher Reid hasn't already been pushing for one. 'I had been attempting to persuade all those the people with an interest in it to do a much more complete Ted Hughes Letters. Not to be edited by me, because I've done my bit with him, but it seemed to me that it would be the ideal project for some young academic who would give 10 years of their life to putting everything in order. But I've given up now because publishers aren't interested, the universities who hold these letters aren't terribly interested. It's the longer vision that's lacking – they can't see beyond the horizon of a couple of years, and the idea of commissioning something that could take much longer than that just doesn't fit with the publishing mentality.'

Should we regret such a shift in values? Or the fact that the *Observer* no longer has a poetry editor? Is Hughes not worthy of the further attention, or is it that we no longer have the appetite, patience or purse for a life in letters in such detail?

'One day it will happen I don't doubt,' Reid says of the grander Hughes project. 'But it will probably be printed online rather than in book form – it's the way it's going.'

---

* Some will never make it to the definitive collection: recently I asked Al Alvarez whether Plath had ever written to him about her situation towards the end. 'Oh yes,' he said. And? 'And I burnt them all after she died, out of respect.' Did he regret this now? 'Absofuckinglutely.'

The Coming Home Question

4232134 SIGMN. BARKER H.C., 30 WING SIGNAL
SECTION, G COMPANY, AIR FORMATION
SIGNALS, CMF.

28 January 1945

Dearest,

The return to writing in ink (and with your pen) is an indication that things are a little more normal. We had a short sea trip from Volos to Athens where we are at present. I have only had a truck ride through the town at the moment. It seems very little damaged.

Athens is only a temporary resting place for us. What happens depends on decisions already taken [that] may be altered in the light of opinion. All the R.A.F. personnel have been informed (in a printed Order which I have seen) that '– as soon as possible you are being returned to Italy and thence to England'. It would be quite unfair for unequal treatment to be meted out to different branches of the service who have suffered precisely the same, and I know that those at home will represent this view as forcibly as possible. It is a little difficult for me to write very well when within me there is the jumping thought that soon – very soon – I may be actually telling you these things. But I will make some attempt and know you will not mind any deficiencies.

You were right in your interpretation of the news para. 'I was there' alright. I spent some bad hours lying with my brother in a shallow trench outside the hotel, while all sorts of fire was [aimed?] in our direction. Mortars were the worst, and when we returned to the hotel an hour before the surrender, we counted ourselves lucky to be alive. We were attacked for a day and a half. Well, when the 'Ceasefire' was given we laid down our warm weapons and came out with our hands raised (just like the pictures!) past a bearded partisan who pleasantly said 'Hail Comrade'. We lost everything. I had £7 or so on me, and my two most desired (I think) possessions – my Overseas Record of Events and my 'Unfamiliar Quotations'. I still have them, and am delighted accordingly.

I have just received your mail, 6 letters and four packets (2 coffee, 2 socks), a bit of luck as had they arrived before 'the day', they would have been lost. More about your dear letters later. I know how you must have suffered. But now it is alright. (The socks seem wonderfully well knitted.) (The photo was great.)

We spent the first ten days marching. About 120 miles, through rain, snow, hail at times, always very cold, always hungry. Our overcoats were taken, and we had no blankets. Jack Crofts, Bert, and I had terrible nights. No sleep, very cold. It was best during the day when we could get some warmth through keeping on the move. The three of us regard ourselves as fortunate in our experiences. Many chaps had very bad times, boots stolen (you can imagine how this affected one, stockinged feet in the snow), underclothes taken, trousers and blouse removed and very thin, ragged clothes given in exchange. You should be wary of believing all that you hear. Many chaps with small minds are anxious to be thought heroes or martyrs or something, and we had enough press correspondents to interview them all. Everyone has a story. Nevertheless, I must tell you that very few people take the same view of the ELAS as myself. As a matter of fact, most of my prisoner colleagues would like to shoot the whole of the Greek population.

I have read your letters and been moved by your concern and the power of your love. Please have no worries concerning my condition. I am not as fit as I was, but my rheumatics are my only complaint and I shall soon control that.

I hope you have been spared the worst of the rocket bombs, which (now that we see the newspapers again) were so active recently, and that your general health is as good as mine. I think of you. I think of you. I think of you. I will write as much as I am able, but bear with me as I have much to do. I love you.

Chris

27 WOOLACOMBE RD, LONDON SE3

3rd February 1945

Dearest,

'How do I feel?' – such a large question sweetheart, oh such a large question! So difficult for me to tell you. When I received your telegram, I sat down and wrote immediately but nothing would really come, I was like a sleep walker suddenly awakened, didn't know where I was, felt all soft and pappy, tremulous and bubbly inside, and today with your letter, oh Christopher, all this warmth melting inside me, that I somehow want to wrap around you, to make up for all your sufferings of the past weeks, it seems a lifetime. I knew you wouldn't be warm enough, or have enough to eat, but I didn't think it would be quite so bad. Oh Chris, I wish I could have a damn good howl, but I can't, I am all het up and tense, wondering whether you might come home.

I like to think we went through that time together, felt the overwhelming desiring need of each other at the same periods, those terrifying moments of I shall go mad if I don't have you. The moments of I want to die if I can't live my life with you, and the dragging dreary days of not thinking coherently at all, but just getting through time, with anxiety permanently gnawing at your innards. I look back at that now, with a 'did that happen to me?', but the soreness has not gone quite, I am taking hold of this happiness slowly, savouring every tiny moment, you have come back to me Christopher, you have come back, you mustn't leave me again, you have my heart, within you it beats, whatever fates there be please do not let us be hurt again, not anymore.

I know how the writing position is, I guess you feel a bit unbalanced by it all, especially with the 'coming home' question being in doubt, I feel a bit haywire and chaotic myself. I keep getting excited twinges in my middle, with my mind trying to keep control of the situation, hence this mixture of anguish and painful uncertain joy. You must, must come home, it would be too cruel, we can't bear it. I love you, love you, love you, more and more and more, this bad period has shown me its depth in a fashion that joy did not know. I need you pretty bad, my body to live, my mind to be stimulated. My heart to melt at your presence. You, Christopher, you must come home. Having it dangled in front of us like this, it's impossible, after all that has happened. I knew I should be content with your safety, but your coming home is swamping everything else, and I can read the terrible anxiety that it may not come off in your letter.

Rockets – well my sweet pet, I honestly haven't given them a thought for many weeks, the last bad period I remember was last November when Wilfred was on leave, I can't recall what has been the position since then, they have been falling, but I am very hazy about the quantity. I woke up to rockets when Iris came back from leave about a week ago. She had been to her sister's in Sheffield and came back feeling a bit scared at having to face up to them again, her agitation made me realise what a coma I'd been in, even rockets had left me cold, I suppose our imaginations can only cope with big fears one at a time. I suppose I shall become rocket conscious again.

I am now going to concoct a couple of letters, and hope. Of course, I will bear with you, I understand that you have much to do.

I Love You.

Bessie*

---

* Although only a handful of Bessie Moore's letters have survived, it is clear from Chris Barker's replies that only a few failed to find him at his various camps. And we know that almost all of his letters made it back to England. This was a remarkable wartime feat. The Post Office began planning for war in 1937, strengthening regional offices in anticipation of the aerial bombardment of London. When war broke out, a great deal of care was taken to establish the Army Postal Service, with letters to and from troops deemed essential to the maintenance of morale.

Domestically, volumes of mail remained steady; the biggest reduction was in the posting of football pools following the cessation of professional matches – the pools coupons accounted for 7 per cent of all letters sent. But the particular problems encountered with overseas letters (not least the closure of regular shipping channels and the impossibility of sending mail through Italy) would hit those stationed in North Africa particularly. Ships were obliged to sail via Cape Town to reach Egypt, and could take two months to arrive; Chris and Bessie devised a numbering system to indicate which letter they were replying to. A limited amount of mail (at an exorbitant minimum rate of 1s. 3d. per half-ounce letter) was also carried in the cargo holds of planes. Bessie could not afford this luxury, but she did take advantage of the 'airgraph' service that had been introduced in 1941. This involved writing a letter on a special sheet, taking it to the post office to be photographed on microfilm, and then transmitted to a receiving post that would print the letter and deliver it to the recipient. More than 135 million letters were sent this way before the end of the war.

Chapter Fifteen

Inbox

Computer nerds were formerly known as computer nicks, and on the evening of 29 October 1969 a couple of nicks sat down to make two computers talk to each other for the first time. One computer was on the third floor of a university building in Los Angeles. Foggy grey and the size of a fridge, it was flown in from Cambridge, Massachusetts, in a padded crate and greeted on arrival by nervous and excitable men with champagne glasses in their hands. The other computer was at Stanford Research Institute (SRI) about 350 miles away in Menlo Park near San Francisco, and had been greeted with slightly less fanfare but comparable trepidation.

The names of the programmers have not become house-hold names, but on that day in California they performed an act every bit as significant as walking on the moon, which had happened a little more than three months before. They built the precursor to the Internet.

Computers had been connected to each other before, but they were like teenagers at a disco in the way they clung to their own. Because they were not mass-produced, there was no common operating system or protocols. A highly complicated set of instructions was required for each individual machine to function at all, and their function tended to be both highly specialised and strictly limited; in the mid-1960s they were still essentially the same machines they had always been – immense filing cabinets used for maths and storage. There were many computer systems grasping at something big (the FBI had a network, as did American Airlines and a data centre calling itself Cybernet), but sharing their information with another computer at another location was a slow, complex and costly procedure, and it was one-way: a mainframe computer at HQ could be accessed via telephone wires, but the nodes couldn't send anything back. And as for the mainframe in one company communicating with the mainframe in another – alien software recognising alien hardware – it would have been easier to learn Martian. There was a reason why so many of the early interactive computer pioneers were bald.

But what would the world look like if its isolated computational powers could be linked with relatively little effort, and if one workload of research could be shared with and measured against another? And how useful would it be if two operators could send this hard-won information thousands of miles without having to print everything out and then put it on a plane? The engineers behind those two computers in different parts of California could have had little notion of what they

Where email began: the BBN office in Cambridge, Massachusetts.

were about to unleash upon the world.

What did the two computers say to each other? Not quite what they intended. The plan was that an engineer at UCLA would key in the word LOGIN one letter at a time, and a researcher at SRI would receive the digital transfer of each letter in code. The letters would be going via a phone line especially leased for the occasion. It began well. 'Did you get the L?' the UCLA guy asked over the audio part of the phone line. 'I got 114,' the SRI guy replied, which was indeed L in computer speak. Then the same with O – it was sent and it was received, correctly, as 117. And then, as G was transmitted from UCLA, the computer at SRI recognised it as the word LOGIN, sent back the G-I-N to be helpful, and the system crashed, because it had been programmed to receive only one letter at a time. Still, that was good going: only two letters completed successfully, but it was enough. The two computers had said L-O. And that was when letter-writing began its slow demise.

The birth of the Internet can seem like ancient history now. It is certainly old enough to have its history mixed alchemically with myth, and the biggest myth of all is that it was designed to save the United States in the event of nuclear attack. Some of its architecture was built on systems developed at the height of the Cold War, and its funding did receive its first boost from the Pentagon, but its ethical inspiration derived from the counterculture, and on a system of experimentation and information sharing. Traditionally, the late 60s was a time regarded by cultural historians as the end of a dream, but the digital evidence of the period suggests it was the opposite.

A great many people and institutions were involved in the building of the first computer network, expanding it from those two university computers, but the body responsible for its overall management was ARPA, the Advanced Research

Projects Agency, part of the Department of Defense. By the end of 1970 the Arpanet had established a nationwide network interconnecting many diverse research centres, with a primary purpose of sharing computer time and files; approximately ten nodes were connected. While the original conception of the network was ARPA's, its operation relied on an architecture designed independently at various institutions, including UCLA, Stanford, IBM and a key private company called Bolt, Beranek and Newman (BBN), which was responsible for the crucial design of the Interface Message Processor (IMP), a sub-network of smaller computers that could link distant mainframes like a daisy-chain.

A few years earlier, a computer visionary and former BBN employer named J.C.R. Licklider had written an influential paper about the possibilities of a digital world, giving his report a name that still equated it with something out of H.G. Wells: 'On-Line Man-Computer Communication'.* Towards the end of 1971, a 30-year-old member of the team at BBN named Ray Tomlinson was trying to go one better, working in a room in Cambridge, Massachusetts, on what may be called online man-computer-man communication. Tomlinson's idea was to enable Arpanet users to communicate with each other in a standard and far simpler way than had previously been possible. He devised a simple network protocol consisting of two parts: SNDMSG for outgoing mail and READMAIL to receive it, and his colleagues developed other tools we now also take for granted each day: a bit of code that enabled messages to be stacked and listed in order, and a way of sending a reply without having to type out the sender's address.

* In another sci-fi inspired phrase (it was still perhaps difficult to see it as anything but space-age), in 1962 Licklider called his vision a 'galactic' network, which we may now appropriate either as the entire Internet or just the Cloud. He got another thing correct too – the concept of a universal common library that would house all the world's knowledge, the first time this had been thought feasible for more than two millennia.

R@y Tomlinson lies back and thinks of his inbox.

But in 2012 it was Tomlinson who was among the first to be inducted into the Internet Hall of Fame, for he had done something more than speed messages through a digital frontier and transform our lives: he also invented a new use for @.

The 'at' sign has been an icon of trade and measurement since at least the sixteenth century (our first documentary evidence, in a letter from the 1530s, finds it used by a Florentine merchant as shorthand for an amount of wine stored in an amphora jar). Tomlinson says he just grabbed it off the keyboard because it wasn't much used for anything else, and it soon became a universal way of separating personal and local emails from global ones in a mailing address.* The content of the first message he sent successfully is as vague as the precise date: it was one of dozens of attempts. It may have been 'hello' or '123 testing' or 'qwertyuiop'. And the two communicating teletype terminals were not in separate states or offices, they were next to each other, with Tomlinson able to roll his chair

---

* He also found a way to deliver a message that didn't require the recipient to be there at the time. In interviews he underlines that this was a personal quest performed 'off the clock' when he should have been concentrating on something else.

between them. And in this humble way a revolution was born (when asked for autographs, Tomlinson signs his name R@y).

By 1973, some three-quarters of all traffic on the Arpanet was email, by far its most useful application (although it wasn't called 'e-mail', much less 'email' for a good while after this: an internal memo about the system still referred to messages or mail).

Ten years later, the Arpanet consisted of more than 550 connected nodes, and many other networks had sprung up that were using their own protocols for email and file transfer. Some sort of governance and security was clearly required to combine and protect them all, and the Internet (and then the world wide web) was slowly made.

For more than 15 years email remained an open academic secret, and the world's postal systems didn't wake up to its realities for a decade beyond that. The word Internet didn't enter common usage until the late 1980s, with the *New York Times* mentioning it only once before 1988. But gradually a new system of communication – something an overheated editor at *Wired* magazine would one day compare to the invention of fire – improved not just the professional interactions between those who collaborated in the building of the Internet, but potentially, eventually, everyone in the world. In 1995, the number of email messages sent in the United States surpassed the amount of paper mail delivered by the Post Office. In April 2012, the Internet Society estimated that 1.9 billion people use email, and we send 300 billion emails every day (about 2.8 million a second, about 90 per cent of them spam).

For many of us, checking emails is the first thing we do in the morning and the last thing we do at night, and something we do continually throughout the day; in the old days, this would be like getting up to check the doormat every few minutes to see if the postman had called, over and over and over again. And of course emails follow us wherever we go, a vital supply line and a relentless chore. But 40 years on, emails still want to be more like letters. Their screen iconography is all postal – tiny symbolic envelopes and in-trays – with paper-clips to denote attachments and paper planes to denote sent mail. The trash icon is still a wastepaper basket.

@   @   @

On 11 April 2013, 425 million people received the same email in their inbox. Astonishingly, the message turned out not to be junk. It was from Google to its Gmail users, and it contained details of how to plan for your digital afterlife.

You know the scenario: you're dying, hopefully a timely and relatively painless demise rather than something tragic and sudden, and you want to leave something to your family. Perhaps you want them to have a record of all your social engagements (Gmail began in 2004, so that's a lot of arrangements for lunch with friends and a lot of cinema seat confirmations). Or perhaps you want them to have a record of all the lovely things you've been writing to your wife and children when work schedules tore you apart. Or maybe this is the time to reveal that double life you've been leading with a completely separate family in a nearby town. So here it is from Google: an option that seemed to cover all the angles.

Andreas Tuerk, the product manager based at Google's HQ in Mountain View, California, began in a sensitive way, but still had the air of an ambulance chaser about him: 'Not many of us like thinking about death – especially our own. But making plans for what happens after you're gone is really important for the people you leave behind. So today, we're launching a new feature that makes it easy to tell Google what you want done with your digital assets when you die or can no longer use your account.'

Perhaps you had never thought of email as a digital asset before, but Tuerk was offering to take care of more besides – in fact, all your digital details from your photos to your You-Tube history. Anything you owned that was digitally still in play could, after your death, or if you were just feeling terribly unwell, be handed over to an assigned trustee. It was like a will, except it was instant, and there were no legal fees. And if you didn't want to hand anything on, Google would also promise to delete everything you had committed to them – three, six, nine or twelve months after your account became inactive. This would ensure no one would keep sending you emails after your demise, and would free up a speck of space on Google's servers. The service was called Inactive Account Manager: 'Not a great name, we know,' Andreas Tuerk conceded, and certainly an insufficient one to denote the obliteration and denial of an entire online existence. But in some ways, Google was just following tradition. Our history is littered with the ashes of burnt writing, a violent act against ourselves, but a common wish. Why shouldn't emails disappear as quickly as they arrive? The most convincing reason is, hopefully, spread over the past 400 pages.

Tuerk's digital death is only one option in a land of email opportunities these days. There are companies who are paid by other companies to clean their employees' email boxes, filtering the worthwhile from the junk and shielding the confidential behind firewalls. There are websites that will tell us how to achieve 'inbox zero', a holy grail in which one has to not only clear one's inbox of all emails awaiting a reply, but to empty it afresh at the end of the every day. To do this one must declare 'email bankruptcy', an admission that one can no longer pay one's digital debts. We want to reply to everything that comes in, both out of interest and courtesy, but this has long since become impossible; our screen life is simply overwhelming. So we have to purge, and the results may be psychologically disturbing. A writer from *Forbes* magazine tried it as a new year's resolution at the start of 2013 and felt unhappy. 'As I gazed into a completely empty inbox for the first time [in] five years, a feeling came over me that took a minute to identify. It was loneliness. I felt as if I was in a lifeboat in the middle of the ocean, surrounded by nothing but flat, featureless ocean on all sides.' It was like what W.H. Auden had written in *Night Mail* in 1936: our heart quickens at the sound of the postman's knock, for who wants to think themselves forgotten? When the man from *Forbes* received his first new email after his purge – nothing personal of course, a daily digest from a digital video site – he felt a little less alone. And then he deleted it, and he felt great.

For those less inundated and less proficient, there are the email-writing guides, the manuals of netiquette. These are not quite as abundant as the letter-writing manuals from centuries past, but they are nonetheless sure of themselves. A Penguin guide from 2005 is primitive but precise: 'Keep your attachments short; never send an empty message; never attach sound effects.' When in an email chain or open discussion list, '*Never* post merely to correct someone's English; don't post merely to express agreement; don't ramble; don't ask technical questions about email or the Internet, or about any aspect of computing; don't repost your message because ten minutes has elapsed and you haven't seen it distributed yet. Wait for a couple of days and then contact the list owner.'

In 2007, the authors of *Send: the How, Why, When and When Not of Email*, had a chapter on 'How to Write (the Perfect) Email', in which there are useful sections on carefully choosing one's tone and language to fit the recipient, common misspellings, and advice to keep your punctuation accurate, your emoticons ironic and your exclamation marks unusually generous. 'Because email is without affect, it has a dulling quality that almost necessitates kicking everything up a notch just to bring it where it would normally be.' So rather than just saying 'thanks', which can appear almost sarcastic, 'thanks!!!!' is perfectly acceptable. 'The exclamation point is a lazy but effective way to combat emails essential lack of tone,' say the authors David Shipley and Will Schwalbe. But they have a cautionary note: 'Don't use exclamation points to convey a negative emotion; they make it sound as if you're having a tantrum!'

In June 2004, 190 people replied to a survey conducted by the Sussex-based Mass Observation Project on the subject of letters and emails. It seemed like a good time to take stock: email and personal computers were now a regular part of our lives. The respondents reported writing fewer letters, and regarded email as useful but limited: they would not trust their intimate thoughts to email, and they often printed them out, uncertain whether they would still be on their computers in the morning.

There was still a fondness for tradition: of the 190 people who replied to the survey, 82 per cent sent in their written answers by post.*

But the behavioural details of the survey provide a valuable anecdotal glimpse into the attitudes of general users at a time when email was becoming part of the fabric of our lives. Nine years since the survey, the replies seem both quaint and touching, but they reveal more than mere nostalgia; the impact of receiving hand-delivered mail clearly extends beyond words on a page.

'I can remember receiving my first mail as a young girl and the thrill it gave me,' wrote a 68-year-old woman from Surrey. 'Sometimes I would send off for something, like a sample of face cream or a film star's picture.' Her first pen pal was an

---

* In 2013, email responses had increased to 45 per cent.

American girl from Pikeville, Kentucky, who sent her Juicy Fruit chewing gum and a subscription to a girl-scouting magazine. Later she wrote to a Swedish boy in Landskrona and a Turkish naval cadet.

An 83-year-old woman from Belfast remembered wistful letters during the war. 'One used to put SWALK on the back of the envelope [sealed with a loving kiss] but my mother and father did not quite approve.'*

A woman from Blackpool received four round-robins every Christmas, 'mostly about people we don't know or care about . . . No-one who sends them seems to have children or grand-children who are *not* brilliant. The minutiae they go into (We rise at 8am with the alarm and I bring tea in bed to F) is amazing. It's especially difficult when someone you don't remember or may not even have known is reported dead.'

A 45-year-old man from Gloucester wrote that 'real letters are quite rare and are usually much appreciated. They do make you feel that someone cares about you.

I especially appreciate the rare letter I receive with beautiful handwriting on it. I do have one friend with lovely writing. It seems a shame to open the envelope, and she doesn't write at all often.

Not so long ago her much-loved husband died very suddenly aged 60, and she sold their house and moved. When she was clearing the cellar, the last cupboard in the farthest corner

---

* The origin of SWALK is uncertain, but the common wisdom attributes it to American soldiers in the Second World War. There are others, with varying geography and spelling:
NORWICH – Nickers Off Ready When I Come Home
ITALY: I Trust And Love You
FRANCE: Friendship Remains And Never Can End
BURMA: Be Undressed Ready My Angel
MALAYA – My Ardent Lips Await Your Arrival
CHINA – Come Home I'm Naked Already
VENICE – Very Excited Now I Caress Everywhere
EGYPT – Eager to Grab Your Pretty Tits

buried behind all sorts of stuff was found to contain both sides of an extremely lurid, passionate (and current) correspondence between her deceased husband and a Russian woman whom he was having a very steamy affair with and of which she was entirely ignorant. He had repeatedly promised to leave his empty marriage of 33 years for her (my friend loved her husband dearly and had thought the marriage, sex and all, to be going really well). The contents of all her husband's meticulously copied love letters were appallingly wounding to her as indeed was the revealed fact of his unfaithfulness, just when she could no longer tackle him about it. Just when she thought things couldn't get any worse.

A librarian from Middlesex believed letters were 'like a luxury, a gift – to be able to spend time thinking what to say to someone and trying to send them something that will cheer up their day.

I hardly ever feel sending letters is an obligation. I find letters of condolence hard to write, but I know how much the recipient will appreciate them [and] I put in the effort.

Often I'm not sure how to sign off. I used to write 'Love' to everyone but guess I'm now more cautious. With someone, e.g. a man, I don't want to give the wrong impression, so I'll end 'best wishes'. Most female friends it's 'love', some it's 'lots of love'. I may or may not put kisses after my name – fundamentally I think it's naff. I miss having pet names, the way I did with my ex – the new incumbent doesn't do that sort of stuff. Shame.

How other people write to me . . . Well, not as often as I'd enjoy. Openly, usually, telling me about their lives, sharing jokes and silly things that have happened. They pick up on things I've said and ask about them. A bit like a long slow game of tennis.

I enjoy reading published letters – especially the Bloomsbury Group, Frances Partridge, Dora Carrington (hers were brilliant,

BERNARD PEYTON WATSON
5035 S. W. 71 PLACE
MIAMI, FLORIDA 33155

4/22/97

Dear Mr. Pietsch,

I'm a math professor down in Miami, Fl. and I've been really enjoying David Foster Wallace's brilliant book, <u>Infinite Jest</u>. One of the math equations on page 1024 is wrong (in both hard back and paper back editions). The second equation on page 1024 reads

$$F(x) dx = F'(x)(b-a)$$

but it should read

this was left off → $\left(\int_a^b \right) F(x) dx = F'(x)(b-a)$.

I'm sure this is a printer's error since Mr. Wallace seems to be sharp in math too. I hope this helps.

Yours truly,
Peyton Watson

P.S. When you find out I'm right I would feel like I actually accomplished something if you send me an acknowledgement.

GAAA! A reader writes to David Foster Wallace's editor.

especially the little sketches she drew), Ruth Picardie (so poignant), Laclos' *Liaisons Dangereuses* is an example of a fantastic collection of (fictional) letters; I was always very fond of the 18th century tradition of the epistolary novel.

I did get a nasty Valentine once, implying I thought I was wonderful and I wasn't. Otherwise the closest to that has been the ones I found my soon-to-be-ex writing to his sister and former girlfriend, where he described me in less than glowing terms and wrote memorably 'The sex was all right but I didn't like the foreplay'. Maybe a little practice, interest or application might have helped?

Love letters. Oh yes . . . In my time I must have written hundreds. The one disconcerting thing is that when I read them now (I have kept copies of a few) I realize that the style and content never varies much.

'My darling X, I was so sorry when you went. I miss you. Today I have been . . . Yesterday I . . . Next week I will . . . I want you so much; I'm longing to see you again. You are so much in my thoughts. All my love.' The sort of letter that I think Tom Lehrer memorably described as 'To Occupant'.

I have kept all the love letters I have ever received, with the exception of those sent me by my ex (now in a landfill site somewhere, or maybe recycled as loo paper – that would be apt). I have re-read some of them – it comforts me a lot to think that yes, I did love and was loved in return, and to think on the whole what nice people they were. It was very strange to find all the love letters my current partner wrote to me when we were together for the first time around. Nice, though, to realise that 25 years on we are back together now. So, despite the potential embarrassment to my son, I keep all my love letters and I hope I always shall.

In the spring of 2013 I spoke to Megan Barnard about how an archivist may secure our historical future. Barnard is assistant director for acquisitions and administration at the Harry Ransom Center at the University of Texas at Austin, and as such is responsible for one of the greatest collections of writers' and artists' papers in the world, particularly of the twentieth century. I'd encountered a few of the acquisitions when I was talking to Glenn Horowitz and Sarah Funke Butler in New York: Norman Mailer, David Foster Wallace, the Watergate papers. But there was rather more than this: some 40 million manuscript pages from the pens and ribbons of Conrad, Joyce, Beckett, Wilde, Eliot, Lawrence (T.E. and D.H.), Golding, Lillian Hellman, Updike, Stoppard, Anne Sexton, James Salter, Toni Morrison and Julian Barnes. These included original drafts, typescripts, diaries and letters, but there was also stuff for non-readers: Robert De Niro's costume collection, a reproduction of Scarlett O'Hara's dress made from the green baize curtains in *Gone With The Wind*, unique photographs by Walker Evans and Edward Steichen, a Mercator globe from 1541. Because the intention of the collection was clear – the best of the best available – and because it was Texas, it made perfect sense, as the Center was proud to point out, that a Gutenberg Bible would lie under the same roof as the first ever photograph (made by Joseph Nicéphore Niépce in about 1826) and the mask of the chainsaw maniac in *The Texas Chainsaw Massacre*.

In 2007, in celebration of the Ransom Center's 50th anniversary, Megan Barnard edited a mouth-watering book about the institution, *Collecting the Imagination*, in which she introduced the documentary evidence of six centuries of creative toil and the lengths to which skilled and privileged people have gone to gather it. There is none of the 'what we stole on our holidays' feeling you sometimes get from visiting the British Museum; the Ransom Center is glass, money and auctioned culture all proudly employed for the air-conditioned inspiration of future generations. At the close of her book the editor anticipates the challenges of receiving the discoveries of the future. But in the six years since it was published, the challenges have hardened: only the obstinate are not on email today; few but the deeply recalcitrant won't send their novels to their editors in Word (which may, if the 'track changes' option is enabled, allow an eye-straining but intricate insight into a manuscript's drafting and editing). The future storage of what archivists call 'born digital' material – that is, emails and documents that don't exist on paper – is a headache not just for storage (preservation, multiple software programs and disk formats, copyright protection) but also for presentation and display.

To ease their pain and share their solutions, Barnard and a group of forward-thinking curators from some of the world's leading institutions – the British Library, the Bodleian at Oxford, the Beinecke at Yale, the Rubenstein Library at Duke and the Manuscript, Archives and Rare Book Library at Emory – have for months been working on a guidance document designed to help themselves, dealers and authors establish a framework for the future management of digital archives. 'The stewardship of born-digital archival collections promises nothing if not routine encounters with the unexpected,' the document reasons. Among the recommendations for dealers and donors was the need to 'avoid manipulating, rearranging, extracting, copying, or otherwise altering data residing in the original source media' before they were offered for sale. There was the issue of intellectual property: 'A computer may be shared by co-workers or by an entire family and contain files created by children and spouses'; there was clearly going to be a problem in spending $1 million on an archive if a proud son was later going to make the same material freely available on a blog. Then there were things best kept quiet all round. 'Donors may want to screen email files for sensitive and/or extraneous messages prior to transfer . . . If a donor is not able or willing to screen for sensitive messages, the repository will need to make a decision, in accordance with policy, regarding whether and to what extent to devote staff time to searching for information above and beyond what a repository is required by law to restrict.' And then there was another problem not previously associated with the acquisition of papers from Emily Dickinson or Virginia Woolf: 'In some cases computer media will have long ago sustained damage. Examples of damage to computers, disks, and tapes include a bent computer chassis or disk drive, a cracked cartridge case, an exposed internal magnetic disk, a scratched optical disk, and a floppy disk that is covered in dust.'

'It's a tricky time,' Megan Barnard told me. She has been at the Ransom Center for 10 years. 'We've been acquiring digital materials for a while, but in rather small quantities. But now that's changed, and every archive that we acquire has a digital component, and that will only continue to grow. The initial question is how to get the material here in the first place. A lot of writers at the moment don't think of their digital files as being a part of their archive. If we ask someone "would you

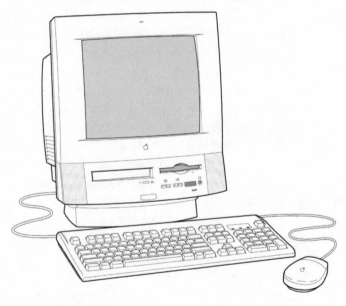

Be your own Salman at this Mac Performa 5400.

be willing to send us all of your emails?" that frightens people.'

At Emory University in Atlanta, Georgia, Salman Rushdie has suggested he has few such qualms. He has not only sold them his emails, but the rest of the contents on his computer too, and for good measure he's thrown in the actual computer. One can now be a virtual Salman: in February 2010, Emory allowed researchers into 'an emulated environment' in which one could sit at Rushdie's 1996 Macintosh Performa 5400, with floppy disc slot and CD-ROM tray (but no USB ports or FireWire and only 8 MB of memory). From here you can access his work files and selected emails and, all being well, write *The Ground Beneath Her Feet.*

The Ransom Center does not, at the time of writing, have any archives made up solely of emails. One collection of correspondence between the novelist Russell Banks and his brother Stephen, four decades strong, is made up of a combination of emails and letters, with the electronic side emerging in 1994, the year Russell observed, 'I just started using it and find it a fast and easy way to stay in touch with lots of people I'd otherwise write to only once in a while.' Megan Barnard has begun to perceive subtle differences. 'The contents still talk about writing, family, what their kids are doing,' she says. 'But the main contrast is that the response time is so dramatically reduced, which I think changes the conversation.' The gap between the letters was sometimes substantial, perhaps a couple of months. The emails are rarely as long as the letters, although when printed out they do look fairly formal. 'He's still a wonderful writer,' Barnard says, 'but the emails are less of a unique, discrete work.'

Not, of course, that this is a bad thing: but it is a different thing. Instead of envelopes with their clues of posting dates and place of dispatch we have electronic date stamps and other concealed forensics. Often, if one ticks the right box in the preference pane, they may automatically store both sides of a correspondence. Reading just one of Russell Banks's emails next to one of his letters one detects slightly less of a literary tone, with afterthoughts quickly appended in the next message. We may assume a certain amount of deletion and back-spacing, because that is how we write emails ourselves; we don't need such a clear head these days, for the same reason we do not need a pencil eraser or a blotter, or even a waste-paper bin: the machine does that for us now. And emails are simply less of an event and less of a struggle; the memory of that terrible aural whining that prefixed itself to any dial-up encounter with America Online and CompuServe is almost as archaic as the rattle of the Spinning Jenny. In the case of the Banks family, it's as if the brothers are speaking to each other from adjoining rooms, and we should acknowledge this for what it is: a great and modern thing. We may miss the formality and pageantry of the post, and the luxury of thinking a little more before we write and send, but the informality and ease of email is our compensation, and few wouldn't accept that as a trade. We now commonly regard email as a hybrid between a letter and a phone call – the pleasure of writing as one speaks, or at least how one soliloquises – the holy grail of letter-writers since Pliny the Younger felt the rumbling of Vesuvius.

At the Ransom Center, and at the Mass Observation archive and the Kleinrock Internet Museum (and all other institutions that safeguard our creative past), a new comparative form of evidence is emerging – not just of the way we write, but the way we think about writing. Could it be, for instance, that our increasingly democratic access to email wherever we go in the world, albeit with some restrictions, has destroyed many centuries of social and political hierarchies? Is this anything but a good thing? And what have we lost, psychologically, by no longer owning our mail in physical form? Is a hand-held, ink-written letter more valuable to our sense of self and worth on the planet than something sent to a fortress of cables in the Midwest that likes to call itself a 'cloud'?

Creatively, the next stage of this thinking is just around the corner: 'It will be interesting to see the correspondence from people who grew up only with email,' Megan Barnard says, 'who have never sent a handwritten letter. What's really interesting is that we have a lot of young interns here, and a lot of them don't even email anymore – they communicate by text or social media. That just seems shocking to me.'

In other words, our current ways may already be history. What if email is just a fleeting distraction from the fact that we no longer want to communicate with each other in the way our parents did, or the way we have communicated for 2,000 years? What if we find that our standard substitute for letter-writing is but a temporary and illusory bridge to not writing at all?

In the Flesh

14232134 SIGMN. BARKER H.C., 30 WING
SIGNAL SECTION, G COMPANY, AIR
FORMATION SIGNALS, CMF.

29th and 31st January 1945

My Dearest One,

I have just heard the news that all the Army men captured by ELAS are to return to their homes. Because of the shipping situation we may not commence to go before the end of February, but can probably count on being in England sometime in March. It may be sooner. I have only just left our Major giving the signal as received from Alexander. It has made me very warm inside. It is terrific, wonderful, shattering. I don't know what to say, and I cannot think. The delay is nothing, the decision is everything. Now I am confirming in my head the little decisions I have made when contemplating just the possibility. I must spend the first days at home, I must see Deb and her Mother. I must consider giving a party somewhere. Above all, I must be with you. I must warm you, surround you, love you and be kind to you. Tell me anything that is in your mind, write tons and tons and tons, and plan our time. I would prefer not to get married, but want you to agree on the point. In the battle, I was afraid. For you. For my Mother. For myself. Wait we must, my love and my darling. Let us meet, let us be, let us <u>know</u>, but do not let us, <u>now</u>, make any mistakes. I

Chris Barker in Rome.

am anxious, very anxious, that you should not misunderstand what I have said. Say what you think – but – please agree, and remember I was afraid, and I am still afraid.

How good for us to see each other before I am completely bald! I have some fine little wisps of hair on the top of my head. It is not much good me trying to write about recent experiences now that I know that I shall be able to tell you everything myself within such a short time. What I have my eye on now is the first letter from you saying that you know I am alright, and the next, saying you know I am coming to you. I must try to keep out of hospital with some of these post P.O.W. complaints. Plan a week somewhere (not Boscombe or Bournemouth) and think of being together. The glory of you. What a bit of luck I got taken P.O.W. When I was captive I used to try and contact you and think hard 'Bessie, my dearest, I am alright. Do not worry.' I never felt that I got through, somehow. But now it is over, and you know that I am alright and going to be with you soon, to join and enjoy. Do not get very excited outwardly. I am conscious of the inner tumult, the clamour, but I am not too much outwardly joyful. Moderation is my advice. Watch the buses as you cross the street.

We are free of duties and yesterday I went to our friends in Athens, taking some of your coffee and cocoa, which they were very pleased to have. Thank you for sending it. We were embraced very excitedly, kissing and so on, continental fashion.

I hope that you will not start buying any clothes (if you have the coupons left), because you think you 'must look nice' for me. I shall be sorry if you do. Just carry on as near as possible to normal. My return at the present time allows us to make public our mutual attachment. I shall tell my family I hope to spend a week away with you somewhere during my leave. My counsel to you is to tell as few people as possible. To someone like Miss Ferguson you can politely reply to her observations that you thought it was your business, rather than hers. Try to avoid preening yourself and saying much. This is my advice, not anything but that. I hope you understand. I do not ever want it to be anything but our affair. Do not permit any intrusion.

I do not know how long leave I shall get. I could get as little as fourteen days, and I may get as much as a month. I am wondering how I shall tell you I am in England. Probably it is still quicker to send a telegram than a letter, and I hope to send you one announcing that I am on the same island. I will send another when I am actually soon to get on the London bound train, and you can ring LEE GREEN 0509 when you think I have arrived there. Tell me how I get to Woolacombe Road, (the number would be sufficient, I shall remember where it is) and I will meet you there, or some other place you may say, as soon as I can. You must bear in mind that I shall be with my brother until we get home. Also, that, having been away from home for so long, my parents will want to see (and have a good case [for seeing]) a lot of me. I hope that everything will work itself out without any unhappiness to anyone. I shall be in great demand from two or three points and it will be difficult to manage without offence.

It is a strange thing, but I cannot seem to 'get going' and write very freely. All I am thinking about is 'I am going home. I am going to see her.' It is a fact, a real thing, an impending event, like Shrove Tuesday, Xmas Day, or the Lord Mayor's Banquet. You have to be abroad, you have to be hermetically sealed off from your intimates, from your home, to realise what a gift this going-home is.

The few letters of yours that I had on me, I burnt the day previous to our surrender, so no-one but myself has read your words. In the first ten days of our captivity I did not think any soft thoughts about you, all I did was concentrate on trying to tell you I was alright. But when we had a few supplies dropped by aircraft (at great risk to themselves in the misty snow-bound Greek mountain villages) and we started hoping we might get sent home upon our release, I was always wondering about you, about us. It is a pity that the winter weather will not be kind to us out of doors. But it will be nice sitting next to you in the pictures, no matter what may be on the screen. It will be grand to know that we have each other's support and sympathy. Won't it be wonderful to be together, really together, in the flesh, not just to know that a letter is all we can send?

I love you.

Chris

27 WOOLACOMBE RD, LONDON SE3

6th and 7th February 1945

Darling, Darling, Darling,

This is what I have been waiting for, your freedom left me dumb and choked up, but now, oh now, I feel released. Oh Christopher, my Dear, Dear Man, it is so, so wonderful. You are coming home. Golly, I shall have to be careful, all this excitement is almost too much for my body. You must be careful too, Darling, all this on top of what you have been through, it is difficult to keep it down, you can't help the excited twinges in your midriff, can you, do keep well, Angel, I shall have to say that to myself as well.

Marriage my sweet, yes I agree, what you wish, I wish. I want you to be happy in this Darling. I make a plea to whatever gods there be to make me greater than myself, so that I can make you as happy as humanly possible, to help you over the bad days, and swing along with you in the good days. Whilst

you are afraid, you will not be happy, we must get rid of those fears between us. Also confidentially, I too am a little scared – everything in letters appears larger than life size, like the photograph, it didn't show the white hairs beneath the black, the decaying teeth, the darkening skin, I think of my nasty characteristics, my ordinariness. Yes, I too feel a little afraid.

Bessie Moore in Blackheath.

Still I can't be bothered with that now, for we are going to meet, does anything else matter Chris?

About what happens on arrival, of course you'll have to spend the first part at home, I suspect I can get my leave when needed, we only have to sign for the actual summer period, otherwise they are very accommodating. Oh Dear Dear Me, plan a week somewhere, bonk, up comes my heart, a week somewhere, by the sea, WITH YOU. Where shall we go, of course I'd choose north Devon, sea, country and air, but March raises the question of weather, might we go to a largish town, I prefer villages normally, but with you I guess I'll do what you want, also I feel that you'll need looking after, don't think you should walk around in the rain, not for awhile, anyway, guess I don't care where, as long as it's the sea, and you, you, you. Inward clangings and bouncings and I wonder how soon.

Glad you managed to give them the coffee and cocoa, our Greek friends I mean, to show them that we wish them well, and hope very strongly that they will get the government they want, though perhaps they live too close to poverty to think of governments, still you'll soon tell me all about it.

I have a few apprehensions floating around, such as the actuality instead of letters. You know I say to myself, 'Bessie my girl, you're not so hot', but I think you may have a similar feeling. I say, how is your digestion, mine's awful, I shall be reduced to taking Rennies or something, a wind remover. My tea at this moment is stuck somewhere in the middle of my chest. So you don't want to get married, well that's a dou[che] of cold water, still I soon shook the water out of my eyes, it seems a bit unimportant, with your homecoming in front of me – I guess most impractical, poor Lamb you hardly know me. 'Do not let us make any mistakes' now underlined. You dear old silly, do you really think you can guard against that, or ensure the future?

I can't help wishing that you won't get these letters, that you'll be on your way, that the time to wait is that short, because my impatience is getting pretty bad, being able to write like we have has been a wonderful thing, but it has always remained only the beginning, the contact for our future and a beginning must change to something else, and now it is changing.

What do you think of the war news? Don't like getting too optimistic, but wouldn't it be wonderful to come home to stay?

I bet Ridgeway Drive is a very joyful place, two sons coming home, crikey. I bet your mother felt slightly flattened out at first, but she'll be bouncing now.

I Love You.

Bessie

Not long after his return home, Chris Barker and Bessie Moore spent a week together in Bournemouth. It was a success, but perhaps not a complete one. The subsequent ardour was a little less explicit, and there was a mysterious incident with fish. We do not have Bessie's letters from this period.

14232134 SIGMN. BARKER H.C., 30 WING, I COY.,
4 AIR FORMATION SIGNALS, C.M.F.

10–28 April 1945

My Dear One,

Our meeting was a wonderful thing, and now we have to put up with the after-effects.

I do not feel in a very good state for writing at the moment, as the ship has been rocking a good deal, and I have succumbed once to the irresistible urge to be sick. We have now got ourselves onto a pretty good job aboard ship, each morning ten of us have to clean out the Ship's Hospital. It gets us out of other jobs, like Mess Orderly, Guards, sweeping the decks, so Bert and I get on happily with our three baths, the lavatory pedestals, and similar number of wash basins. I am not too keen on doing the Scabies bathroom, but never mind. Three weeks ago, when I was a temporary gentleman, the chap in Lyon's 'wash and brush up' washed out my wash basin, now I am doing the same

I wondered on leave, over a number of things. I wonder now if you would like to wear an engagement-ring. If you would like one, and it was not unlucky or something, how do you feel about getting one. I think they are jewellers' blessings, but if wearing one would make you the least bit happier I'd prefer it. What do you think? I am a blunderer, but you must excuse me. I am starting to feel more normal again, though like you, find our days together 'dream-like'.

I hope you did not weep too much (if you did weep). And, if ever you do so again, let it be only at the hardness of our separation, never in despair of our future meeting and life together. Of course, my senses having thrilled and luxuriated in you, I have become more than a little woebegone at our post-war hopes of a home, by ourselves. The figures lead me to think that it will be ten years before we get the chance to choose. I expect you will have to be discreet in what you say to your Dad, but it seems to me that we shall be forced to live at 27 after I return for a little while, in order to prospect for a place. When the war is over I know you will buy what you can to ensure we do not have many troubles in equipping our own home, and, if you can manage, to start house [hunting]. Shall I write my Mother telling of our plans, and asking her to let you have what money you want? As you know, I have £350, and you nearly the same, so we could raise £700 for a first payment. I wish we need to not only feather our nest, but to acquire one also. Remember that I have a regular saving of £3 weekly, for the purpose of repayments or anything else you may think necessary. I am sorry you are alone in your searches.

Do you know, I can't help feeling triumphant at our relationship. It seems so wonderful to possess your regard, and possess you. I do not think I have any of the slave-owner mentality when I confess I am infinitely joyful at owning you, and I feel that I do. I want you absolutely, entirely, wholly. I hope you are feeling all of this too, and that you know in your bones I will do anything for you.

You say I said enough while on leave. I am disgusted how little I said, about ourselves, and about my impressions of 'life abroad' and the Army. I am not very happy about my deficiencies as a sweetheart – I think I teased you too much. I should have been on my knees before you, confessing my utter dependence on you, imploring your interest though I may seem to have it, telling you always that without the hope of you, I should starve and thirst. I could have been so much more eloquent, yet my stutterings satisfied you. I am sorry we wasted those five nights at Bournemouth, it seems to be beside the point that there will be many more. I am sorry about the error of judgement regarding salmon. I'll catch a whale for you on my return journey.

I hope you are getting [on] alright with your spring-cleaning. Personally, I think far too much is made of this event. A properly run house would be ashamed to admit it needed a really good clean-up once a year. It is a suburban blight. But you enjoy yourself, don't mind me. (I bet this 'gets' you!)

[A few days later] I am now once again in Italy, and everything is going as expected. Please write me, always, just what comes into your head, for I want what comes into your head, not the contents of Habits and Manners of Good Society or the Daily Mirror's idea of what the Young Man Abroad wants to hear about from Home. I do not <u>like</u> 'damn, blow, blast, bugger', but I prefer that to something that is not you.

I hope you can have some time with [your brother] Wilfred when he is on leave, but I think that 'celebration' is at least premature while the Japanese are so strong and the fighting is likely to last for so long. And what shall we celebrate? That the Fascists are vanquished? That there is freedom in Germany, and everywhere else? I shall be inclined to celebrate when fighting everywhere has ended, and the people seem apparently to be taking the first steps in controlling their own destinies.

Last night I was on guard, a kind of stroll round the tents (remember the hessian being pinched from our earlier latrine?). I was on 11.50PM–1.30AM, 5.30AM–7.30AM, and thought of you sleeping peacefully, while I patrolled the almond trees and listened to the barks of distant dogs, and the 'perlip, perlip' and 'whirrip whirroo' of the birds around here. A feeling was with me that distance doesn't matter. In one of your letters you say your heart beats within me. That is good. I will look after your heart. Please always try to be happy because of future prospects, rather than sorrowful because of present separation. I know it's grim, because my hands, my lips, are very conscious of their idleness.

I love you.

Chris.

2nd May 1945

Dearest,

I had just addressed the front when someone called out 'News Flash', we all rushed to 'the tent with the wireless', and heard the announcement that the German armies in Italy had surrendered unconditionally. Coming on the same day as the 7A.M. announcement (which I heard) that Hitler was reported dead, and Rundstedt captured, it gave us a certain extra elation and hope that other Germans will also surrender rather than make it necessary for our chaps to get killed unnecessarily. We have again been warned that sobriety is expected of us when the great announcement is made. For us, I don't expect the change to mean anything except more spit, and more polish, more parades, more guards, more sickening routine and regulation.

I think I stand a good chance of returning to U.K. for good in a year.

3rd–9th May 1945

I am very glad that the rockets have finished. What is it like to be able to go unthinkingly to bed, and to know you will be undisturbed?

Your comments about my greatness over my Greek experiences are very welcome, but they are by no means correct. I am not a great man nor have I ever behaved like one. I am a very little man, with his ear close to the ground.

I hope you <u>will</u> buy clothes. Don't wait for my approval. If you want to save, consider again the smoking habit. I thought of an idea. Suppose you smoke 20 a day now, carry on smoking 20 each day for a week, then smoke 19 each day. At the end of that week, reduce to 18 for the next seven days, and so on.

It would take nearly six months to reduce to nothing, but it might be the way out, to slowly slide away from it. You say you wish you were thoughtful like me – well, I'm not thoughtful, only artful! I have no doubt that between us we share all the faults and vices human beings are heir to . . . Question is how often we display them. I think we'll rub along together very well indeed. I feel fairly certain we have both sufficient intelligence not to try to make the other unhappy.

I think I would like you to say, about the ring, that the money could be more wisely used and that we don't need to conventionally demonstrate our undertakings to the world. We do not need a symbol, and our love is strong. A point I had in mind was that the Ivy-type of mind might be saying 'Ah, Chris has been home, but I see that Bessie is still on the shelf.' Or something cheap and silly like that.

The events in Europe are less and less meaningful, the staggering waste of our lives – and what I must do in the meantime – is sickening. Oh, for 8 hours' work a day, 6 days a week! I imagine it will be many months before any large number of chaps start discarding khaki for colours of their own choice, but with no blackout, sand-bagged windows, or A.R.P., things generally should be easier. I imagine that your Foreign Office task will cease, and that most of the wireless stations will close down.

I heard a broadcast record by Bevin yesterday, in which he said there would be a short standstill period before chaps started demobilising. Some of our chaps with low numbers are not happy about that! We just listen in, and imagine things to suit our own cases.

I am still in a glum state and I believe that only the news that Japan have surrendered also would be sufficient to un-glum me. I am very thankful that the end of the war in Europe has come at last, and all the terrible things that war involves

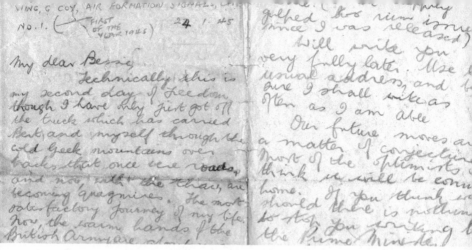

Another magical record: Chris Barker's letters preserve the past.

will now cease there. But I am very conscious that the people generally have suffered much, and I do not believe we are any nearer a decent state of society. On top of all my general mix-up of confused thought and regret is a more acute realisation that we are not together, and the chance of being so is remote. I know that it doesn't make you happy to have me fed-up (and I _am_ that) but I do not feel like a song and a dance just at present. It's grim.

We put up a tent. We take it down. We are told there will in future be no trucks to the village (a quarter of an hour's walk). Today and tomorrow we _must_ ride in a truck (because of possible trouble with celebrations, I suppose). We exhibit our kit daily so that all the dust can blow on it. We must take Mepacrine tablets daily. We must have our mosquito nets down by 1800 hours daily. We must roll our tent walls up by 0000. We must not perform our ablutions outside our tents. Ordinarily you just grin, curse and bear it. At the moment, I am not very happy about such things.

We have again been reminded we mustn't get drunk. Chaps are getting 1½ bottles of beer this week. I was going to have mine just now, but remembered I had already promised it a bloke. It is horrible stuff (light ale) I'm told.

We had a sing-song, and I joined in a few of the songs. It was not easy to get 'order' for the King at 9P.M., but I was near the wireless and heard all he said. What an ordeal for him it is every time, and how, of recent years, he has become adept at just avoiding a wrong word. I bet he is glad it is over. I thought there might have been greater mention of his Allies in the struggle, but otherwise it was a reasonable effort. If only everyone would recall that we are at peace in Europe only because of the death and mutilation of literally millions of our fellow countrymen (and women) and of our fellow world citizens. Yet, if 'private enterprise' had its way, the air raid shelters that are being dismantled in England would be sold at a handsome profit to Japan. They will need them alright.

There hasn't been any real relief here because of the end of the war. Most chaps are much too aware of the time that will elapse before they return home, and some are now more than ordinarily apprehensive about SEAC [South East Asia Command], which we all call Burma. I can quite understand the feelings at home and that much of the enthusiasm is synthetic, cultivated by the flag-selling interests. Remember that I saw the paper flags Woolworths were selling when on leave. But anyhow, I'd like to see them all waving around Blackheath at the moment!

I wonder if next Spring we shall be doing the cleaning together? I hope so. I hope we shall both be really living, really living together by then. I want to explore, to voyage, to investigate, to discover and to know. I want to hold you tight and tell you you are mine and I am yours.

I LOVE YOU.

Chris

Epilogue: Dear Reader

In 2004, three years before he died at the age of 93, Chris Barker asked his son Bernard what to do with his war letters. 'Should I throw these away, or will you take them?' They reached an agreement: the letters would be saved, but his father insisted on an injunction that they wouldn't be read until he and Bessie were both dead. 'I asked why,' Bernard remembers, and he said: "I say what I'd like to do with her".'

Bernard Barker, a professor of education at the University of Leicester, began to read the letters properly in 2008. 'There were many more letters, and many more words, than I expected.' There were 501 letters totalling 525,000 words.

His parents, Chris and Bessie, were married in October 1945. He was born the following August, two months after his father finally returned to England from Italy and resumed his work in the London Post Office. They lived in Blackheath, a suburb of south-east London, where they soon had another son, Peter, in 1949. Chris Barker worked his way up to executive level, wrote regularly for several Post Office journals, and after his retirement in 1973 he remained active in the local Labour Party and the Campaign for Nuclear Disarmament. Bessie also resumed her work at the Post Office, and at home developed her talents for painting, enamel firing and gardening.

'Both my parents were to me transparently emotional, passionate people,' Bernard notes, 'but their feelings were under such adamantine self-control that it is a surprise now to read these open statements of their shifting wartime emotions, written long ago. Their love for one another was so complete, always, that it was difficult for my brother and I in childhood and adolescence to relate to each of them as a single person. Even so, this early love at a distance was, perhaps, the best because they found one another through their ability to write about what was really important in life and to imagine a happy future with home and children.'

I spoke to Bernard Barker in May 2013, a few weeks after he donated his father's letters to the Mass Observation Archive at Sussex University, of which I am a trustee. The letters were part of a wider archive, including Chris Barker's journalism for various Post Office journals, photographs, and a collection of documents relating to his family stretching back to the 1890s. They were beautifully and painstakingly presented, a testament to a life lived through paper. Many other documents in Chris Barker's life were either lost or burnt, including the majority of Bessie's letters, of which only 16 survive. But we have enough to appreciate the flowering of a full and lasting relationship during the most challenging times – a battle triumphant.

In the written introduction to his father's archives, Bernard Barker remarks how 'our life capsules spin at painful speed towards and away from even our friends and the closest members of our family. We catch parts of one another, disclosed fragments of a greater whole, before hastening to another time and place. We think the years have gone but we ourselves are lost to each other in the end.'

The wartime correspondence between Bernard Barker's parents ended with these lines on 7 June 1946, with Chris Barker writing to his new wife:

> Darling, tonight I spend my last night in the Army. Tomorrow I spend the night in the train. As you go to sleep on Wednesday night, think of me speeding along the rails towards you, sleeping

this final separate sleep. And remember that when you awaken in the morning, it will be to hear my voice and see me. Dearest, Darling, Only One, thank you for all that you have been to me through these years, and be sure we shall overcome with our love, any difficulties there may be later on . . . I can never be as good as you deserve, but I really will try very hard . . . We shall be collaborators, man and woman, husband and wife, lovers.

Great miserabilist that he was, Philip Larkin was spot-on with his famous line from 'An Arundel Tomb', as right with Chris Barker and Bessie Moore as with you and me: what will survive of us is love. Letters fulfil and safeguard this prophecy. Without letters we risk losing sight of our history, or at least its nuance. The decline and abandonment of letters – the price of progress – will be an immeasurable defeat.

When will it come, that monumental day, that last proper letter through the door? Next Wednesday? A year from today? Five years? The last letter will appear in our lifetime. It will be personal, emotional, maybe even handwritten, but crucially it will be physical, the evidence of human connection. It will have travelled along a definable route, perhaps not far from the journey we'd have taken to deliver it ourselves. We will not know it was the last until months or years later, when we have glanced back to acknowledge a passing, like the last hair to whiten, or the last lovemaking.

And what can we do to stave off this terrible event? We could write more letters, unwieldy as this seems. We could write to a few of the people we now email, a longer and less urgent transaction, and one that may create a certain amount of alarm amongst our recipients. The quality would probably be better, the physical effect memorable, the pleasure more.

We could sign off in haste and run to catch the post. Our grandchildren and historians may thank us. And then there would be the unusual pleasure of receiving a letter back.

We could join a letter-writing club. Recently I talked to a woman in Leeds who ran one in local pubs and reported new members every week; they wrote to relatives and friends they had lost touch with, and occasionally to each other. They liked the process of writing, the self-expression, but they also liked the camaraderie – the same pleasures one might derive from a book club or knitting circle. There is also the very pink online site called MoreLoveLetters.com, in which a caring bunch (more than 10,000 have signed up) send love letters to strangers to brighten their day (they leave them in fitting rooms, coat pockets, library books). I think the main purpose of it may be to make the letter-writers feel cute about themselves, but no harm in that.

Or we could pay for a letter subscription. In April 2013 I emailed the American writer and filmmaker Stephen Elliott to ask him about a project he had started a year before called Letters in the Mail. This was an adjunct to Elliott's leftfield culture website The Rumpus, and had about 1,500 subscribers, each of whom were paying $5 per month (in the US) and $10 (overseas) to receive a photocopied letter through the post every fortnight. The letters are usually written by a novelist, or an artist of some type, among them Margaret Cho, Rick Moody and Aimee Bender, and they write about whatever takes their fancy – their next novel, a failed relationship, their mother – either handwritten or typed, and some with illustrations. They mail their letter to The Rumpus, and The Rumpus photocopies it 1,500 times and puts it in 1,500 envelopes. There is usually a return address from the writer, and recipients are welcome to write back. It's for people who miss real letters – a photocopy being the closest many of us will get these days. 'The inspiration was just that I was sending out these daily emails and I got into a conversation about letter writing,' Elliott told me. 'I missed writing letters. I decided to do Letters in the Mail that day and announced it the following morning.'

Some of the letters are a bit self-conscious, but some are terrific – revelatory, funny, full of news, thought-provoking. I got one from a woman called Alix Ohlin about what letters had meant in her life, including those from her dad and some from a stalker who had somehow tracked her changing addresses through five states. The stalker letters would open with history and philosophy, but then descend into incoherence. He (Ohlin assumes it was a he) has stopped writing now, and Ohlin is no closer to knowing the stalker's identity. She found the letters perplexing and annoying rather than threatening. Initially she thought they might be from a shy ex-boyfriend or would-be boyfriend, but towards the end she just envisaged someone lonely and angry. She was reminded of

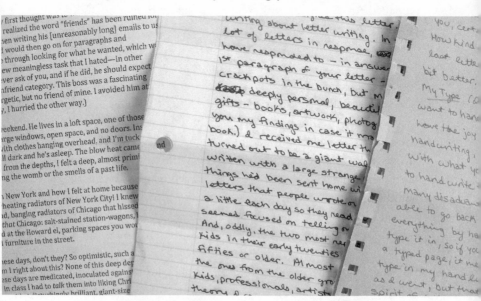

Letters from a loft: Deb Olin Unferth keeps a tradition alive.

Emily Dickinson: 'This is my letter to the world / That never wrote to me'.

I also received a letter from someone named Melissa who wrote from the hipster Thunderbird hotel in Marfa, Texas. She was looking out from her room onto blue skies and wild grasses, listening to the whistle of passing trains. She was supposed to be working on a new book idea, but she had just spent the last few days having sex with her girlfriend instead, and now she was running out of time. She wrote of how she was reminded of Sylvia Plath, how she wanted 'to live and feel all the shades, tones and variations of mental and physical experience' that life had to offer. 'And I am horribly limited.'

Another letter I really liked came from a woman called Deb Olin Unferth, who wrote from Connecticut of her life as a writer and a teacher. 'I'm staying at my partner's this weekend,' she explained.

> He lives in a loft space, one of those democratic constructions with large windows, open space, and no doors. Instead of a closet he has this cubby hole with clothes hanging overhead, and I'm tucked in here writing this because it's still dark and he's asleep. The blow heat came on and woke me, and in my emergence from the depths, I felt a deep, almost primitive longing for radiators, like missing the womb or the smells of a past life.

Not exactly earth-shattering, but I could imagine that place, and there was an appealing tone to her writing (I discovered later that Unferth was a university English professor and novelist/memoirist). I read on:

> Oh radiators! My first winter in New York and how I felt at home because of the radiators, the outrageous overheating radiators of New York City! I knew them from growing up in Chicago, the loud, banging radiators of Chicago that hissed and clanged and leaked. I lived in that Chicago: salt-stained

station-wagons, black slush, heat lamps that never worked at the Howard el, parking spaces you would dig out of snow and 'save' with old furniture in the street.

Much of her letter focused on a video she had been given by her mother after graduation – something she refers to emblematically as The Movie – a film that taught her something about self-worth and self-image. She also wrote fleetingly about the death of a brother and a nephew, about teaching in a maximum security prison, and of feeling alone.

It was an oddly personal and brave letter to send out to people you didn't know, and a reader could never be sure of its veracity. But I trusted her, and a week later, I wrote back. I wrote about this book, about the loss of letters, a little about my family. I wrote the letter over several days, and discovered a depth I had previously neglected in emails: I would analyse things more, and make more connections between things that happened. I was intrigued by the possibilities of our new writerly relationship. Then I did something I regretted. 'I did briefly Google you and now wish I hadn't,' I admitted to her.

Not because I found anything that was even fractionally unappealing, but because I found out anything at all, when I should have just let a correspondence run its natural course. The temptations and remorse of the Internet. So if you can resist Googling me, I'll tell you something that people always enjoy: if it hadn't been for the Nazis, my dad wouldn't have changed his name from the original Garfunkel, which means I'd be Simon Garfunkel. But of course I probably wouldn't, because I'd have rushed to change it on the morning of my 18th birthday. (Lacking the courage to use it as my calling card, the way people have clung to names like Laurel Hardy even as celebrity events overtake them.)

I'm 52, so old enough to have lived many of my romances through correspondence. I have the shoeboxes. I have the proof of naiveté and the rush of lust and over-cleverness, and I can remember even a slight sense of predictability and boredom when letters from my first proper girlfriend used to arrive almost every day, quite fat envelopes with the contents in a beautifully rushed hand, probably lots of things about what happened at school (we were 17/18), most of which she'd already told me the afternoon before when we met for coffee. Sometimes I think she even got the last post on her way home, after we'd just met. It's the best history of that time that I have. Her lovely letters. I used to write back every two or three days, and I think I grew up a bit with each one.

And like you I'm not unfamiliar with family bereavements. You wrote about your brother and sister's son. My brother died when I was 18 and he was 23. My mother a year later from breast cancer. I still have the condolence letters, too difficult to read then and now, most of them no doubt beginning how difficult it was to put anything into words. But of course one tried, and still does – the condolence letter the last letter to fall, the one that one still has to find a decent sheet of paper and envelope and proper grammar for.

A few weeks later, Unferth wrote back. And so it has continued, a new friendship through the mail. There was no other way: we didn't have each other's telephone numbers or email addresses; I'm not on Facebook, and tweets would have been insubstantial. I wrote to her of how my eldest son Ben (now 25) recently told me of meeting a woman he liked on holiday in Lisbon. They wanted to keep in touch, and so resolved to write. Ben vaguely envisaged some sort of old-fashioned penpal correspondence through the post involving envelopes and stamps, but things being what they are, they began writing by email instead. The problem was, this was all too instant. He would write, she would reply, and then he'd be obliged to write again, probably on the same day. But there was nothing significant to report, and so the whole thing fizzled out almost as soon as it began.

I wrote to Unferth about the pleasures of snail mail, and about the origin of the phrase. There's an understandable assumption that it began as a negative comparison to email, or, if its roots were earlier, it first appeared as a contrast to airmail in the 1940s. But there is at least one earlier reference, now almost a century old, and fittingly it appears in a letter. In 1916, an Austrian woman named Christl Lang was in regular correspondence with her fiancé Leopold Wolf on the southern front between Italy and Austria-Hungary. But in December of that year, her letters suddenly failed to reach him. 'I can hardly wait for you to answer my letters,' she wrote to him. 'It should be called the Snail Mail, not the Military Mail!'*

Unferth wrote that I was far from the only person to reply to her.

> In fact, I received an awful lot of letters in response, many more than I could have responded to, and there were indeed a few crackpots in the bunch, but most of them were fascinating, deeply personal, beautifully written letters and included gifts – books, artwork, photographs, bookmarks. I received one letter that arrived as a package and it turned out to be a giant wall-hanging letter that he'd written with a large strange pen that he'd found in a box of things he'd been sent home with when he lost his job. I had letters that people wrote over a period of two weeks, adding a little each day so they read like journals, and ones that seemed focused on telling one story and leaving it at that. And, oddly, the two most represented age groups seemed to be kids in their early twenties and men and women in their fifties or

---

* I am grateful for this quotation to Christa Hammerle's essay 'You Let a Weeping Woman Call You Home?' in *Epistolary Selves*, edited by Rebecca Earle, Ashgate, Aldershot, 1999.

older. Almost no one in their 30's or 40's! And the ones from the older group were mostly married with kids, professionals, artists. Really excellent letters. The theory I came up with about that group is that those people know how to write letters, they grew up writing letters, they sort of miss writing letters, they can communicate that way with ease and grace. They know what a letter is for. The younger group – excellent letters too – but, well, who isn't a little lost in their early 20's? It seems like they mostly wrote because they feel a little lost and are hoping for some adult wisdom or guidance (haha, right).

I wrote back with a few examples of my favourite letters – both famous and not. I told her I had always been fascinated by the letter Elvis Presley had sent to President Nixon in 1970 when he wanted a badge from the federal narcotics agency. Presley already had other police badges, but he hoped that this one would allow him to carry guns and drugs into any country as he pleased. He wrote the letter by hand during a flight from LA to DC (it's on American Airlines notepaper), and you won't find a finer example of the persuasive power of celebrity. Elvis talks about the scourge of drugs amongst America's youth, and how he wants to do anything he can to help. He ends with a PS – 'I believe that you, Sir, were one of the Top Ten Outstanding Men of America also.' (The letter worked: he met Nixon at the White House, and he did get his badge. He then went on to take a lot more drugs.)

I explained that I am also a big fan of Jessica Mitford's letters, not least her battles with her sisters and her unrelenting fire against bullies wherever she found them. I am not alone: in a book review, J.K. Rowling revealed that she loves them too, praising their rebelliousness, bravery, adventurousness, humour and irreverence.* Rowling noted how her cor-

---

* *Decca: The Letters of Jessica Mitford*, ed. Peter Y. Sussman, Weidenfeld & Nicolson, 2006. J.K. Rowling's review appeared in the *Sunday Telegraph*.

respondence provided a much fuller picture of the writer than her autobiographies, 'as letters usually do'. Rebellion, bravery, adventure: not attributes one commonly assign to emails.

But perhaps my favourite single letter hangs above my desk. I have very little idea of what it actually says (and it is not the original letter, but a photo of it). It was written by Edouard Manet in 1879 to the art collector Albert Hecht, and the words are certainly less significant than what sits alongside them – two beautiful little colour sketches of plums and cherries. I have always coveted letters with illustrations – Edward Lear and Beatrix Potter sent fine ones with drawings of some of their most famous creations, while other artists such as Magritte drew sketches and cartoons they would never exhibit; another loss to email. I first saw the Manet letter at the Frieze art fair in London, and for a brief caffeinated moment thought I might buy it. It's a small thing, about 25cm × 15cm, elaborately framed, and I thought I would spend a bit of my book advance on it, although I didn't quite know how much the gallery, Stephen Ongpin, was asking. I figured maybe £5,000–£8,000, but how I dreamt up this figure I'm not sure. I made an enquiry. They wanted £180,000.

In April 2013, Unferth wrote that she had married her boyfriend with the loft space, and she had an update on her Letters in the Mail postbag.

> I am still receiving letters from strangers! I just received one from Australia yesterday. I'm only getting a trickle now (You know, you should write a letter for them, for Rumpus). All the people I wrote postcards to wrote me back. One kid, who had written a very sad letter about feeling life was meaningless and about feeling suicidal – I wrote him a postcard with a list of things to do and he wrote me back with a photocopy of the postcard and a list of ways he was trying all the things I suggested.

I'm writing this in my small house in Cornwall. The place is called The Old Post Office Garage, and is built on the land where the St Ives post office used to maintain its delivery vans. It was converted in about 2000, and when I bought it a few years later it still had, under the stairs, one of those large wicker baskets with GPO (General Post Office) on the side. It used to contain bags holding thousands of letters, and now contains beach stuff like boogie boards and fishing gear, none of which I use but one of my kids occasionally roots around in. One might regard this as symbolic.

Earlier today postwoman Tracey rang the doorbell to ask whether the Royal Mail could install a sort of staging post somewhere on my driveway where she and her colleagues could store their letters midway through their rounds, so that they wouldn't have to carry the whole lot on their backs or in trolleys. By 'letters' I think she meant to include Amazon parcels, other online purchases and junk mail. What it entails is erecting a grey steel box by a side wall on a concrete plinth, apparently all fully removable in a flash. There's no money in it, but I get some sort of reward in stamps, and a warm feeling for contributing to the smooth running of the local postal service. I said yes.

There does appear to be a greater awareness these days of the value of letters as items of instruction and delight. I'm

Manet's fruit stall from 1879.

Lundi

Mon cher Jacques,

Je rentre d'un séjour d'une semaine à la mer, au coq pour préciser et je trouve ton appel en rentrant – C'est cruel comme coïncidence, mais ni toi ni moi n'en sommes responsables. Ne trouveras-tu pas le moyen de passer tout de même 1 jour ou 2 à Bruxelles ? Pendant mes vacances trop courtes comme toujours j'ai pensé à ceci :

et à une bâche couchée dans une prairie. Sur les clos et les fleurs de la hête se trouve posé l'inévitable : un château fort – et à un sujet de petit récit : un pauvre père avec une dizaine de jeunes enfants se promenant – une petite fille désire une crème à la glace)

'Ceci n'est pas un ballon a air chaud': Magritte writes to a friend.

cheered by the huge number of online hits at Letters of Note, and by the enthusiasm for the recently published collections of P.G. Wodehouse, Kurt Vonnegut, Benjamin Britten, and the correspondence between Paul Auster and J.M. Coetzee. But the future for letters looks bleak. The apparatus is changing – the privatisation of the Royal Mail was announced in 2013, the US Postal Service is planning to end Saturday deliveries – and who knows what will happen to communication now that emails are seen by the young as old hat, and tweets and instant messaging compel us to keep everything brief? When, in the not too distant future, email correspondence is published as an ebook, the ebook will look just like our inbox.

Recently at a dinner party I sat opposite a young bookseller who told me that one of her favourite books was – perhaps unsurprisingly – *84 Charing Cross Road* by Helene Hanff. She'd also seen the brown and melancholy film with Anthony Hopkins and Anne Bancroft, and she'd liked that too. Hanff's is the one book of letters almost everyone I know seems to have read: a true account of the postwar correspondence between a single bookish television writer in New York (Hanff) and the staff at a London booksellers called Marks & Co, located at the address in the title. She's bullish and generous, and ever eager for clean, readable, affordable copies of Plato, Austen and the like, and the booksellers are erudite, proper, and keen to fulfil her wants list as best they can. In particular she strikes up a touching relationship with a man in the shop responsible for dealing with her demands called Frank Doel, who clearly likes his new client's reading habits and forthrightness. And reading it now, of course, with Marks & Co long gone and the book trade undergoing another of its life-long uncertainties, it has an added poignancy. I like to think I'm maintaining that grand transatlantic airmail tradition with my new correspondent in Connecticut, albeit without the exchange of slightly foxed Hazlitts and austerity hams.

What accounts for the grand appeal of the book? Its brevity and simplicity play a part, as does its wistful elegy to a lost world. *84 Charing Cross Road* is compelling because it's about love: a love for reading, a love for writing, a love for the divergences of class and culture in what was perhaps the last period (the 1950s) when the Anglo-American divide meant more than just the missing 'u' in color. But it is also a love affair served up in a way only letters can – subtly, cerebrally, gradually. The book is an old-fashioned courtship, and its slowness engenders thoughtfulness and an honesty born of care; it makes us care, too, for in these letters we recognise ourselves.

Not long ago my editor noticed an interesting thing while watching *Postman Pat* with her kids. (For those without kids I should explain that *Postman Pat* is a preschool television classic, running since the early 1980s, a felt stop-go animation in which nothing really happens: so long as *Postman Pat* and his black and white cat are on their daily rounds averting tiny crises and spreading good cheer through the village then they are spreading good cheer throughout all villages, and, by karmic extension, the whole world.) In the most recent series, Pat's world has been updated in small ways (he now carries a mobile phone). But most things are as they were, with only a small amendment to the famous theme tune. A while ago, the Royal Mail decided it didn't want to be associated with Mr Pat anymore, as his show no longer fitted its go-ahead corporate image. So every child's favourite postman saw the way the wind was blowing and changed the words to his song. In the new version he no longer brings 'letters through your door', but rather 'parcels to your door'. And thus do empires crumble.

The decline in personal letter-writing has clearly acceler-

The way it's going: a letter box pageant in Somerset.

ated in the last decade.* But the sense of the decline is nothing new: we have already seen how it had been remarked
upon frequently in the decades before. In the mid-70s, in one
of his letters to Kingsley Amis, Philip Larkin, writing from
Hull University where he ran the library, says how good it
was receiving a letter from him. 'I don't get many letters now,

---

* There are no precise figures; it would be impossible to calculate the commercial
traffic of the personal letter (as opposed to a business one or a circular). A letter
with a handwritten address may provide a pointer, but the national postal services do not track such things through automated systems. The Royal Mail, does,
however, maintain records of the number of personally addressed letters posted
annually, defining a letter as anything that is not a parcel (the figure thus includes
marketing mail). The figures have increased steadily since 1980–81, from 9.96 billion in that year to 12.53 billion in 1986–87 and 16.36 billion in 1992–93. The peak
was reached in 2004–05 with 20.19 billion, followed by a steady decline. The figure
was 18.04 billion in 2008–09 and 16.64 billion in 2009–10. In 2011–12 it was 15.14
billion. The preliminary result for the year ended 31 March 2013 was 13.86 billion.

except ones threatening to cut off the gas or the telephone, or wanting £5,000 by 1st July 1976.' What he wanted was a letter from one of the queen's servants offering a new job in charge of the library at Windsor, where he would be given a house in the grounds. Better still would be a letter that began: 'I am directed to inform you that under the will of the late Mr Getty . . .'

In his introduction to *Counting One's Blessings*, the collected letters of the Queen Mother, the editor William Shawcross remarks that in 1964, when Roger Fulford was editing the correspondence between Queen Victoria and her daughter Victoria two phrases he heard all over the place were 'Nobody writes letters nowadays' and 'The art of letter writing is dead.'

The letters of the Queen Mother are surprisingly amusing, tracking the British century in a unique way. Her later correspondences, including one with Ted Hughes, are full blooded and feisty, but perhaps the best of all are her thank-you notes for diplomatic and exotic gifts, which serve as fine examples to kids having to reply to unusual birthday presents. The last letter in the book is a thank-you note to Prince Charles for a set of large fluffy bath towels for her 101st birthday, in which she luxuriates in the thought of the towels wrapping her entire body ('heavenly') and reflects upon the shininess of the sea and sun in Scotland. And when, on an earlier occasion, she received a lavish box of chocolates, one would assume that a cursory 'delicious chocs!' would do, but no: they were 'too excellent for words' (perhaps the Queen Mum is being sarcastic here, not a regularly acknowledged Windsor trait). She then insists she has never had a box like them. 'The extraordinary thing is, that they are all so good.' (I can't shake the image of her eating them in bed, propped up Cartland-style on a hundred frilled pillows, going 'Mmmm! Caramel! Another winner!')

The letters also track a century of brilliant valedictory sign-offs. Her first letter, from February 1909 to her father Lord

Strathmore, when she was eight, mentions a 'donky' on an Italian holiday and ends with 'Xxxxxxxxxxxxx Ooooooooooo'. (I had assumed that the hugs suggested by 'o' were a fairly recent thing, but apparently not – I do know that the 'x's on a letter developed from the practice of drawing a cross on a document in medieval times as an act of god-fearing sincerity and faith, and then kissing it; the 'x' just became shorthand.) Writing to her mother seven years later, in the middle of the war, having just that morning taken some exams in Hackney (travelling by bus and tram, seven years from becoming a duchess) Elizabeth still ends with 'oooooooxxxxxxxxx'. And gradually, as her responsibilities deepen and her letter duties increase, we get the spread of 'I am, Yours very sincerely' (to Churchill) and 'Ever yours affect' (to Prince Paul of Yugoslavia) and 'your sincere friend' (to Eleanor Roosevelt). But the best sign-off of all – now famous I think, or if not it should be – came in the midst of war in February 1941. Elizabeth was in Buckingham Palace, writing to her friend Elizabeth Elphinstone, a nurse who had recently lost a brother in the conflict. The queen sends her sympathy, and admits she is as frightened of bombs and gunfire as she was at the beginning of the war, and how her heart still 'hammers' at the sound. And then she says goodbye. But it is not just any farewell. It is:

> Tinkety tonk old fruit, & down with the Nazis
>
> Always your loving
>
> Peter

No idea what the Peter thing is about, but she may have picked up 'tinkerty tonk', with an 'r', from P.G. Wodehouse.

Katherine Mansfield once wrote to a friend, 'This is not a letter but my arms around you for a brief moment,' and perhaps all personal letters should feel like that at the end.

So how to close a book about letters? You can't go wrong

with the simple 'Yours' of course, and 'Farewell' has survived intact for more than 2,000 years. But I think I'm going with the Queen Mum on this one.

So tinkety tonk old fruit, and down with the Nazis forever. It's been a pleasure writing to you.

Acknowledgements

Thank-you letters are among the last to disappear. Here is mine. I owe a considerable debt to those who have helped me explain the true and lasting worth of correspondence. In a general survey such as this, an author necessarily relies upon a great deal of scholarship to provide both context and expert detail, and I am grateful to all the authors listed in the bibliography. If you require further illumination, it's the perfect place to start.

A number of people also shared their wide-ranging experience and analysis in person, and the book would have been much poorer without them. In addition to those interviewed and mentioned in the text, I would like to thank Stephen Carling, Craig Taylor, Paul Tough, Lenka Clayton, Michael Crowe, Lucy Norkus, Simon Roberts, Richard Tomlinson, Suzanne Hodgart, Richard Ferraro, Emma Banner, and Geoff Woad.

The remarkable wartime narrative threaded through the book is testament not only to the power of letters, but to the rigours of careful stewardship. Chris Barker and Bessie Moore are responsible for the first act, and Bernard Barker and Katy Edge for the second. The latter pair not only recognized the letters for what they are (ie a significant and highly entertaining read), but they have ordered and transcribed them into a form that has made them accessible to all. I only stepped in once this initial legwork had been done, and without it I may have found my own editing role far too daunting a task. The letters you have read should be regarded as merely a taster of the whole correspondence; perhaps in the near future a longer version will reveal further rewards. Chris Barker's papers (the letters and many other documents) have found the ideal home at the Mass Observation Archive, University of Sussex, where they are under the watchful stewardship of Fiona Courage, Jessica Scantlebury and their colleagues.

This book has benefitted greatly from the inspiration of three main custodians at Canongate. I would like to thank Nick Davies, Anya Serota and Jenny Lord for their careful suggestions and creative editorial stewardship – it's been a pleasure working with three such talented and inspiring individuals. Natasha Hodgson has proved a tireless editorial assistant in securing permissions and illustration rights, and Vicki Rutherford has guided the manuscript through every process with seemingly effortless grace. I also wish to thank Jenny Todd for her long-range vision, Anna Frame for her publicity nous, Rafaela Romaya for the beautiful cover design, Sîan Gibson for her sales knowledge and Caroline Gorham and Laura Cole for managing production. And then there's Jamie Byng, a force of nature and a force for irrepressible literary good. Thanks for making me feel instantly at home.

In the United States, Gotham has again proved itself the perfect transatlantic companion. In particular I wish to thank Bill Shinker, Jessica Sindler, Charlie Conrad, Lisa Johnson and Beth Parker.

I've been blessed once again with the witty inventiveness of James Alexander at Jade Design, while Seán Costello saved me from multiple embarrassments with his painstaking copyediting. I have always relied on the staff and the shelves at the London Library to lead me to the best material, but never more so than with this subject. My agent Rosemary Scoular at United Agents has become a true friend.

I met my wife, Justine Kanter, at a point where love emails and texts had already taken over from love letters, so this book is an attempt to reverse the process.

Select Bibliography

Abelard and Heloise, *The Letters of Abelard and Heloise*, translated by Betty Radice (Penguin Books, London, 1974)

Bannet, Eve Tavor, *Empire of Letters: Letter Manuals and Transatlantic Correspondence*, 1688–1820 (Cambridge University Press, Cambridge, 2005)

Beale, Philip O., *England's Mail: Two Millennia of Letter Writing* (Tempus, Stroud, 2005)

Beard, Mary *Confronting The Classics* (Profile Books, London, 2013)

Bishop, Elizabeth, *Words in Air: the Complete Correspondence between Elizabeth Bishop and Robert Lowell* (Faber and Faber, London, 2008)

Bowman, Alan.K. et al., *Oxyrhynchus: A City and Its Texts* (Egypt Exploration Society, London, 2007)

Bowman, Alan K., *Life and Letters on the Roman frontier: Vindolanda and Its People* (British Museum, London, 2003)

Bradford, May, *A Hospital Letter-Writer in France* (Methuen, London, 1920)

Brown, Richard D., *Knowledge Is Power: The Diffusion of Information in Early America 1700–1865* (Oxford University Press, Oxford, 1989)

Campbell-Smith, Duncan, *Masters of the Post: the Authorized History of the Royal Mail* (Allen Lane, London, 2011)

Chartier, Roger et al., *Correspondence: Models of Letter-Writing from the Middle Ages to the Nineteenth Century* (Polity Press, Cambridge, 1997)

Cicero, *Letters of Cicero*, translated by Evelyn S. Shuckburgh (George Bell and Sons, London, 1899)

Creswell, Harry B., *The Honeywood File* (Architectural Press, London, 1929)

Daybell, James, *The Material Letter in Early Modern England: Manuscript Letters and the Culture and Practices of Letter-Writing, 1512–1635* (Palgrave Macmillan, London, 2012)

Dearborn, Mary V., *The Happiest Man Alive: a Biography of Henry Miller* (HarperCollins, London, 1991)

Decker, William Merrill, *Epistolary Practices: Letter Writing in America before Telecommunications* (University of North Carolina Press, Chapel Hill and London, 1998)

Earle, Rebecca, ed., *Epistolary Selves: Letters and Letter-Writers, 1600–1945* (Ashgate, Aldershot, 1999)

Freeman, John, *The Tyranny of E-mail: the 4,000-year Journey to Your Inbox* (Scribner, New York, 2009)

Garfield, Simon, *The Error World* (Faber and Faber, London, 2008)

Hafner, Katie and Lyon, Matthew: *Where Wizards Stay Up Late: the Origins of the Internet* (Touchstone, New York, 1996)

Hanff, Helene, *84, Charing Cross Road* (Andre Deutsch, London, 1971)

Henkin, David M., *The Postal Age: the Emergence of Modern Communications in Nineteenth-Century America* (University of Chicago Press, Chicago, 2006)

Hughes, Ted, *Letters of Ted Hughes* (Faber and Faber, London 2007)

Keats, John, *Selected letters of John Keats*, edited by Grant F. Scott (Harvard University Press, Cambridge, Mass., 2002)

Kerherve, Alain, ed., *The Ladies Complete Letter Writer* (Cambridge Scholars Publishing, Newcastle upon Tyne, 2010)

Klauck, Hans-Josef and Bailey, Daniel P., *Ancient Letters and the New Testament: a Guide to Context and Exegesis* (Baylor University Press, Waco, Texas, 2006)

Lewins, William, *Her Majesty's Mails: The British Post-Office* (Samson and Marston, London, 1864)

Little, Peter, *Communication in Business* (Longmans, London, 1965)

Mallon, Thomas, *Yours Ever: People and Their Letters* (Pantheon, New York, 2009)

Meyer, Jessica, *Men of War: Masculinity and the First World War in Britain* (Palgrave Macmillan, London, 2008)

Mitford, Jessica, *Decca: The Letters of Jessica Mitford*, edited by Peter Y. Sussman (Weidenfeld & Nicolson, London, 2006)

Motion, Andrew, *Keats* (Faber and Faber, London, 1997)

Mossiker, Frances, *Madame de Sévigné: A Life and Letters* (Alfred A. Knopf, New York, 1983)

Mullan, John, *What Matters in Jane Austen?* (Bloomsbury, London, 2012)

Nin, Anaïs and Miller, Henry, *A Literate Passion: Letters of Anaïs Nin & Henry Miller*, edited by Gunther Stuhlmann (Harcourt Brace & Company, San Diego, 1987)

Oldfield, Sybil, ed., *Afterwords: Letters on the Death of Virginia Woolf* (Edinburgh University Press, Edinburgh, 2005)

The Paston Letters, edited by Norman Davis (Oxford University Press, Oxford, 1983)

Petrarch: The First Modern Scholar and Man of Letters, introduced and selected by James Harvey Robinson (G.P. Putnam & Sons, New York and London, 1909)

Plath, Sylvia, *Letters Home* (Faber and Faber, London, 1975)

Pliny the Younger, *The Letters of the Younger Pliny*, translated by Betty Radice (Penguin Books, London, 1963)

Poster, Carol and Mitchell, Linda C., eds, *Letter-Writing Manuals and Instruction from Antiquity to the Present* (University of South Carolina Press, Columbia, South Carolina, 2007)

Richlin, Amy, ed., *Marcus Aurelius in Love* (University of Chicago Press, Chicago, 2006)

Roberts, William, *History of Letter-Writing: From the Earliest Period to the Fifth Century* (William Pickering, London, 1843)

Robertson, J, *The Art of Letter Writing* (University Press of Liverpool, Liverpool, 1942)

Rosenmeyer, Patricia A., *Ancient Epistolary Fictions: The Letter in Greek Literature* (Cambridge University Press, Cambridge, 2001)

Rotunno, Laura *Victorian Literature and Culture* (Cambridge University Press, Cambridge, 2005)

Rummel, Erika, ed., *The Erasmus Reader* (University of Toronto Press, Toronto, 1990)

Seneca, *Selected Philosophical Letters*, edited by Brad Inwood (Oxford University Press, Oxford, 2007)

Sévigné, Madame de, *Selected Letters* (Penguin Books, London, 1982)

Stanhope, Philip (Second Earl of Chesterfield), *Some Short Observations for the Lady Mary Stanhope Concerning the Writing of Ordinary Letters* (Farmington, Conn., 1934)

Stanhope, Philip (Fourth Earl of Chesterfield), *Letters to His Son and Others* (Dutton, London, 1986)

Thomas, Katie-Louise, *Postal Pleasures: Sex, Scandal and Victorian Letters* (Oxford University Press, Oxford, 2012)

Tingey, John, *The Englishman Who Posted Himself and Other Curious Objects* (Princeton Architectural Press, Princeton, 2010)

Vaughn, Sally N., *St Anselm and the Handmaidens of God* (Brepolis, Turnhout, 2002)

Whyman, Susan E., *The Pen and the People: English Letter Writers, 1660–1800* (Oxford University Press, Oxford, 2009

Woolf, Virginia, *Leave The Letters Till We're Dead: The Letters of Virginia Woolf, Vol VI*, edited by Nigel Nicolson (Hogarth Press, London, 1978)

Picture Credits

While every effort has been made to contact copyright-holders of illustrations, the author and publishers would be grateful for information about any illustrations where they have been unable to trace them, and would be glad to make amendments in further editions.

p6 Courtesy of the British Postal Museum and Archive, London, UK/© Royal Mail Group Ltd./The Bridgeman Art Library; **p8** Courtesy of the British Postal Museum and Archive, London, UK/© Royal Mail Group Ltd. /The Bridgeman Art Library; **p16** Courtesy of Bloomsbury Auctions; **p22** Courtesy of Private Collection/Photo © Christie's Images/The Bridgeman Art Library **p33** Courtesy of the Vindolanda Trust; **p35** ©Adam Stanford and the Vindolanda Trust; **p36** © the Vindolanda Trust; **p39** © the Vindolanda Trust; **p50** Source: Wikimedia Commons; **p56** Courtesy of De Agostini Picture Library/A. Dagli Orti/The Bridgeman Art Library **p63** Courtesy of Private Collection/Photo © Agnew's, London, UK/The Bridgeman Art Library; **p67** Used with kind permission of Bernard Barker; **p73** Courtesy of De Agostini Picture Library/G. Nimatallah/The Bridgeman Art Library; **p75** ©Jim Linwood; **p83** Photography © The Art Institute of Chicago; **p84** Courtesy of Universal Studios Licensing LLC; **p87** Courtesy of Private Collection/© Look and Learn/The Bridgeman Art Library; **p96** Courtesy of Universal History Archive/UIG/The Bridgeman Art Library; **p103** Courtesy of Private Collection/The Bridgeman Art Library; **p107** © The British Library Board (General Reference Collection C.40.b.35); **p123** Courtesy of British Library, London, UK/© British Library Board. All Rights Reserved/The Bridgeman Art Library; **p125** Courtesy of Universal History Archive/UIG /The Bridgeman Art Library; **p128** Courtesy of Palazzo Barberini, Rome, Italy/The Bridgeman Art Library; Courtesy of Hever Castle, Kent, UK/The Bridgeman Art Library; **p130** © The British Library Board. (Add. 22587, f.22v); **p135** Courtesy of Private Collection/The Bridgeman Art Library; **p140** ©Simon Annand; **p151** Courtesy of Musee de la Ville de Paris, Musee Carnavalet, Paris, France/Giraudon/The Bridgeman Art Library; **p163,167,178,182,185,188** Courtesy of Private Collection/Photo © Christie's Images/The Bridgeman Art Library; **p191** Photo © Neil Holmes/The Bridgeman Art Library; **p192** Courtesy of Private Collection/© Look and Learn/The Bridgeman Art Library **p194** ©Bonhams; **p199** Courtesy of The Albert Einstein Archives, The Hebrew University of Jerusalem, Israel/Private Collection/Photo © Christie's Images/The Bridgeman Art Library/; **p208** Courtesy of Photo Pierpont Morgan Library/Art Resource/Scala, Florence; **p210** Courtesy of Private Collection/The Bridgeman Art Library; **p213** Courtesy of Private Collection/The Bridgeman Art Library; **p217** Courtesy of Private Collection/The Stapleton Collection/The Bridgeman Art Library; **p218** © The British Library Board. (C.71.cc.8); **p227** Courtesy of The Royal Mail/The British Postal Museum; **p229** Courtesy of Private

Permission Credits

Index